ASTON VILLA REVIEW 1994

ASTON VILLA F.C.

PREPARED

Published by Sports Projects Ltd

ACKNOWLEDGEMENTS

Aston Villa Review 1994
First published in Great Britain in June 1994
by Sports Projects Limited

© 1994 Sports Projects Limited
188 Lightwoods Hill, Smethwick, Warley,
West Midlands B67 5EH.

ISBN 0 946866 19 8

Printed and bound in Great Britain
by The Bath Press, Avon

Editor: Dennis Shaw

Statistics: Trevor Hartley

Photographs: Bernard Gallagher, Sports Projects
and Terry Weir

Design, layout and graphics: Bernard Gallagher,
Trevor Hartley, Phil Lees and Nadine Goldingay

Special thanks to: Steve Stride and Frank Beach

KEY

❏	Player booked
■	Player sent off
32	Figure in goals column indicates time of goal
†56	First substitute and time of substitution
†	First player substituted
‡56	Second substitute and time of substitution
‡	Second player substituted

Notes:

● *Players are listed in order of position, goalkeeper, defenders, midfield and then forwards.*

● *The first named substitute is always the substitute goalkeeper.*

● *In friendly games, where several substitutes may have appeared, additional symbols are used in the following order: #, §, ††, ‡‡, ##, §§, ≠.*

A return to European action and winners at Wembley

Volume Two of Aston Villa Review follows precisely the pattern established in the successful first publication a year earlier.

Collectors of the series will be the proud possessors, year by year, of the ONLY complete annual record of the club's playing affairs ever published.

Once again the reports of each match take the reader through the season, virtually kick-by-kick while also providing a permanent work of reference. The statistics, compiled by Trevor Hartley of Sports Projects, cover every aspect of the club's playing affairs with nothing of true relevance left out.

For the season 1993-94 there is, of course, two crucial differences: European football was restored and the Coca-Cola Cup was won in thrilling style. Wembley victory in the Final over Manchester United was widely regarded as one of Wembley's most entertaining matches.

Likewise, the two-legged semi-final against Tranmere Rovers, with its Villa Park penalty shoot-out, captivated its live audience and the nation's TV viewers.

All this is faithfully recorded in both descriptive and analytical fashion. Where it lacks the visual impact of video screening it scores in its factual recording, all available at the flick of the pages.

Goals, goal times, outstanding performances, oddities, attendances, pre-match build-up, traumas, triumphs, yellow cards, red cards, comings and goings... all are to be found in the following pages.

Those who purchased last year's copy will not wish to have missed No.2 and those who missed No.1 can at least start now.

The facility for supporters to order their copy in advance, and thus have their name printed for posterity in the Subscribers' Roll Call, was a most popular one and has been continued in this latest instalment.

This style of season-by-season, factual and descriptive chronicle of events, was a pioneering initiative by Villa in its first year. Maybe other clubs will follow suit. If so the archives of the game for future generations will be the better for all the information and observation compiled and condensed in this type of package.

Aston Villa Review 1994 sits on the bookshelf alongside 1993, two years of club progress recorded in book series fashion.

Dennis Shaw
June 1994.

CONTENTS

CONTENTS

Saturday 14th August 1993 • Villa Park • 3.00pm

ASTON VILLA 4 QUEENS PARK RANGERS 1

Half-time 1-1 • *Attendance* 32,944

Referee Kelvin MORTON (Bury St. Edmunds)

Linesmen K.J. HAWKES and C. JONES

Claret Shirts with Blue Stripes, White Shorts		Goals	Black Shirts and Shorts with Red Trim		Goals
1	Nigel SPINK		1	Tony ROBERTS	
2	Earl BARRETT		18	Karl READY	
4	Shaun TEALE		3	Clive WILSON	
5	Paul McGRATH		5	Darren PEACOCK	
3	Steve STAUNTON	90	21	Tony WITTER	
7	Ray HOUGHTON †		7	Andrew IMPEY	
14	Andy TOWNSEND		14	Simon BARKER	
6	Kevin RICHARDSON		4	Ray WILKINS	
7	Tony DALEY		8	Ian HOLLOWAY †	
10	Dalian ATKINSON	38, 86	9	Les FERDINAND	44
9	Dean SAUNDERS	61	10	Bradley ALLEN	
	Substitutes			*Substitutes*	
30	Michael OAKES		13	Jan STEJSKAL	
15	Gordon COWANS †58		19	Devon WHITE †83	
22	Guy WHITTINGHAM		15	Rufus BREVETT	

BEFORE	P	W	D	L	F	A	pts	AFTER	P	W	D	L	F	A	pts
Villa	0	0	0	0	0	0	0	1 Villa	1	1	0	0	4	1	3
QPR	0	0	0	0	0	0	0	22 QPR	1	0	0	1	1	4	0

FACTFILE

Andy Townsend signs in with a stormer... Whittingham, the £1.1m new Guy, watches from the bench... Gordon Cowans starts his third period with the club... Dalian Atkinson scores on the opening day for a third successive year... Premiership players now wear squad numbers and names on their shirts.

Goal blast raises the new roof

Football is pure theatre, the romantics have it. If they are right then Villa Park is rapidly becoming the classic auditorium.

During the summer of '93 work has gone on ceaselessly to bring the stadium up to the demands of the Lord Justice Taylor report. Off the field the task is to improve on runners-up place, prepare for the UEFA Cup and make a determined assault on the two domestic cups.

As fans hurry back, even the short close season is too long for those who can't bear the break, they are greeted by the framework of the new Witton Lane stand, now two-tier and mighty impressive.

"It blows your mind, the way it has transformed the ground. Next to Old Trafford Villa's must be the best in the country," says Ron Atkinson, not one to minimise his club's many qualities. "Somehow, it levels the sides with the Holte End, makes everywhere look higher and will be very intimidating for visiting teams when it's full."

Big Ron's re-built section of the club looks pretty good, too. There in midfield is Andy Townsend, at £2.1m from Chelsea, the very kind of midfield powerhouse lacking last season. But the other two newcomers, Guy Whittingham a £1.1m striker from Portsmouth, and Gordon Cowans back on a free from Blackburn Rovers, have to welcome in the new season impatiently on the bench.

An air of high-expectancy is almost tangible as Ron Atkinson's third season leaves the traps against a Rangers side shorn of Andy Sinton who is on the move, probably to Arsenal.

All the pre-season conjecture has been about how the strike force of Dean Saunders and Dalian Atkinson will recover from their blank finish to the previous season.

Dalian, plagued by injury and failure to regain his explosive streak, had got stuck on 13 since his two at Sheffield Wednesday on December 5, eight long months ago.

To massive relief that famine survives for only 38 minutes into the new season. The kind of run through midfield which prompted such a large fee for a 30-year-old sees Townsend feed Atkinson for a magnificent finish.

Yet Villa are not instantly into a smooth pattern and Rangers have had their share of the ball and, a minute before the half-time whistle is due, make good use of it in carving out the opening for a dynamic strike from the edge of the area by England cap, Les Ferdinand.

With an hour gone Deano signs in with a nicely worked opening and a precise right-foot finish. That goal arrived within moments of Cowans being sent from the bench to smooth things out in midfield and as 90 minutes approaches the large crowd will be happy to settle for the narrow victory. Then, as though a bottle of fizzy pop has been well shaken, the cork pops and out pours an effervescent finish of two goals in a brief but ecstatic injury time.

First, Atkinson explodes with one of his Goal of the Month-bidding moments to surge forward and almost rip out the net for 3-1. But he then discovers it's not even the Goal of the Match. This description must be applied to Steve Staunton's grand finale, a curving blast of a drive greeted by a roar which almost removes that new Witton Lane Stand roof.

Three points and a 'plus' goal difference of three. Welcome 93-94...

New boy Andy Townsend milks the applause of the Holte End as scorer Dean Saunders is mobbed

Wednesday 18th August 1993 • Hillsborough • 7.45pm

SHEFFIELD WEDNESDAY 0 ASTON VILLA 0

Half-time 0-0 • Attendance 28,450

Referee Peter FOAKES (Clacton-on-Sea)
Linesmen R. PEARSON and M.A. RILEY

Blue and White Striped Shirts, Blue Shorts	Goals	Claret Shirts with Blue Stripes, White Shorts	Goals
1 Chris WOODS		1 Nigel SPINK	
2 Roland NILSSON		2 Earl BARRETT ❑	
12 Andy PEARCE		4 Shaun TEALE	
17 Des WALKER		5 Paul McGRATH	
18 Phil KING		3 Steve STAUNTON	
16 Graham HYDE		11 Tony DALEY	
11 John SHERIDAN		14 Andy TOWNSEND †	
4 Carlton PALMER		6 Kevin RICHARDSON	
3 Nigel WORTHINGTON		12 Steve FROGGATT	
7 Paul WARHURST		9 Dean SAUNDERS	
9 David HIRST †		10 Dalian ATKINSON	
Substitutes		*Substitutes*	
13 Kevin PRESSMAN		13 Mark BOSNICH	
10 Mark BRIGHT †85		15 Gordon COWANS †27	
14 Chris BART-WILLIAMS		22 Guy WHITTINGHAM	

BEFORE		P	W	D	L	F	A	pts	AFTER		P	W	D	L	F	A	pts
6	Villa	1	1	0	0	4	1	3	6	Villa	2	1	1	0	4	1	4
18	Wednesday	1	0	0	1	0	2	0	17	Wednesday	2	0	1	1	0	2	1

FACTFILE

Villa again avoid defeat at Ron Atkinson's former club... Steve Froggatt makes his first appearance since February... Andy Townsend limps off... Deano has a 'goal' ruled out for offside - TV evidence seems to suggest otherwise... England international Des Walker makes his home debut for Wednesday.

Froggy returns to test the Owls

Before the opening match Ron Atkinson expressed the view that some of the team's best football of 92-93 came with Steve Froggatt in the side. The young winger had, however, been out since February with a knee problem which had finally been put to right by intensive recovery work during the summer.

At Hillsborough Froggy is recalled to the action in place of Ray Houghton who was withdrawn during the opening day win over QPR and not chosen to face Wednesday.

Although Cowans, sub against QPR, went out again, he was quickly needed when Andy Townsend limped off after only 27 minutes with a minor hamstring strain.

Wednesday also have their injury problem, in the shape of the loss of Phil King for ten-minutes of the first half with a head injury, subsequently heavily-bandaged, after a collision with Paul McGrath.

A summer of intensive work in the transfer market has seen Trevor Francis kick-off with a squad enhanced by the signing from Italy of Des Walker and the retention of Carlton Palmer and Paul Warhurst about whose future doubts had been expressed.

As a result Wednesday have been one of the teams named by pundits for, at the very least, a challenging season, views which are to be strengthened subsequently with the arrival from QPR of Andy Sinton.

Earl Barrett - booked for kicking the ball away

Much of Villa's football is up to the best levels of last season, though the defence is sometimes rather less composed. Wednesday feel that, after successive Villa wins at Hillsborough, they owe their former manager a lesson or two.

This is not to be. Both sides miss chances in a game of massive energy and all-out effort but Wednesday appear to take the lead when John Sheridan side-foots past Spink.

Mercifully for Villa the move is adjudged offside and as Wednesday continue to press, Earl Barrett receives a rare booking for booting a dead ball away to give a few moment's respite.

Although Wednesday do more of the first-half attacking the best chance falls to Dalian Atkinson who, fed by Dean Saunders, finds Chris Woods blocking his shot.

During a match which never gives up its intensity the England keeper also denies Tony Daley and Kevin Richardson.

Froggatt is earning his place by supplying a well-judged cross or two, one of which leads to Woods making another save, this time from a glancing Deano header.

In the second-half both Sheridan and David Hirst waste good chances while Daley has missed an opportunity to put Villa ahead.

A minute later Daley releases Saunders who cracks the ball confidently past Woods. Offside flags a linesman. Dubious decision!

However, the moment which could have given the tightly-fought contest a 1-0 scoreline in Villa's favour arrives seven minutes from time. Atkinson releases the ball into space just right for Deano to connect with his right foot.

Unfortunately the Welsh international is afflicted by what golfers call 'a slice' and the chance is gone. "I thought we did enough to have won," mused Big Ron.

"They would be more relieved than us to get away with a draw."

Even so, two points have gone while Manchester United, Villa Park visitors next Monday, have six out of six.

Saturday 21st August 1993 • Selhurst Park • 3.00pm

WIMBLEDON 2 ASTON VILLA 2

Half-time 1-1 • Attendance 7,533

Referee Jim BORRETT (Great Yarmouth)

Linesmen W.M. JORDAN and D.C. MADGWICK

Dark Blue Shirts with Yellow Trim, Dark Blue Shorts		Goals	Claret Shirts with Blue Stripes, White Shorts		Goals
1	Hans SEGERS		1	Nigel SPINK	
17	Roger JOSEPH		2	Earl BARRETT	
5	Dean BLACKWELL		5	Paul McGRATH	
15	John SCALES		4	Shaun TEALE	
35	Alan KIMBLE		3	Steve STAUNTON	82
7	Andy CLARKE †		7	Ray HOUGHTON	
20	Lawrie SANCHEZ		6	Kevin RICHARDSON	17
8	Robbie EARLE		15	Gordon COWANS	
2	Warren BARTON		12	Steve FROGGATT	
9	John FASHANU	85	9	Dean SAUNDERS	
10	Dean HOLDSWORTH ▢	38	10	Dalian ATKINSON	
	Substitutes			*Substitutes*	
37	Perry DIGWEED		13	Mark BOSNICH	
14	Gerald DOBBS †66		17	Neil COX	
18	Steve TALBOYS		22	Guy WHITTINGHAM	

BEFORE		P	W	D	L	F	A	pts	AFTER		P	W	D	L	F	A	pts
6	Villa	2	1	1	0	4	1	4	10	Villa	3	1	2	0	6	3	5
7	Wimbledon	2	1	1	0	3	1	4	11	Wimbledon	3	1	2	0	5	3	5

FACTFILE

Steve Staunton scores direct from a corner... Villa's 3,700 following makes up almost half of the gate... Ray Houghton plays his 50th game for the club... The introduction of squad numbers in the Premiership is already becoming farcical as Wimbledon have numbers 35 and 37 in their 14 on duty.

Fash the Bash makes his point

Pressure on players to recover from injuries quicker than nature intended has already arrived with only two matches played.

Both Andy Townsend and Tony Daley have fairly minor hamstring problems arising from the nil-nil draw at Hillsborough, but are desperate not to miss games.

"After all my problems of last season I would play on one leg to avoid losing my place," said Daley, but in the event he can't make it to hop out at Selhurst Park. Nor can Townsend.

Consequently, Ray Houghton returns on the right side of midfield with Gordon Cowans staying in at left centre.

Wimbledon have a matching record to Villa's of one win and one draw from the first two games though the Dons have hit the headlines for the wrong reason, namely their chairman Sam Hammam's graffiti-writing on the dressing room wall at West Ham the previous week.

If Villa skipper Kevin Richardson has any negative vibrations remaining from his crucial FA Cup penalty shoot-out miss at this venue last season they are quickly dispelled.

As Villa take a measure of control early on Richardson gives a neat demonstration of the art of finishing in the 17th minute as Houghton and Cowans combine to unhinge the Dons' defence.

Blessed with such a positive opening Villa promise to settle into their most enterprising mood and Hans Segers is the goalkeeper under siege rather than Nigel Spink. But no team is ever safe against the Wimbledon style of counter-attacks by the short route and one such break seven minutes before the interval sees Dean Holdsworth equalise with a near-post header.

The second half features Villa resuming their confident attacking football but the necessary clinical finish is missing. It was here, last season, that Dalian Atkinson scored his spectacular 'Goal of the Season'.

This time, according to Bryon Butler in the Daily Telegraph, he 'billowed one chance over the bar, dragged another wide and volleyed a third into the upper executive tier of gin and tonics at the supermarket end of Selhurst Park'.

It is left to Steve Staunton to thread in an 82nd minute corner for what seemed a likely winner.

Unfortunately for Villa one key element remains in the shape of the rugged physical battle which had been constantly fought out between penalty area warriors John Fashanu, Shaun Teale and Paul McGrath.

Bumps and bruises have been dispensed in full measure. "I've got a sore ear," said Teale. "And I'm sure Fash has got a sore eye. When he hits you he says: 'sorry, baby'."

Not a sincere sentiment, one imagines, as Fash the Bash ensures that Villa's second lead survives only three minutes. The Wimbledon hard man meets a cross by climbing higher than Teale who just gets a touch on the ball, but Fashanu's looping header evades Spink.

Ron Atkinson is not in the mood to speak to the press afterwards. The lead has been allowed to slip twice, good chances have been created and wasted, two points which were there for the taking have gone.

Well done Steve - Villa take the lead for the second time with just eight minutes left.

Monday 23rd August 1993 • Villa Park • 8.00pm

ASTON VILLA 1 MANCHESTER UNITED 2

Half-time 1-1 • *Attendance* 39,624

Referee David Elleray (Middlesex)

Linesmen J. McGRATH and P.M. ROBERTS

Claret Shirts with Blue Stripes, White Shorts		Goals	Black Shirts, Black Shorts		Goals
1	Nigel SPINK		1	Peter SCHMEICHEL	
2	Earl BARRETT		2	Paul PARKER	
5	Paul McGRATH		4	Steve BRUCE	
4	Shaun TEALE		6	Gary PALLISTER	
23	Bryan SMALL		3	Denis IRWIN	
7	Ray HOUGHTON ‡		14	Andrei KANCHELSKIS ❏	
6	Kevin RICHARDSON		8	Paul INCE	
8	Garry PARKER ❏		16	Roy KEANE	
3	Steve STAUNTON ❏ †		5	Lee SHARPE	17, 74
9	Dean SAUNDERS		11	Ryan GIGGS	
10	Dalian ATKINSON	44	10	Mark HUGHES	
	Substitutes			*Substitutes*	
13	Mark BOSNICH		13	Les SEALEY	
12	Steve FROGGATT †78		9	Brian McCLAIR	
22	Guy WHITTINGHAM ‡80		18	Darren FERGUSON	

BEFORE		P	W	D	L	F	A	pts	AFTER		P	W	D	L	F	A	pts
3	United	3	2	1	0	6	1	7	1	United	4	3	1	0	8	2	10
10	Villa	3	1	2	0	6	3	5	10	Villa	4	1	2	1	7	5	5

The meeting of last season's top two sees United gain revenge for their two Villa Park defeats in 92/93... Guy Whittingham makes his Premier League debut... The game is shown live on Sky Sports... Les Sealey makes his first return to Villa Park since rejoining United on a free transfer.

A match of the highest quality

The biggest game of the season, anywhere in the country so far, packs Villa Park to capacity despite the presence of Sky cameras for live transmission.

Villa Park is the only place to be. And two hours before kick-off, and more, the streets around the ground are filling up fast. The reigning champions versus the runners-up is not a fixture to be missed by the true enthusiast and the atmosphere produced by nearly 40,000 fans with one common aim is, to use Ron Atkinson's word 'ELECTRIC'.

Villa are still without the injured Andy Townsend and Tony Daley while United have neither Eric Cantona, who was on World Cup duty for France the previous day, nor suspended Bryan Robson.

When United emerge they look menacing, indeed, in their all-black strip and this impression merely deepens as the action starts. Unmistakeably the champions are better than ever enhanced by the arrival of Roy Keane from Forest in midfield alongside Paul Ince.

The passing football of both sides is first-class and is played at awesome pace, though United have that extra dimension in sheer physical presence and supreme confidence in all they do.

In 18 minutes Villa are a goal down and though it could have been prevented no-one can complain. Ince exchanges passes with Ryan Giggs who is up front alongside Mark Hughes.

The slender, profoundly talented young Welshman shows the 'feel' of a genuine artist as he touches the ball forward to perfection for Ince running on. Shaun Teale goes into a frantic tackle in front of goal, the ball deflects out to the United left, Earl Barrett looks a shade casual and unaware of Lee Sharpe, who is on his blind side and living up to his surname, and United are one up.

Before that Peter Schmeichel had saved from a Dalian Atkinson header when Dean Saunders had gone for the same ball and unintentionally got in the way.

The Villa crowd's reaction to United's lead is to turn up the volume to deafening proportions and as half-time beckons it is as though they will the equaliser.

Atkinson gets possession down the left and with Paul Parker momentarily adrift swerves forward and inward before unleashing one of his stunners. Schmeichel is crouched a yard or two from his right hand post in readiness but the Dalian blast is so powerfully accurate that the 'keeper can only get a token touch as the thunderously-struck ball finds its narrow target.

With adrenalin flowing freely after going in at 1-1 Villa dominate the start of the second half with some terrific football to embellish a match of the very highest quality.

Deano looks to have claimed the lead with a left-footed volley but Schmeichel leaps to claw it for a corner. From the flag kick Kevin Richardson leaves the Dane in statuesque relief as his drive thunders against an upright.

Giggs beats Nigel Spink in similar fashion at the other end and also strikes the woodwork but then, calamity for Villa. With the industrious 'feed' man Richardson temporarily down injured, Ince strikes a long, snaking forward pass which ought to be cut out.

Instead it pierces midfield where Richardson might otherwise have been, beats a back four caught square and static and Sharpe is allowed to run through and claim the winner.

"One of the best games since I've been at the club," said United's Alex Ferguson. "The best United display I can recall," said Ron Atkinson.

"We had our money's worth. And the better team won," admitted supporters, most of whom felt that, perhaps, they had just seen the 1993-94 champions in action.

Saturday 28th August 1993 • Villa Park • 3.00pm

ASTON VILLA 1 TOTTENHAM HOTSPUR 0

Half-time 0-0 • *Attendance* 32,498

Referee Keith COOPER (Pontypridd)

Linesmen R.E. BUDDEN and D.C. RICHARDS

Claret Shirts with Blue Stripes, White Shorts	Goals	White Shirts, Navy Blue Shorts	Goals
1 Nigel SPINK		1 Erik THORSTVEDT	
2 Earl BARRETT		2 Dean AUSTIN	
5 Paul McGRATH		5 Colin CALDERWOOD	
4 Shaun TEALE		6 Gary MABBUTT	
3 Steve STAUNTON ❑	71 pen	23 Sol CAMPBELL	
7 Ray HOUGHTON		4 Vinny SAMWAYS	
6 Kevin RICHARDSON		14 Steve SEDGLEY	
8 Garry PARKER		12 Jason DOZZELL	
11 Tony DALEY †		15 David HOWELLS †	
9 Dean SAUNDERS		8 Gordon DURIE	
10 Dalian ATKINSON		10 Teddy SHERINGHAM ❑	
Substitutes		*Substitutes*	
13 Mark BOSNICH		12 Ian WALKER	
22 Guy WHITTINGHAM †81		20 Darren CASKEY †58 ‡	
17 Neil COX		9 Darren ANDERTON ‡69	

BEFORE		P	W	D	L	F	A	pts	AFTER		P	W	D	L	F	A	pts
7	Tottenham	4	3	0	1	4	2	9	9	Tottenham	5	3	0	2	4	3	9
11	Villa	4	1	2	1	7	5	5	10	Villa	5	2	2	1	8	5	8

FACTFILE

A rare sight in the Premiership since the introduction of squad numbers as Villa field numbers 1 to 11... Number 3 Steve Staunton scores his third goal of the season... The last three Villa Park meetings between these sides had ended goalless... Mark Bosnich makes his 50th appearance for the club.

Stan's the man for Villa

Both of the Premier League fixtures with Spurs last season proved a contradiction in that, for all the attacking football served up, they provided 180-minutes without goals.

A continuation of that particular trend would not go down too well with home supporters on the heels of an exciting display against Manchester United which had brought only defeat.

The pre-match news is only half good... Tony Daley is fit again after his hamstring injury but Andy Townsend is still missing with a similar problem.

Spurs have won 2-1 at Liverpool in midweek, both goals coming from Teddy Sheringham, one of them from the penalty spot.

On the eve of the game Ron Atkinson has taken the unusual step, for him, of singling out part of his team for a public roasting. The manager's verbal attack is aimed straight at the back four for having allowed United the luxury of winning with goals that were virtually gifts.

It was not just the United defeat Atkinson had in mind when he talked of defensive lapses. The lead had twice been surrendered to Wimbledon in similar fashion.

Quickly it becomes apparent that this is not going to be a classic though there is a fair smattering of good passing football from both teams. Equally, though, it is clear that soft goals are less likely to be conceded.

There are few openings for either side and shots on target are a rarity, a fact which is to be highlighted by John Motson on BBC Match of the Day later.

England boss Graham Taylor, watching from the stand in the final stages of his squad selection for the World Cup qualifier against Poland at Wembley in ten days time, sees an accomplished display from Earl Barrett who is subsequently named.

Nigel Spink has been disturbed only once, when he has to dive in spectacular fashion to block a Steve Sedgley header which deflects off Paul McGrath. Erik Thorstvedt has rather more to contend with including a header from Dean Saunders which he keeps out with an acrobatic bound.

The winner arrives in the 72nd minute as in-form Kevin Richardson cruises onto a perfectly-placed forward chip by Parker. Richardson is about to shoot from a good position when his legs are scythed away by defender Dean Austin. Ray Houghton puts the loose ball in the net but the referee has already awarded a penalty.

This is the moment Villa have increasingly needed as their escalating second-half superiority threatens to be wasted. Steve 'Stan' Staunton takes on the responsibility of making it pay, which he does with a firmly-struck drive low to Thorstvedt's left for his third goal of the season.

Scorer Staunton

Guy Whittingham gets just nine minutes of action this time, as substitute for Daley, again not enough time to seriously threaten the security of Saunders or Dalian Atkinson. He does, however, manage to register his first on-target shot in Villa colours, a long-range effort which causes the Spurs 'keeper to concede a corner.

Overall, a moderate performance by Villa which just deserves the welcome victory but more than acceptable after playing far better but dropping those valuable, early points.

Tuesday 31st August 1993 • Goodison Park • 7.30pm

EVERTON 0 ASTON VILLA 1

Half-time 0-1 • Attendance 24,022

Referee Allan GUNN (Sussex)

Linesmen I. BLANCHARD and A. STREETS

Blue Shirts, White Shorts		Goals	Green, Black and Red Striped Shirts, Black Shorts		Goals
1	Neville SOUTHALL		1	Nigel SPINK	
10	Barry HORNE		2	Earl BARRETT ❏	
2	Matthew JACKSON		5	Paul McGRATH	
6	Gary ABLETT		4	Shaun TEALE	
3	Andy HINCHCLIFFE		3	Steve STAUNTON	
8	Graham STUART †		6	Kevin RICHARDSON	
7	Mark WARD		15	Gordon COWANS	
14	John EBBRELL		14	Andy TOWNSEND	
11	Peter BEAGRIE		9	Dean SAUNDERS †	
9	Tony COTTEE		10	Dalian ATKINSON	
15	Paul RIDEOUT ‡		22	Guy WHITTINGHAM	32'
	Substitutes			*Substitutes*	
13	Jason KEARTON		13	Mark BOSNICH	
16	Predrag RADOSAVLJEVIC †55		17	Neil COX †86	
19	Stuart BARLOW ‡82		8	Garry PARKER	

BEFORE		P	W	D	L	F	A	pts	AFTER		P	W	D	L	F	A	pts
8	Everton	5	3	0	2	7	5	9	4	Villa	6	3	2	1	9	5	11
10	Villa	5	2	2	1	8	5	8	8	Everton	6	3	0	3	7	6	9

FACTFILE

Guy Whittingham scores the winner on his first 'start'... Tony Daley is transfer-listed on the day of match... Manager wields the axe to re-shape the midfield and strike force... Villa wear the new green and black away kit for the first time in a competitive match and the referee is forced to change his colours mid-match.

Debut Guy hits the winner

The trip to Goodison Park inevitably revives memories of a year earlier when Villa were far the better footballing side yet lost 1-0 to a late Mo Johnston goal. A chance to square the account...

Again Everton have started the season on a high note before faltering a shade, so this time Villa are fancied for the first away win of the season. Before the game it emerges that Tony Daley, left out of the team in a re-shuffle after being withdrawn on Saturday, has requested a move.

Ron Atkinson won't stand in his way. But the price will be around £2m. "I know the prices I get asked when we go in for players," stresses the Villa manager. "We had to pay Chelsea £2.1m for Andy Townsend and he's 30. We shall want something similar for Daley. We're certainly not going to give him away."

Despite Saturday's deserved victory over Spurs changes are made, the most notable being the inclusion of Guy Whittingham for his first 'start' since his £1.1m signing from Portsmouth.

Andy Townsend is also back after injury while Gordon Cowans is recalled in a changed formation from 4-4-2 to 4-3-3 with Whittingham, Dean Saunders and Dalian Atkinson looking a formidable strike force.

Ex-soldier Whittingham, released from the bench at last, is gunning to prove that he can reproduce his 47-goal First Division form of last season in the higher grade.

In little more than half-an-hour he offers an encouraging

Winner Whittingham

clue that, perhaps, he can do just that. Moving powerfully onto a loose ball he goes past two defenders and, as Neville Southall advances, he steers the ball past him from near the 18-yard line.

The goal has all the single-minded stamp of the genuine article, a player whose one consuming purpose is to constantly build on his strike rate.

But Villa are not getting things all their own way in a fairly even game. Winger Peter Beagrie, a trickster who can deceive the best of defenders, cuts out Earl Barrett to fire a drive which rebounds off the inside of Nigel Spink's far post.

Almost immediately Villa escape again when Tony Cottee goes around Spink yet contrives to shoot wide when needing only to beat Steve Staunton covering the 'keeper on the goalline.

This unsuccessful double Everton assault on the Villa goal came just before Cowans' long delivery led to the first score on Whittingham's Villa account.

Judging by the coldly clinical way he takes that chance No.1 when it arrives there will be many more. "I didn't see Southall until the last moment. Then I just stuck my foot out and poked the ball past him," Whittingham tells the media afterwards. "It was important for me to get going at this level. It has been frustrating waiting but I knew it would be a challenge."

The reversal is a body blow to Everton who must have fancied themselves to get ahead themselves but they rarely threaten to get back on terms.

Ex-Villa man Paul Rideout tests Spink but as the excitement builds Villa hold on comfortably. Can it be that those defensive errors of the opening games have been permanently eradicated?

Saturday 11th September 1993 • Villa Park • 3.00pm

ASTON VILLA 0 COVENTRY CITY 0

Half-time 0-0 • Attendance 31,181

Referee Martin BODENHAM (Looe)
Linesmen R.H. ANDREWS and J. LEECH

Claret Shirts with Blue Stripes, White Shorts	Goals	Sky Blue Shirts, Sky Blue Shorts	Goals
1 Nigel SPINK		1 Steve OGRIZOVIC	
2 Earl BARRETT		32 Lloyd McGRATH	
5 Paul McGRATH		4 Peter ATHERTON	
4 Shaun TEALE		20 Phil BABB	
3 Steve STAUNTON		3 Steve MORGAN	
6 Kevin RICHARDSON		17 Roy WEGERLE ‡	
14 Andy TOWNSEND		16 Willie BOLAND	
15 Gordon COWANS		6 David RENNIE	
9 Dean SAUNDERS		12 Peter NDLOVU	
10 Dalian ATKINSON		7 John WILLIAMS †	
22 Guy WHITTINGHAM †		10 Mick QUINN	
Substitutes		*Substitutes*	
13 Mark BOSNICH		13 Martin DAVIES	
7 Ray HOUGHTON †75		15 Paul WILLIAMS †65	
17 Neil COX		19 Tony SHERIDAN ‡72	

BEFORE		P	W	D	L	F	A	pts	AFTER		P	W	D	L	F	A	pts
4	Coventry	6	3	3	0	11	4	12	4	Coventry	7	3	4	0	11	4	13
6	Villa	6	3	2	1	9	5	11	5	Villa	7	3	3	1	9	5	12

FACTFILE

Villa have now gone 324 goalless minutes against Coventry... The Sky Blues have still never won at Villa Park... Guy Whittingham makes his full home debut ... Steve Staunton, Andy Townsend, Ray Houghton and Dean Saunders return from mid-week World Cup action with Ireland and Wales.

It's a game of frustration

Due to the weekend and mid-week off to make way for World Cup qualifers there has been an eleven-day break from the action and the 1-0 win at Everton in the previous game seems a long way back.

Not too far, however, for Ron Atkinson to recall that Guy Whittingham made his full debut and scored the winner in a change of format to 4-3-3.

So with Steve Froggatt and Dwight Yorke both still injured the team remains unchanged though, pre-match, the manager makes it clear that he intends using his improved squad to give players a rest and 'keep them fresher'.

The visit of Coventry, who have started the season well and are above Villa in the league has prompted unhappy recollections of last season when Sky Blues restricted Villa to one point out of six.

There is a degree of unspoken anxiety in the Villa camp and maybe an unconscious awareness that the first journey into Europe lies ahead.

Supporters of the two clubs ringing in to the Friday local radio phone-ins have made much of the fact that Coventry have never won at Villa Park and that, equally, Villa have been finding Coventry difficult to score against.

Amazingly, the 90 minutes confirms that scenario right down to its 0-0 scoreline in a disappointing game for

Gordon Cowans

a large crowd which has, again, gone over the 30,000 mark.

Coventry concentrate on a largely defensive display with players packed into their own half in large numbers. Despite this Villa's superior football creates several scoring chances.

Whittingham is operating from the left side of the front three while Dean Saunders is as busy as ever in a more free-running role.

The Welsh cap causes problems galore in front of the Sky Blue goal but once again his finishing is neither precise nor clinical.

When the final whistle arrives Deano can reflect on four headers which have failed to find the mark. A scoring record which raced to 15 in his first 26 appearances after he moved in from Anfield has tailed off, sadly, to only three in 25 since December.

Sheer frustration is the name of the game since Saunders has played extremely well otherwise in finding ways past the solid defensive pairing of Peter Atherton and Phil Babb.

Dalian Atkinson also has an unproductive 90 minutes, wasting a couple of good chances as Coventry defend their record as one of only two unbeaten teams in the Premiership.

The 'plus' side of the two dropped home points is that Coventry are rarely allowed to threaten a tight defence on the break and are never going to win it, while Andy Townsend and Gordon Cowans produce some splendid midfield play.

Whittingham has a quiet first home start and is withdrawn in the second half in order to allow Ray Houghton to attempt to supply greater width.

"I could have played in our goal in the second half," says Ron Atkinson though he admits that Saunders' goal drought has become a problem. With away goals required in Bratislava four days hence the manager must have team changes on his mind.

Wednesday 15th September 1993 • Tehelné Pole • 2.45pm (GMT)

SLOVAN BRATISLAVA 0 ASTON VILLA 0

Half-time 0-0 • Attendance 10,886

Referee Marcello NICCI

Linesmen D. NICOLETTI and A. RANGHETTI

Officials from Italy

Blue and White Patterned Shirts, Blue Shorts	Goals	Claret Shirts with Blue Stripes, White Shorts	Goals
1 Alexander VENCEL		1 Nigel SPINK	
2 Tomas STUPALA		2 Earl BARRETT	
3 Marian ZEMAN		5 Paul McGRATH	
4 Ondrej KRISTOFIK		4 Shaun TEALE	
5 Vladimir KINDER		3 Steve STAUNTON	
6 Dusan TITTEL		7 Ray HOUGHTON	
7 Robert TOMASHEK		6 Kevin RICHARDSON	
8 Ludovit LANCZ †		8 Gordon COWANS	
9 Stefan MAIXNER		11 Andy TOWNSEND	
10 Fabio NIGRO		9 Dean SAUNDERS	
11 Jaroslav TIMKO ‡		10 Dalian ATKINSON	
Substitutes		*Substitutes*	
Juraj KAKAS (Gk)		13 Michael OAKES (Gk)	
Pavol GOSTIC ‡45		12 Garry PARKER	
Ladislav PECKO †59		14 Tony DALEY	
Miroslav CHVILA		15 Guy WHITTINGHAM	
Erik CHYTIL		16 Neil COX	

FACTFILE

Villa open their seventh European campaign, Slovan their 16th... Slovan are the only Czechoslovakian club to have won a European trophy, having defeated Barcelona in the 1969 Cup-winners' Cup final... Slovan qualified by virtue of finishing in third place in last season's Czechoslovakian League, but now play in the newly formed Slovakian League... All but Nigel Spink, Paul McGrath and Gordon Cowans make their Euro debuts for Villa... The game is 'live' on ITV.

Spink dents Slovan's spirits

The return to European conflict takes Villa to Bratislava, capital of the new Republic of Slovakia, former 'home' of ex-Villa manager Jozef Venglos.

Ron Atkinson decides to spend the minimum time possible on the trip, flying his team out on a chartered air bus, loaded with fans, on Tuesday mid-day and returning them straight after the match, and home for supper.

Housed in a large, modern hotel on the banks of the River Danube, the team take the whole thing in a most matter-of-fact way despite the disappointment of Saturday's disappointing result, with no signs of pressure.

Guy Whittingham returns to the subs bench and Andy Townsend is played on the left side of midfield with Ray Houghton returning on the other side.

The climate on the day is that of a fresh Spring afternoon back home, with warm sunshine and fleecy clouds. Slovan's wide-open Brick Fields stadium is sparsely populated due, Venglos believes, to the club's decision to increase the price of tickets from the equivalent of less than a pound to between three pounds and five pounds, the top price being roughly a day's pay for the average worker.

Villa, perhaps are a shade too 'laid back' and in the opening ten minutes they could be two goals down as Slovan open brightly. In only the second minute Ondrej Kristofik slices wide of a yawning target after being allowed a clear unchallenged shot.

Five minutes later it is Stefan Maixner's turn and Villa are left relieved that Slovan have sold their star turn, Peter Dubrovsky, to Real Madrid, as another excellent chance is squandered.

Then, as Slovan remain in control with some thrustful football, Nigel Spink has to dive hur-

riedly to deny a Vladimir Kinder long shot. This proves the turning point as Slovan become discouraged and less assertive while Villa get their act together.

Mid-way through the half Dalian Atkinson is released encouragingly and his pace takes central defenders by surprise. Dalian dallies too long, however, veers out to the right, passes too late and too far right for Dean Saunders who is left with far too narrow an angle.

But the moment which might have left Villa with a useful lead and an away goal to take back to Villa Park arrives after 55 minutes.

Atkinson is clear again and as goalkeeper Alexander Vencel comes out the Villa forward nicks the ball past him towards an unguarded goal. Total silence descends on the ground as Vencel crashes into Atkinson, off the ball which has passed him, for what looks a one-hundred-percent penalty.

Silence is followed by gasps of disbelief as the Italian referee declines a spot kick. Atkinson's version on the decision later is that the referee would have had to send the 'keeper off for a professional foul to prevent a goal and ducked out of the dual decision.

Now Villa are a trifle discouraged and Slovan, given extra menace up front by the appearance of substitute Ladislav Pecko causing problems down the left of Villa's defence.

Throughout the game Gordon Cowans has distributed passes with precision and persistence but in the closing stages Spink takes over as the star man with three result-saving saves.

"There was a lot of sound performances out there, " said Ron Atkinson. "I thought the experience of our international players showed itself well."

His opposite number, Slovan coach Dusan Galis, apologises to Villa for the 'lack of atmosphere'. He, too, possibly feels that the price increase has been counter-productive.

Back at Villa Park Big Ron will not have to return that 'no atmosphere' apology...

Saturday 18th September 1993 • Portman Road • 3.00pm

IPSWICH TOWN 1 ASTON VILLA 2

Half-time 1-1 • *Attendance* 16,617

Referee Lawrence DILKES (Mossley)
Linesmen G.T. PEARSON and A. SCHNEIDER

Blue Shirts with White Sleeves, White Shorts		Goals	Claret Shirts with Blue Stripes, White Shorts		Goals
1	Craig FORREST		1	Nigel SPINK	
2	Mick STOCKWELL		2	Earl BARRETT	
3	Neil THOMPSON		5	Paul McGRATH	
15	Phil WHELAN		4	Shaun TEALE	
5	John WARK		3	Steve STAUNTON	
6	David LINIGHAN		6	Kevin RICHARDSON	
7	Geraint WILLIAMS		15	Gordon COWANS	
18	Steve PALMER †		14	Andy TOWNSEND	55
4	Paul MASON ‡		9	Dean SAUNDERS	19
10	Ian MARSHALL	9	10	Dalian ATKINSON ‡	
11	Chris KIWOMYA		22	Guy WHITTINGHAM †	
	Substitutes			*Substitutes*	
13	Clive BAKER		13	Mark BOSNICH	
14	Steve WHITTON †45		11	Tony DALEY †61	
9	Bontcho GUENTCHEV ‡79		7	Ray HOUGHTON ‡87	

BEFORE		P	W	D	L	F	A	pts	AFTER		P	W	D	L	F	A	pts
6	Villa	7	3	3	1	9	5	12	3	Villa	8	4	3	1	11	6	15
11	Ipswich	7	3	2	2	7	7	11	12	Ipswich	7	3	2	3	8	9	11

FACTFILE

Dean Saunders is back in scoring business after seven games without a goal... Ian Marshall ends Villa's run of 385 minutes without conceding a goal... Andy Townsend scores his first competitive goal for Villa... On-offer Tony Daley returns as substitute.

Handy Andy stuns Ipswich

Ron Atkinson's policy of making team adjustments to keep players fresh continues as Guy Whittingham comes in for Ray Houghton.

However, it is difficult to escape the feeling that the best blend of players has not yet emerged and that team-work has reached only about eighty-percent its optimum capability.

Villa go into the game with a run of clean sheets behind them, which they look capable of preserving against a struggling team, and an attacking policy which promises to produce an early lead.

Football is never quite that predictable, however, and it is the home team who take the lead, after only nine minutes, albeit against the shape of the game.

Striker Ian Marshall is sent on a forward run, Nigel Spink advances to block his first attempt but has no chance when the Ipswich man gets a second bite.

It is, however, a misleading and precarious lead for Ipswich who hold on only briefly. Ten minutes on they are split asunder by a magnificent through ball from Steve Staunton, rapidly emerging as the man of the match.

That pass is to mark the end of Dean Saunders' goal drought. As it beats the defence the Welsh cap controls the ball confidently and rams his shot into the net.

At last! Deano is back in scoring action...

The second half sees Villa at something approaching their best and, after the game, Ipswich manager Mick McGiven confesses that his players were in awe at the quality unfolded before them.

Andy Townsend ought to have made it 2-1 almost as soon as the second half starts but he makes amends for his miss ten minutes later. And how.

Moving in powerfully from the right he launches a 30-yard shot which curves in flight and hits the far corner of the net, an unstoppable blast fit to settle any game.

"We don't feel we have been playing as well as we can," says manager Atkinson as his team move into a challenging third place behind Manchester United and Arsenal.

"The front three haven't gelled yet," he confesses.

In fact, the three-striker formula has been disturbed again as Whittingham, with a slight breathing ailment, is replaced by Tony Daley in little more than an hour.

Things are now taking shape steadily. Birmingham City, Villa's next opponents, please note.

Andy Townsend's first league goal for the club was a spectacular winner

Tuesday 21st September 1993 • St. Andrew's • 7.45pm

BIRMINGHAM CITY 0 ASTON VILLA 1

Half-time 0-0 • Attendance 27,815

Referee Keren BARRETT (Coventry)

Linesmen A. BUTLER and P. HARDING

Blue Shirts, White Shorts		Goals	Claret Shirts with Blue Stripes, Black Shorts		Goals
1	Kevin MILLER		1	Nigel SPINK †	
2	Scott HILEY		2	Earl BARRETT	
5	Richard DRYDEN		4	Shaun TEALE	
15	Chris WHYTE		5	Paul McGRATH	
3	John FRAIN		3	Steve STAUNTON	
28	Carl SHUTT		6	Kevin RICHARDSON	83
4	George PARRIS		15	Gordon COWANS	
11	Dave SMITH		14	Andy TOWNSEND	
18	Louie DONOWA		9	Dean SAUNDERS	
9	Andy SAVILLE		10	Dalian ATKINSON	
12	Paul PESCHISOLIDO †		22	Guy WHITTINGHAM	
	Substitutes			*Substitutes*	
13	Richard STEADMAN		13	Mark BOSNICH †30	
10	Ted McMINN †86		7	Ray HOUGHTON	
8	Paul TAIT		8	Garry PARKER	

Mark Bosnich saves a penalty within six minutes of replacing the injured Nigel Spink - "I saw Frain was left footed and decided to dive to my left. You could call it a bit of a detective's hunch!"... All but Spink and Gordon Cowans in the Villa side are playing in their first Birmingham 'derby'... The game is the fifth between Villa and Blues in the League Cup. The first two were in the 1963 final when Blues won 3-1 at St Andrew's and drew 0-0 at Villa Park. The last two were in the second round five years ago when Villa won 2-0 away and 5-0 at home to complete an impressive aggregate scoreline.

FACTFILE

Bozzie gives Frain the blues

New generations of fans who have never experienced the old-style Brum derby welcome this match with relish as St Andrew's is packed to the limits imposed by the police.

Villa arrive at the fixture in a calm and confident mood having, in the last week, drawn 0-0 in Bratislava in the UEFA Cup and won at Ipswich in the Premiership. Blues' most recent form has not been too impressive in the shape of a home draw with Grimsby Town.

Atkinson retains his 'three-strikers' formation with Guy Whittingham keeping his place alongside Dean Saunders and Dalian Atkinson.

A massive police operation is mounted to ensure law and order is preserved and this proves effective in a trouble-free derby on and off the field. There are some 40 arrests but these are largely for drink-related offences outside the ground and in the City.

The first half, although goalless, is an exciting affair with Villa getting marginally the better chances and Blues acquitting themselves with honours. The opposition's new danger man, Paul Peschisolido, finds the higher-grade

Guy Whittingham pressures Scott Hiley

central defensive work of Paul McGrath and Shaun Teale more difficult to break down than the average First Division back line. He is troublesome enough, however, for McGrath to be booked for an illegal challenge on him.

Both sides play good passing football and it leads to first Kevin Richardson and then Andy Townsend striking shots against the City woodwork. However the big moment of the first half comes in the 36th minute when Atkinson, chasing back, fells Andy Saville in front of goal. TV replays show it to be a fair penalty decision and, afterwards, Atkinson confirms the referee's judgment.

Villa have just seen Nigel Spink depart injured to be replaced by Mark Bosnich and the Australian, by way of signing in, moves smartly to save the spot kick struck to close too him and at a convenient height by Brummie John Frain. Blues are declined two further penalty appeals. One of them when Paul McGrath handles to keep the ball away from David Smith, is regarded as a definite offence by Ron Atkinson who declares: "I thought Macca had taken up Gaelic football...!"

The second half is less entertaining than the first though Villa fans are not complaining about the game's finale. Eight minutes from time Steve Staunton hurls a long curving pass which, at last, fully deceives the solid central defence of Chris Whyte and Richard Dryden.

Richardson, influential throughout, glides in unnoticed to meet the ball at just the right moment and touch it delicately past the approaching Kevin Miller.

On Central TV Jimmy Greaves expresses the view that Villa's front three are too similar in that all three are forward runners while none of them 'hold the ball up' when they receive it, in order to 'feed' the other two.

Again it seems clear that Villa are getting favourable results without achieving maximum potential from their strikers. "It's not over yet..." stresses a 'gutted' Blues boss, Terry Cooper.

Saturday 25th September 1993 • Boundary Park • 3.00pm

OLDHAM ATHLETIC 1 ASTON VILLA 1

Half-time 1-0 • *Attendance* 12,836

Referee Howard KING (Merthyr Tydfil)
(replaced by P. Rejer of Tipton at half-time)
Linesmen E.G. HANNAH and P. REJER
(Reserve official N.Doherty took over as linesman in second half)

Blue Shirts, White Shorts	Goals	Claret Shirts with Blue Stripes, White Shorts	Goals
13 Jon HALLWORTH		13 Mark BOSNICH	
2 Craig FLEMING		17 Neil COX	
5 Richard JOBSON		4 Shaun TEALE ❏	
6 Steve REDMOND		5 Paul McGRATH ❏	
15 Andy BARLOW		3 Steve STAUNTON	
11 Paul BERNARD		7 Ray HOUGHTON	
12 Neil ADAMS ‡		6 Kevin RICHARDSON	
10 Mike MILLIGAN		15 Gordon COWANS	
7 Gunnar HALLE ❏	14	14 Andy TOWNSEND ❏	
8 Andy RITCHIE †		9 Dean SAUNDERS	51
14 Graeme SHARP		22 Guy WHITTINGHAM	
Substitutes		*Substitutes*	
1 Paul GERRARD		30 Michael OAKES	
19 Roger PALMER †66		19 Stefan BEINLICH	
17 Darren BECKFORD ‡66		16 Ugo EHIOGU	

BEFORE		P	W	D	L	F	A	pts	AFTER		P	W	D	L	F	A	pts
3	Villa	8	4	3	1	11	6	15	3	Villa	9	4	4	1	12	7	16
20	Oldham	8	1	2	5	5	15	5	20	Oldham	9	1	3	5	6	16	6

FACTFILE

Injuries and illness force Nigel Spink, Earl Barrett and Dalian Atkinson to miss their first games of the season, Mark Bosnich and Neil Cox start their first, Stefan Beinlich and Ugo Ehiogu are in the 14 for the first time in 93/94... Paul McGrath makes his 200th appearance for Villa in league and cups.

Red faces in the commentary box

Being confronted by the the fourth successive away game, and their second on consecutive Saturdays, further demonstrates how the fixture pattern has changed from the former predictable pattern.

Mark Bosnich remains in goal, having replaced the injured Nigel Spink as substitute in the win at St Andrew's but there are two enforced changes. Neil Cox replaces Earl Barrett, who has an ankle injury, while Dalian Atkinson is down with a heavy cold. Manager Ron Atkinson decides on a change of pattern, with Ray Houghton returning to a four-man midfield behind Dean Saunders and Guy Whittingham.

As always Villa's midfield work is good to watch and gives hope of chances being offered to the front men but it is Oldham who dictate the game's destiny by forcing a 15th minute lead. Villa lose possession to Mike Milligan near the half-way line, and Graeme Sharp finds space to act as the link man for Norwegian cap Gunnar Halle to rifle his shot wide of Bosnich.

From then on Villa dominate much of the play, prise open Oldham's foot-of-the-table defence and make enough openings to take a clear lead.

Dean Saunders is his familiar mixture of mobile and enterprising forward play and occasional frustrating shortage of accuracy with his finishing.

Two possible equalisers are wasted before, for a fleeting moment, it seems that Guy Whittingham has squared it. In the 36th minute he firmly heads home a centre for Steve Staunton and as he ends up in the arms of celebrating fans

behind the goal he is momentarily unaware that a linesman's flag has ruled it 'off-side'.

Whittingham and the fans are not the only ones who miss the linesman's flag and the ref's 'no goal' decision. The XTRA AM commentators broadcasting live from the press box give it out to the masses back home that Villa are now 1-1, and it's several minutes before the red-faced duo inform listeners of the bad news.

So, the nagging worry about a damaging defeat remains until the 52nd minute when Deano gets a richly-deserved reward for his tireless efforts.

A throw-in by Kevin Richardson is collected by Houghton who exchanges passes with Saunders to pierce the static back four. Houghton smartly delivers a well-flighted pass to the far post for the Welsh international to equalise with a diving header.

The final half-hour becomes a niggly affair as Oldham doggedly defend their point and Villa go vainly in search of a win. There are cautions for Shaun Teale, Andy Townsend and Paul McGrath from substitute referee Paul Rejer who replaced Howard King, taken ill at half-time.

Certainly not a satisfying display by Villa and undoubtedly a case of two points lost rather than one gained. Ron Atkinson, untypically, misses the usual post-match press conference.

His deepest thoughts were perhaps better left unspoken, though a run of four consecutive away games in three competitions, without defeat, completed a reasonable ten-day period.

Saunders lingered just long enough after the game to express an opinion that was no doubt in his boss's mind, namely that, to win the title, teams like Oldham have to be left for dead.

Neil Cox

Wednesday 29th September 1993 • Villa Park • 7.45pm

ASTON VILLA 2 SLOVAN BRATISLAVA 1

Aggregate 2-1 • Half-time 2-0 • Attendance 24,461

Referee Peter MIKKELSEN

Linesmen C.J. CHRISTENSEN and J.P. STAERK

Officials from Denmark

Claret Shirts with Blue Stripes, White Shorts		Goals	Blue and White Patterned Shirts, Blue Shorts		Goals
1	Nigel SPINK		1	Alexander VENCEL	
2	Neil COX		2	Tomas STUPALA	
5	Paul McGRATH		3	Marian ZEMAN	
4	Shaun TEALE		4	Ondrej KRISTOFIK †	
3	Steve STAUNTON		5	Vladimir KINDER	
7	Gordon COWANS		6	Dusan TITTEL	86
6	Kevin RICHARDSON		7	Ladislav PECKO	
8	Andy TOWNSEND	21	8	Robert TOMASHEK	
11	Guy WHITTINGHAM		9	Miroslav CHVILA	
9	Dean SAUNDERS		10	Fabio NIGRO ❏	
10	Dalian ATKINSON	14	11	Jaroslav TIMKO ‡	
Substitutes			*Substitutes*		
13	Michael OAKES (Gk)			Juraj KAKAS (Gk)	
12	Ray HOUGHTON			Pavol GOSTIC ‡45	
14	Ugo EHIOGU			Erik CHYTIL	
15	Tony DALEY			Ludovit LANCZ †28	
16	Bryan SMALL			Frantisek KLINOVSKY	

FACTFILE

*Neil Cox and Guy Whittingham make their European debuts...
Ron Atkinson retains unbeaten home record in Europe... Villa
stretch unbeaten league and cup record, home and away, to eight
games... Second round draw pairs Villa with Spanish club
Deportivo La Coruña.*

Neil Cox - first taste of European action

Over the first European hurdle

No-one at Villa Park under-estimates the difficulty against the Slovakian team, despite the 0-0 draw in Bratislava. The tie is still balanced on a knife-edge, with even a 1-1 draw being fatal since the Slovaks would go through on the strength of an away goal.

There is also the danger of extra time and penalties via a 0-0 scoreline but Ron Atkinson has resisted any pre-match penalty practice on the grounds that slotting them in on the training ground bears no comparison to the tension of the real thing.

His pre-match message to the players is to get it over without such a danger. "You had to work hard last season to earn this European place," he tells them. "Now make sure we stay there."

Nigel Spink passes a fitness test to avoid Mark Bosnich taking up one of the three 'non-national' places but Earl Barrett misses the fitness deadline. Dalian Atkinson returns after missing the 1-1 draw at Oldham last Saturday and Ray Houghton reverts to substitute.

All the early signs are good when the action gets underway. Although Bratislava's technique and control is good they put Villa under only token pressure and after just 21 minutes a safe-looking 2-0 home lead has been set up. Friday's second round draw looms invitingly and the crowd relax in anticipation of more goals before half time.

Visiting goalkeeper, Vencel, looks distinctly ill-at-ease from the start and this is confirmed in the 14th minute. The 'keeper

Euro-debutant Guy Whittingham in action

fails to cut out Neil Cox's cross from the right, Andy Townsend heads it on towards Guy Whittingham whose overhead kick is knocked down by Vencel for Dalian Atkinson to volley home.

Another eight minutes and Townsend connects with a left-footed curler from outside the box on Villa's left and Vencel can only get a vain touch of the ball is it goes across him into the far corner.

After that, however, the merit of the performance declines as chances are missed and Villa give the impression of settling for their two-goal advantage.

Also, Vencel's contribution improves in the shape of fine saves from Kevin Richardson and Whittingham who is eagerly searching for the first goal of his career in European competition.

Dean Saunders gives an inspirational display of mobility and enthusiasm up front but lacks the necessary accuracy to push the tie out of Slovan's reach.

But it is Richardson who seems to have the ideal chance when, from a few yards out, he heads an Atkinson centre from the left flank across goal and wide of the far post.

A 3-0 scoreline would have effectively ended the tie. As it is there remains a scary last four minutes for Villa and their supporters.

The excellent libero, Tittel, fires a long shot past Spink, helped by a deflection, and suddenly the few hundred visiting fans, who travelled overland by coach, sniff the chance of a sensational come-back.

Their team is, indeed, lifted by the goal and Villa live dangerously until the relief of the final whistle. "We've come through a difficult task against an experienced, quality side in Europe," said a relieved Villa boss.

Saturday 2nd October 1993 • Villa Park • 3.00pm

ASTON VILLA 0 NEWCASTLE UNITED 2

Half-time 0-0 • *Attendance* 37,336

Referee Paul DURKIN (Dorset)

Linesmen J.A. ELWIN and M. STOBBART

Claret Shirts with Blue Stripes, White Shorts	Goals	Black and White Striped Shirts, Black Shorts	Goals
1 Nigel SPINK		30 Mike HOOPER	
17 Neil COX		2 Barry VENISON	
4 Shaun TEALE		19 Steve WATSON	
5 Paul McGRATH		5 Kevin SCOTT	
3 Steve STAUNTON		3 John BERESFORD	
6 Kevin RICHARDSON		7 Robert LEE	
15 Gordon COWANS ‡		10 Lee CLARK	
14 Andy TOWNSEND		4 Paul BRACEWELL	
9 Dean SAUNDERS		8 Peter BEARDSLEY	
10 Dalian ATKINSON		9 Andy COLE	80
22 Guy WHITTINGHAM †		21 Malcolm ALLEN	46 pen
Substitutes		*Substitutes*	
13 Mark BOSNICH		1 Pavel SRNICEK	
11 Tony DALEY †55		11 Scott SELLARS	
7 Ray HOUGHTON ‡63		15 Brian KILCLINE	

BEFORE		P	W	D	L	F	A	pts	AFTER		P	W	D	L	F	A	pts
3	Villa	9	4	4	1	12	7	16	6	Newcastle	10	4	4	2	15	10	16
11	Newcastle	9	3	4	2	13	10	13	7	Villa	10	4	4	2	12	9	16

FACTFILE

Villa's first defeat in nine league and cup games... Newcastle extend their unbeaten run to eight league games and record their first win at Villa Park since 1985-86... The Magpies' substitute goalkeeper Pavel Srnicek was in the Banik Ostrava side which came to Villa Park in the UEFA Cup three years ago.

Geordies rise to the occasion

The seventh fixture in 21 days and one which is to prove the season's first major disappointment with a totally unacceptable display and result.

On the eve of the game Ron Atkinson names the squad which beat Slovan Bratislava in midweek but talks of considering introducing 'some fresh legs'.

In the event, with Earl Barrett still unfit, the same line-up starts the game against the newly-promoted Geordies who continue to flourish under Kevin Keegan's managership.

Atkinson describes Keegan as 'the natural successor' to Graham Taylor when the reigning England boss decides to call it a day.

With the multitudes spilling down from the North-east and Villa fans looking for a strengthening of the title challenge Villa Park is virtually full. The stage is set for another Villa spectacular.

Newcastle, spurred on by the major challenge of it all and probably lifted more than Villa by the big atmosphere and sense of occasion look to have the greater appetite.

Peter Beardsley is more influential in midfield than any of the Villa contingent and leading scorer Andy Cole a constant menace.

Villa's line-up, with their trio of strikers in Dean Saunders, Dalian Atkinson and Guy Whittingham, simply doesn't gell, a fact which is obvious to all when a 0-0 half-time arrives.

Newcastle's slick football is quicker and more incisive than Villa's and they ominously increase in confidence.

The Villa manager publicly displays his discontent by pulling Whittingham off ten minutes into the second half to send on Tony Daley in an attempt to introduce more width.

Less than ten minutes after that he pulls off Gordon Cowans to introduce Ray Houghton into what is now effectively a 4-4-2 or 4-2-4 formation.

Now there are 'fresh legs' but no noticeable improvement, Newcastle having taken the lead from a penalty within a minute of the restart.

The spot kick arose when Robert Lee collected a failed clearance by Shaun Teale and was floored by Steve Staunton. Malcolm Allen converted the penalty and Villa rarely look likely to pull one back though Nigel Spink makes several saves.

Ten minutes before the end Beardsley deceives Villa's advancing back-line to release Cole for the second and decisive goal.

Manager Atkinson is unable to conceal his wrath at the poor display and reveals that he had offered any players who felt affected by the heavy fixture programme the chance to stand down for a rest.

Nobody took him up on the opportunity yet there had been a suspicious hint of staleness in the manner of the emphatic defeat.

"We are not going to throw everything away because of one defeat but I saw things I didn't like out there. We were an absolute disgrace, an embarrassment," said Atkinson.

Hot-shot Andy Cole took his tally to eleven goals in eleven games so far this season

Wednesday 6th October 1993 • Villa Park • 7.45pm

ASTON VILLA 1 BIRMINGHAM CITY 0

Aggregate 2-0 • Half-time 0-0 • Attendance 35,856

Referee Gerald ASHBY (Worcester)
Linesmen V.J. REED and M.L. SHORT

Claret Shirts with Blue Stripes, White Shorts		Goals	Yellow Shirts with Blue Stripes, Blue Shorts		Goals
13	Mark BOSNICH		1	Kevin MILLER	
17	Neil COX		2	Scott HILEY †	
4	Shaun TEALE		5	Richard DRYDEN	
5	Paul McGRATH		15	Chris WHYTE	
3	Steve STAUNTON		3	John FRAIN	
6	Kevin RICHARDSON ❑		29	Lyndon HOOPER	
15	Gordon COWANS		8	Paul TAIT ■	
14	Andy TOWNSEND †		11	Dave SMITH	
11	Tony DALEY		18	Louie DONOWA ‡	
9	Dean SAUNDERS	82	6	Paul MARDON	
10	Dalian ATKINSON		28	Carl SHUTT	
	Substitutes			*Substitutes*	
1	Nigel SPINK		13	Richard STEADMAN	
7	Ray HOUGHTON †45		14	Richard SCOTT †48	
22	Guy WHITTINGHAM		20	Paul FENWICK ‡72	

FACTFILE

Lyndon Hooper makes his Blues debut... Andy Townsend is replaced at half-time with a recurrence of his hamstring problem and it keeps the Ireland captain out of the subsequent World Cup qualifier against Spain... Blues have now failed to score in any of their six Villa Park cup ties - against Villa in the FA Cup (0-1), League Cup (0-0, 0-5 & 0-1) and Full Members' Cup (0-6) and against West Bromwich Albion in an FA Cup semi-final (0-2) in 1968.

Kevin Richardson - pushed into the Trinity Road seats by Paul Tait

Deano slides in the winner

Blessed with their one-goal lead from the first leg Villa appear to be runaway favourites for the third round but it proves to be no easy ride.

Blues have been given a faint scent of success by last Saturday's result against Newcastle when Villa were overturned by a team going at them hard. Terry Cooper can't claim to have a line-up to match Kevin Keegan's but he is well capable of winding his men up into a death-or-glory display and that proves to be the case.

Villa knowing that a quick goal would virtually see an end to City's challenge also seem conscious of the fact that a Blues goal would leave it all-square and anybody's tie.

In the event it is the First Division side who go for it with the greater gusto and there are some uncomfortable moments for Villa.

Carl Shutt is the chief threat as he breaks forward in threatening runs on several occasions.

Three times he finishes it off with scoring attempts and just before the break Mark Bosnich makes the game's crucial stop by diving with huge courage and perfect timing at the ex-Leeds forward's feet.

Dean Saunders is the Villa equivalent of Shutt making similar, equally unsuccessful attempts to break the deadlock of this tense second leg.

For just over an hour Villa's passage into the next round remains in doubt but then Blues are reduced to ten men in a moment of self destruction. Midfielder Paul Tait, making tracks along their left touchline is scythed down by Kevin Richardson in what is clearly a foul tackle which misses the ball and takes the feet.

As the two players scramble to their feet off the field of play Tait squares up aggressively to Richardson. First he makes a head-butting gesture without contact.

Then, as Richardson holds up his arms to avoid getting involved, Tait pushes him in the chest and the Villa skipper tumbles backwards over the advertising boards and into an empty seat.

The referee has no hesitation in producing his red card, though Cooper insists afterwards that it was a harsh verdict in a 'blood and thunder' local derby. Richardson is booked for his tackle.

That incident undoubtedly undermines City's efforts and, eight minutes from time, Saunders is released from the half-way line by a Richardson pass.

The Welsh cap races clear of the visiting defence, veers wide of goalkeeper Kevin Miller, and slides in the winner. Amid endless TV re-runs the argument, voiced by Cooper, rages on about whether Deano was offside, though in slow-motion it does appear he began his run from his own half.

Ron Atkinson is unmoved by all the fuss. "I thought he was onside," he said. "And you have to give full credit to the little man. If you keep buying a ticket you'll eventually win the prize."

"Full marks to them," Atkinson added. "They did very well until the kid got sent off. He had been playing well. The game didn't live up to my expectations but it is the early rounds and what matters is we are through."

Dalian Atkinson takes on Dave Smith and Chris Whyte

Saturday 16th October 1993 • Upton Park • 3.00pm

WEST HAM UNITED 0   ASTON VILLA 0

Half-time 0-0 • *Attendance* 20,425

Referee Stephen LODGE (Barnsley)

Linesmen S.G. CLINGO and W.M. JORDAN

Claret Shirts with Blue Sleeves, White Shorts	Goals	Green, Black and Red Striped Shirts, Black Shorts	Goals
1 Ludek MIKLOSKO		13 Mark BOSNICH	
2 Tim BREACKER		17 Neil COX	
4 Steve POTTS		4 Shaun TEALE ❑	
12 Tony GALE		5 Paul McGRATH ❑	
33 David BURROWS		23 Bryan SMALL	
8 Peter BUTLER		7 Ray HOUGHTON	
14 Ian BISHOP		6 Kevin RICHARDSON	
34 Mike MARSH		14 Andy TOWNSEND	
16 Matt HOLMES		11 Tony DALEY	
25 Lee CHAPMAN		9 Dean SAUNDERS	
9 Trevor MORLEY		10 Dalian ATKINSON	
Substitutes		*Substitutes*	
13 Gerry PEYTON		1 Nigel SPINK	
17 Steve JONES		8 Garry PARKER	
23 Keith ROWLAND		22 Guy WHITTINGHAM	

BEFORE		P	W	D	L	F	A	pts	AFTER		P	W	D	L	F	A	pts
7	Villa	10	4	4	2	12	9	16	7	Villa	11	4	5	2	12	9	17
17	West Ham	10	3	2	5	6	13	11	17	West Ham	11	3	3	5	6	13	12

FACTFILE

Upton Park success evades Big Ron again... Villa continue unbeaten away record... Tony Daley could be on the verge of £2m move to Italy... Villa have not won at West Ham in seven league and cup visits since 1984-85... Paul McGrath plays the 400th league and cup of his career.

Bozzie nearly throws it

Against a background of national gloom over the World Cup disappointments Ron Atkinson has been named among possible future candidates for the England job but he has solidly pledged himself to stay with Villa.

For the Upton Park visit team selection has been complicated by Earl Barrett being joined on the injury list by fellow full back Steve Staunton plus doubts about Andy Townsend who missed the Irish Republic qualifier against Spain.

Hammers have scored only three home league goals out of six games so far this season while Villa have not lost away in any competition. Thus the opportunity to take three points seems to be there.

"We must stay in touch with the leading pack," says Atkinson. "Manchester United are looking good but that is not to say they will remain there all season. Our job is to stay in the chase."

Unfortunately, as an uninspired game fails to reach any degree of attacking conviction from either side a goalless draw is always on the cards. Villa are visibly lacking the necessary zest, an indication possibly that this fixture precedes departure for La Coruña and Tuesday night's next UEFA Cup fixture against Deportivo.

Whatever the cause Villa's form is never more than lukewarm. They are blessed with an escape when Bosnich redeems himself with a flying one-handed save after the

Aussie goalkeeper has seemingly gifted Lee Chapman with a West Ham lead when he slips in trying to dribble the ball clear.

Otherwise West Ham threaten very little going forward and are fortunate to emerge with a point. "It was a good result for us," confessed their manager, Billy Bonds.

Not so good for Villa, though, who should have taken all three. Daley is in for Guy Whittingham who, after scoring on his debut as sub at Everton, failed to find the net in six full appearances.

Daley, now wanted by the Italian club Udinese, is playing a deep-lying left wing role and looks the liveliest and most threatening of Villa's attackers. The former England cap repeatedly unhinges the home defence to create chances, mainly for Dalian Atkinson who is twice denied by goalkeeper Ludek Miklosko.

Dean Saunders also sets up a shooting chance for his strike partner and though Miklosko's one-handed save propels the ball across the face of a unguarded goal there is no Villa man there to finish it off.

Tony Daley - Villa's liveliest attacker

Oddly, Ron Atkinson has never taken any of his teams to West Ham and won there and one theory for this is that Big Ron's teams tend to play a similar passing style to Hammers and they simply cancel each other out.

The Villa manager's biggest satisfaction afterwards is that Daley looks to be getting some of his best form back. As a prelude to the UEFA Cup-tie he urges him, if he wants his £2m move to go through, to use the European stage, and TV coverage throughout the Continent, to show what he can do.

Tuesday 19th October 1993 • The Riazor Stadium • 9.00pm

DEPORTIVO LA CORUÑA 1 ASTON VILLA 1

Half-time 0-0 • Attendance 27,500

Referee Marc BATTA
Linesmen P. CROCHEMORE and A. CHIAB
Officials from France

Blue and White Striped Shirts, Blue Shorts	Goals	Claret Shirts with Blue Stripes, White Shorts	Goals
1 Francisco LIAÑO		1 Mark BOSNICH	
2 Salvador Gonzalez 'VORO' †		2 Earl BARRETT	
5 Miroslav DJUKIC		5 Paul McGRATH	
4 José Luis RIBERA		4 Shaun TEALE	
7 Luis LOPEZ RIKARTE		3 Bryan SMALL ❑	
6 MAURO SILVA		6 Kevin RICHARDSON	
8 DONATO		8 Gordon COWANS	
3 Fernando Martinez 'NANDO'		7 Andy TOWNSEND	
10 Francisco Javier Gonzalez 'FRAN'		10 Dalian ATKINSON	
9 Javier MANJARIN ‡		9 Dean SAUNDERS	78
11 BEBETO		11 Tony DALEY	
Substitutes		*Substitutes*	
13 José Alejandro Sánchez 'ALEX' (Gk)		13 Nigel SPINK (Gk)	
12 MARIANO		12 Garry PARKER	
14 JOSÉ RAMON		14 Guy WHITTINGHAM	
15 MARCO VALES †67		15 Ray HOUGHTON	
16 PEDRO RIESCO ‡77	87	16 Neil COX	

FACTFILE

Mark Bosnich saves a 3rd minute penalty from Bebeto on his European debut... Bryan Small is also playing his first game in European competition... Deportivo, unbeaten in the Spanish League this season, qualified for their first European campaign by finishing third behind Barcelona and Real Madrid. In the first round they disposed of AAB Aalborg 5-1 on aggregate, after losing the first leg 1-0 in Denmark.

Bozzie's save of the century

All the intelligence filtering to Villa Park from this craggy North-Westerly tip of Spain has suggested that this tie is tougher even than the previous round.

Deportivo, boasting several internationals including the prolific-scoring Brazilian, Bebeto, have been the nation's surprise team over the past three years.

La Coruña is a larger and more attractive seafront location than most of the visiting party had realised while the Raizor Stadium, with its ornamental tower is of an unusual design.

With Steve Staunton injured Ron Atkinson elects to use up the vacant non-national place by selecting Mark Bosnich in goal, an inspired decision as events are to dramatically confirm.

Deportivo are both skilled and comfortable on the ball and sharp and aggressive with their forward thrusts.

It takes only three minutes for Villa's defence to become ominously unhinged. Paul McGrath is unable to get control of the ball near the corner of the penalty area, allowing Manjarin, a skilled replacement for the injured Claudio, to take possession and advance on goal. Shaun Teale lunges into a sliding tackle but takes the player's legs for an undeniable penalty.

Bebeto is the one to place the ball on the spot confident no doubt of accepting a home lead.

"My advice to goalkeepers is always to wait and watch the taker before making a late decision on which way to go, rather than to guess and go early," said Ron Atkinson. "And they (Bosnich and Bebeto) were like gunslingers staring each other out."

Deano and Dalian celebrate

The tactics work to almost miraculous effect. Bebeto strikes his shot firmly, at around waist height well to the 'keeper's left. Bosnich, who seemingly doesn't move a muscle until the ball is struck, throws himself almost horizontal to claw the ball away.

"That save was unreal," said the Villa boss. "It was the best I have ever seen."

Had the brilliant young Aussie not made that save, the damage to the team's morale could have been incalculable.

Still the Spaniards keep pressing forward but Villa's confidence and performance grows as the game progresses. Dalian Atkinson makes a number of surging runs from midfield, Tony Daley and Dean Saunders use their pace and mobility to stretch defenders and the action crackles along entertainingly.

Bosnich pulled another save, from Fran, and was later rounded by Manjarin who then fired into the side-netting from a narrow angle.

In the home goal Liaño is threatened by an Andy Townsend strike which he deflects away for a corner but he can do nothing when Villa's best attack arrives eleven minutes from the end.

Atkinson powers forward in a way which has worried Deportivo defenders earlier. This time he holds the ball just the right amount of time before feeding Saunders, moving in on his right, and the Welsh cap buries his chance with delight.

That looks like being the only goal of the game but with just three minutes to go a rather untidy assault ends with substitute Pedro Riesco rescuing his side with an equaliser.

"Bosnich is possibly the World's No.1," Big Ron told the Spanish Press after the game before boarding the coach for transportation to the airport 40 minutes away, and a 4am arrival in Birmingham.

Saturday 23rd October 1993 • Villa Park • 3.00pm

ASTON VILLA 1 CHELSEA 0

Half-time 1-0 • *Attendance* 29,706

Referee David ALLISON (Lancaster)
Linesmen T.A. ATKINSON and J. BARLOW

Claret Shirts with Blue Stripes, White Shorts		Goals	Blue Shirts, Blue Shorts		Goals
13	March BOSNICH		1	Dmitri KHARINE	
2	Earl BARRETT		12	Steve CLARKE	
16	Ugo EHIOGU		15	Mal DONAGHY ‡	
4	Shaun TEALE		20	Glenn HODDLE	
14	Andy TOWNSEND		35	Jakob KJELDBJERG	
10	Dalian ATKINSON	6	26	Andy DOW	
15	Gordon COWANS		6	Frank SINCLAIR	
6	Kevin RICHARDSON		27	David HOPKIN	
11	Tony DALEY		18	Eddie NEWTON	
9	Dean SAUNDERS		19	Neil SHIPPERLEY	
22	Guy WHITTINGHAM ❑ †		16	Robert FLECK †	
	Substitutes			*Substitutes*	
1	Nigel SPINK		13	Kevin HITCHCOCK	
8	Garry PARKER †64		9	Tony CASCARINO †77	
17	Neil COX		5	Erland JOHNSEN ‡81	

BEFORE		P	W	D	L	F	A	pts	AFTER		P	W	D	L	F	A	pts
7	Villa	11	4	5	2	12	9	17	7	Villa	12	5	5	2	13	9	20
15	Chelsea	11	3	4	4	10	10	13	15	Chelsea	12	3	4	5	10	11	13

FACTFILE

Dalian Atkinson's first league goal since August... Paul McGrath fails a late fitness test and misses his first game of the season, deputy Ugo Ehiogu plays his first.. Andy Townsend faces Chelsea for the first time since leaving them in the summer and plays in an unfamiliar left-back role.

Fade out after a bright opening

Back to league action after the exertions of the UEFA Cup in Spain in mid-week, Villa seemingly face the prospect of losing Tony Daley to Italian club Udinese for £2m.

The danger of an adverse reaction to the trip is uppermost in manager Ron Atkinson's mind as he urges his players to forget Europe and concentrate on league position.

The stresses and strains of going for three competitions, with two matches a week and internationals involved in World Cup calls, are beginning to have an effect. Dean Saunders has been off-colour with a virus infection while Steve Staunton shows little sign of recovering from his deep groin injury. Glenn Hoddle's Chelsea are without their skipper, Dennis Wise.

"A lot of talk has been focussed on our spell of games in the Coca Cola and UEFA Cups, but it is important for us to put together some back-to-back league victories," says Ron Atkinson with memory of the home defeat by Newcastle fresh in mind.

Six minutes is all it takes for Villa to lay the foundation of the much-needed victory with a cracking goal by Dalian Atkinson, his first in the Premiership since Manchester United on August 23.

Daley who, wrongly it transpires, believes this could be his farewell to Villa Park, delivers a peach of a centre to stretch the visiting defence after being released by a pin-point Cowans ball.

Moving in full of menace, Atkinson connects with his head to resist Andy Dow's aerial challenge and beat goalkeeper Dmitri Kharine to post a 1-0 lead and supporters settle down in anticipation of what they believe will be the best home display since opening day against QPR.

For 20 minutes or so, with Gordon Cowans supplying the inspirational passes, such a prospect looks in store as Deano goes looking for a second goal. Unhappily, however the tempo gradually eases off and although Chelsea are unable to capitalise on Villa's fall-off the danger always exists in a disappointing display.

Michael Ward, in the Birmingham Post, wrote afterwards: "...it was as if some mystery virus suddenly invaded the Villa ranks to sap inspiration from minds and strength from the legs. Instead of the anticipated jackpot we had nothing more than a lottery of misplaced ideas and passes."

Many of the players, especially Saunders, begin to look a little jaded as hope of more goals fades. From spraying passes around in their most entertaining manner early on Villa are reduced to a mundane last hour when they seem satisfied with their 1-0 lead.

Fortunately Chelsea have little to offer in attack though Ugo Ehiogu, deputising for injured Paul McGrath, lets in Robert Fleck for a 58th minute chance which he drives wide.

Nine minutes from time Hoddle's team threaten again but this time Mal Donaghy's header is off-target. Bosnich's only serious threat was in the 18th minute when he dived to deny Andy Dow.

"We began brightly, scored a super goal and then lost our way," confessed Ron Atkinson. Whether the UEFA Cup trip in mid-week had anything to do with it, I don't know but at least we got the three points. Sometimes you can play really well and get nothing."

Dalian Atkinson heads the winner

Tuesday 26th October 1993 • Roker Park • 7.45pm

SUNDERLAND 1   ASTON VILLA 4

Half-time 0-2 • Attendance 23,692

Referee Allan FLOOD (Stockport)
Linesmen J. BILLINGHAM and P. KITSON

Red and White Striped Shirts, Black Shorts		Goals	Claret Shirts with Blue Stripes, White Shorts		Goals
1	Alec CHAMBERLAIN		13	Mark BOSNICH	
16	Martin GRAY ‡		2	Earl BARRETT	
6	Kevin BALL		5	Paul McGRATH	
19	Andy MELVILLE		4	Shaun TEALE	
3	Richard ORD †		23	Bryan SMALL	
7	Gary OWERS		8	Garry PARKER	
22	Martin SMITH		6	Kevin RICHARDSON	33
9	Gordon ARMSTRONG		14	Andy TOWNSEND	
15	Brian ATKINSON		10	Dalian ATKINSON	27, 89
10	Phil GRAY	47	22	Guy WHITTINGHAM †	
8	Don GOODMAN		11	Tony DALEY	
	Substitutes			*Substitutes*	
13	Tony NORMAN		1	Nigel SPINK	
4	Gary BENNETT †19		7	Ray HOUGHTON †74	75
24	James LAWRENCE ‡72		16	Ugo EHIOGU	

FACTFILE

Dean Saunders misses his first game since joining the club 13 months ago, he's kept out by chickenpox... Ray Houghton scores with his first touch of the ball after replacing Guy Whittingham... There have been three previous League Cup meetings between these sides. In the 1962/63 semi-final Villa won 3-1 at Roker and drew 0-0 in the home leg and three seasons later Villa won a 3rd round away tie 2-1... The fourth round draw gives Villa another away tie at either Norwich or holders Arsenal.

Ray Houghton

Brilliant Bozzie silences Roker

There has been a problem or two in the build-up to the game with Dean Saunders' 'virus' confirmed as chickenpox and Neil Cox having asked for a transfer.

On the 'credit' side, Paul McGrath is fit to return in the centre of defence for the potentially intimidating atmosphere of Roker Park where Leeds United lost in the previous round.

Ron Atkinson, disappointed that Cox, who was signed by Jozef Venglos for £400,000 three years earlier, should want a move has placed a £1.5m price tag on his head.

Cox would have been in the squad but is pulled out by the Villa boss who stresses: "If he wants a move he can have one but if he seriously believes he can find a better club than Aston Villa then good luck to him."

Twenty-two-year-old Cox, who was the subject of an inquiry by Norwich in the summer, and is unsettled because of his limited first team opportunities, explains: "I can't be a substitute and a reserve team player for ever."

Saunders' absence means another chance for Guy Whittingham after three games on the bench but it is Mark Bosnich who takes centre stage in spectacular fashion.

On the eve of his departure for Australia's World Cup qualifier against Argentina in Sydney Bosnich is sensational in denying Sunderland any reward for a series of first-half assaults.

"They battered us early on but Bosnich was like a trapeze artist," said manager Atkinson. "He made one save that, from where I was sitting could only go in, but he is like that."

In the opening 27 minutes Villa are barely able to cross the half-way line as Sunderland besiege Villa's goal but then a sudden counter-attack conjures a 1-0 lead.

Industrious Kevin Richardson threads a pass forward and Dalian Atkinson leaves defenders in his path and powers in on goal to drive his shot wide of goalkeeper Alec Chamberlain and stun the Roker Park into disbelieving silence.

Again Sunderland launch a wave of attacks and again Bosnich frustrates their every scoring attempt. Now, with their own defence exposed, Sunderland are even more vulnerable to counter-attack and it takes a mere five minutes for Villa to go a remarkable 2-0 up.

This time Tony Daley is the provider for Richardson to finish it off. Two minutes into the second half Sunderland finally manage to get one past Bosnich, a volley from inside the box by Phil Gray.

By now, however, Sunderland's attacking aggression is beginning to ease off with Bosnich rather less active as the game progresses towards a Villa victory. This becomes inevitable the very moment Whittingham is replaced by Ray Houghton in the 74th minute.

Within seconds of the Irish international's arrival a goalmouth deflection rebounds over the line off Houghton's shin and there is no way back for the shell-shocked Wearsiders.

In the final minutes Dalian Atkinson adds his second goal of the match and his seventh of the season to finalise a scoreline which totally contradicts the shape of the game.

"We owe this win to our goalkeeper," said two-goal Dalian. "You have to feel sorry for Sunderland. They probably won't play better than that all season."

Mark Bosnich - the star of the show

Saturday 30th October 1993 • The County Ground • 3.00pm

SWINDON TOWN 1 ASTON VILLA 2

Half-time 1-1 • *Attendance* 16,530

Referee Keith BURGE (Mid Glamorgan)
Linesmen E.W. GREEN and R.J. HARRIS

Red Shirts, Red Shorts		Goals	Green, Black and Red Striped Shirts, Black Shorts		Goals
1	Fraser DIGBY		1	Nigel SPINK	
2	Nicky SUMMERBEE		2	Earl BARRETT	
5	Luc NIJHOLT		16	Ugo EHIOGU	
26	Terry FENWICK †		4	Shaun TEALE	43
3	Paul BODIN	pen 32	12	Steve FROGGATT	
8	Ross MacLAREN ‡		7	Ray HOUGHTON	
6	Shaun TAYLOR		6	Kevin RICHARDSON ❏	
7	John MONCUR		8	Garry PARKER	
16	Kevin HORLOCK ❏		14	Andy TOWNSEND ❏ ‡	
9	Jan Aage FJORTOFT		10	Dalian ATKINSON	68
25	Andy MUTCH		22	Guy WHITTINGHAM †	
	Substitutes			*Substitutes*	
23	Nicky HAMMOND		30	Michael OAKES	
14	Adrian WHITBREAD †45		11	Tony DALEY †67	
10	Martin LING ‡79		24	Dariusz KUBICKI ‡83	

BEFORE		P	W	D	L	F	A	pts	AFTER		P	W	D	L	F	A	pts
7	Villa	12	5	5	2	13	9	20	5	Villa	13	6	5	2	15	10	23
22	Swindon	12	0	5	7	10	28	5	22	Swindon	13	0	5	8	11	30	5

FACTFILE

Mark Bosnich is away on World Cup duty with Australia... Steve Froggatt is back after a 14-game absence... Dariusz Kubicki appears for the first time this season... Shaun Teale scores his first goal of 93/94... Ugo Ehiogu concedes the penalty after a foul on Andy Mutch... Swindon still seek their first win in the top division.

Dalian does the business again

The absence of Roker hero Bosnich, now in Australia for the World Cup qualifier, means a recall for Nigel Spink at Swindon.

He has been sub for the previous five games and is well aware that, apart from possibly European games, he is now No.2 'keeper.

"There's no way I can follow Mark's display at Sunderland," Spink admits as he gets his recall. "I'm on a hiding to nothing.

"I've not asked for a move and I can understand the gaffer wanting me available for the European games but I feel it is inevitable that I shall move on."

This is the reliable keeper's 434th appearance for Villa and, with Southampton possibly interested in him as a replacement for Tim Flowers, it could be his last, though Ron Atkinson is not keen to let him go.

With the UEFA Cup second leg against Deportivo coming up on Wednesday this is an awkward fixture as Swindon look for their first league win since promotion to the Premiership.

A large squad of players has travelled to Wiltshire with Paul McGrath again troubled by his hamstring injury. Ugo Ehiogu replaces McGrath, Ray Houghton keeps his place as does Guy Whittingham but Steve Froggatt comes in for his first appearance since August. Pole Dariusz Kubicki is in the fourteen for the first time this season, as sub, and gets a brief ten minutes action, replacing Andy Townsend.

Dean Saunders is still out of sorts with chickenpox and a query hangs over his availability for the Deportivo game.

The game proves, predictably something of a bread-and-butter slog with the basic need to collect three points more pressing than the manner of so doing.

The back four has an unusual look with Ehiogu alongside Shaun Teale in the centre and Froggatt at left back. Both players fill in admirably but for ten minutes of the first half Swindon harbour hopes of recording that first win.

This is after Paul Bodin has beaten Spink from the penalty spot in the 33rd minute when Ehiogu fouls Andy Mutch in an aerial challenge for possession.

The equaliser is hooked in by Teale, his first goal of the season and only his second in the league in Villa colours, just before the break. But still Villa live with the danger of a result which would affect their place near the top.

Skipper Kevin Richardson, although booked for a foul tackle, is Villa's outstanding performer on the day but the match-winner proves to be Dalian Atkinson with his fourth goal in three games.

The goal follows instantly upon a substitution as Tony Daley replaces Whittingham for an impressive twenty minutes or so. The former Portsmouth player continues to find the kind of chances which brought him 47 goals last season, difficult to come by.

Daley is still the subject of reported interest from Italian club Udinese though doubts are now creeping in as to whether the £2m deal will actually go through.

The player, however insists he is flying to Italy on Thursday after the Euro game to complete the move.

Steve Froggatt

Wednesday 3rd November 1993 • Villa Park • 7.15pm

ASTON VILLA 0   DEPORTIVO LA CORUÑA 1

Aggregate 1-2 • Half-time 0-1 • Attendance 26,737

Referee Jürgen WEBER
Linesmen H.G. FÜLLBRUNN and W. WERTHMANN
Officials from Germany

Claret Shirts with Blue Stripes, White Shorts		Goals	Blue and White Striped Shirts, Blue Shorts		Goals
1	Mark BOSNICH		1	Francisco LIAÑO	
2	Earl BARRETT		2	Salvador Gonzalez 'VORO'	
5	Paul McGRATH		5	Miroslav DJUKIC	
4	Shaun TEALE		4	José Luis RIBERA	
3	Bryan SMALL		10	Francisco Javier Gonzalez 'FRAN'	
8	Gordon COWANS †		7	Luis LOPEZ RIKARTE	
6	Kevin RICHARDSON ❑		8	DONATO	
7	Andy TOWNSEND ❑		3	Fernando Martinez 'NANDO'	
10	Dalian ATKINSON		6	MAURO SILVA	
9	Dean SAUNDERS		9	Javier MANJARIN †	36
11	Tony DALEY		11	BEBETO ‡	
	Substitutes			*Substitutes*	
13	Nigel SPINK (Gk)		13	José Alejandro Sánchez 'ALEX' (Gk)	
12	Garry PARKER		12	MARIANO	
14	Guy WHITTINGHAM		14	JOSÉ RAMON	
15	Ray HOUGHTON †61		15	MARCO VALES ‡81	
16	Ugo EHIOGU		16	PEDRO RIESCO †75	

FACTFILE

Ron Atkinson suffers the first-ever home defeat by one of his teams in Europe... Mark Bosnich has returned from World Cup duty but he can't save Villa this time... Steve Staunton is still out and needs surgery... Deportivo are knocked out by Eintracht Frankfurt in the next round, losing both legs 1-0, but go on to have another excellent season in the league. A last minute penalty miss in the final game of the season robs them of the title, which again goes to Barcelona.

The agony of a European exit

Playing the second leg at home, with a 1-1 draw from the away leg, has given Villa what appears to be the possibility of a winning advantage.

A 0-0 scoreline would be enough to earn a place in the third round draw on Friday and only the continued absence of injured Steve Staunton undermines optimism.

That plus the knowledge that the Spanish club team have skilled players in all departments and, though new to European competition, have several internationals.

Gordon Cowans is recalled to midfield with instructions to 'put his European head on' in terms of using his experience to help Villa dominate the pace and pattern.

Also, Ron Atkinson has called for the crowd to make Villa Park an intimidating arena for the opposition and, presumably to this end, the rousing strains of *Jerusalem* echoes around the ground before the start. This is followed by *Land of Hope and Glory* yet, when the action starts, it has a rather lukewarm feel about it.

Villa seem content to play a possession game, moving the ball around with ground passes but Cowans's accuracy is below its normal excellence. Dalian Atkinson gets the chance of an early shot at goal but sends it a shade too high and wide in Villa's only attacking offering of an uneventful opening 36 minutes.

Then possession is lost near the half-way line down Villa's left and Deportivo make dramatic use of it. Switching the point of attack across midfield to the other side, Nando is left unmarked down the right of Villa's defence. His centre is met at the far post by Manjarin as Paul McGrath attempts to clear it off the line, and the situation is turned on its head.

Mark Bosnich, the penalty-save hero of the first leg, has been to Sydney and back for Australia's World Cup qualifier with Argentina, and has recovered from jet lag. However, he is beaten by the ball in flight and has no chance of keeping his team all-square.

Now Villa need a goal to stay alive but Deportivo's strangulation tactics, with excellent close marking and covering in midfield, prove an effective game plan. Apart from a volley over the top by Dean Saunders, back after chicken pox, and a goodish shot by Tony Daley, which is going wide as Francisco Liaño makes a spectacular 'save', Villa never remotely look able to turn the scoreline around. Daley is thought to be playing his last Villa game before an intended £2m move to the Italian club Udinese but this proves to be not the case.

As Villa go for the necessary equaliser the strains of a bugle rallying call, sounding repeatedly over the public address system, prompts some increased reaction from the disappointed crowd but the team remain oddly uninspired.

Their style has changed from ground passing to a more direct high route but there remains a sad lack of shape about the entire display.

Ron Atkinson is scathing about his team after his first-ever home defeat in European competition. "I was more disappointed by the performance than the result," he said. "We were not a good advert for English football."

Asked how the players felt about it he replied: "They should feel ashamed."

On TV, immediately after the game, the Villa boss shows his reaction to the poor display in a prickly interview with ITV's Jim Rosenthal when he storms away without answering the final question.

On such a disappointing European exit what else was there to say..?

Ron Atkinson

Saturday 6th November 1993 • Highbury • 3.00pm

ARSENAL 1 ASTON VILLA 2

Half-time 0-0 • *Attendance* 31,773

Referee Martin BODENHAM

Linesmen M.K. BULLIVANT and M.G. WRIGHT

Red Shirts with White Sleeves, White Shorts	Goals	Green, Black and Red Striped Shirts, Black Shorts	Goals
1 David SEAMAN		13 Mark BOSNICH †	
2 Lee DIXON		2 Earl BARRETT	
14 Martin KEOWN		5 Paul McGRATH	
6 Tony ADAMS		4 Shaun TEALE	
3 Nigel WINTERBURN		23 Bryan SMALL	
15 Anders LIMPAR		7 Ray HOUGHTON ‡	
22 Ian SELLEY		6 Kevin RICHARDSON	
17 John JENSEN ❏		14 Andy TOWNSEND	90
10 Paul MERSON		9 Dean SAUNDERS	
8 Ian WRIGHT	58	10 Dalian ATKINSON ❏	
7 Kevin CAMPBELL		11 Tony DALEY	
Substitutes		*Substitutes*	
13 Alan MILLER		1 Nigel SPINK †51	
11 Eddie McGOLDRICK		22 Guy WHITTINGHAM ‡65	74
12 Steve BOULD		16 Ugo EHIOGU	

BEFORE	P	W	D	L	F	A	pts	AFTER	P	W	D	L	F	A	pts
3 Arsenal	13	6	5	2	12	6	23	3 Villa	14	7	5	2	17	11	26
5 Villa	13	6	5	2	15	10	23	6 Arsenal	14	6	5	3	13	8	23

FACTFILE

Mark Bosnich completes a hat-trick of penalty saves, pushing Ian Wright's 43rd minute spot-kick onto the post... Villa's unbeaten away record continues... Arsenal end their four-game premiership goal drought, another blank would have completed their worst league scoring run in 83 years.

Robbery at Highbury

If ever the club and supporters needed a lift today is the day, though Highbury is hardly the ground to go looking for favours!

In mid-week Gunners have rattled seven past Standard Liege to suggest that their goal-scoring problems are over but home fans are not convinced. Should Arsenal fail to score today it will give them a run of five consecutive goalless displays in the league, their worst run for 83 years.

For Villa, the depression of UEFA Cup exit has not yet been lifted though Ron Atkinson is placing the emphasis heavily on a forward-looking attitude, with the need to stay in touch with the leaders now the priority.

Steve Staunton remains unfit and is joined on the injury list by Steve Froggatt so Bryan Small remains at left back where he is to get a hard time from Anders Limpar. Ray Houghton retains Gordon Cowans' midfield place.

Villa, battling to shed the mental and physical reaction to last Wednesday night's defeat spend most of the first hour under siege.

In that period goalkeeper Mark Bosnich is thrust right back into the limelight, two minutes before the interval. Ian Wright has been sent on a dangerous run into the Villa area by Limpar and is tripped by Shaun Teale.

It's a penalty, no argument about that and, predictably, it is Wright who steps forward with relish to take it. The England-capped striker who, perhaps, has not done his homework strikes the ball to Bosnich's left.

Goalscorer Guy Whittingham

So, for the third penalty against him in succession, the acrobatic Aussie is able to dive to what appears to be his favourite spot and complete a hat-trick of spot kick saves.

This one is arguably even better than the one against Deportivo, Wright's shot being only at about knee height and well wide of Bosnich.

In making that dive Bosnich injures his hip and six minutes into the second half has to limp off to be replaced by Spink.

More and more pressure is applied by Arsenal as Wright gives Spink an early warning with a 20-yard drive which clears the bar by a fraction. In the 58th minute Arsenal's No.1 striker, who missed the seven-goal victory, gets his reward for persistency.

Fed by Limpar, he evades Paul McGrath's challenge and beats Spink with a low cross-shot. Arsenal's superiority has been translated into the lead and Villa look well beaten.

Yet an Alfred Hitchcock-type finale is on the cards after Houghton is withdrawn and replaced by Guy Whittingham with Dalian Atkinson pulled back into a wide midfield berth.

Less than ten minutes after the change Atkinson pierces a pass through into Whittingham's path and the ex-Portsmouth striker advances to

shoot past David Seaman for the equaliser.

As this 'injury time' drags on Dean Saunders goes full pelt in pursuit of a 'lost cause' ball near the corner flag, beats Nigel Winterburn, and crosses for Andy Townsend to smash in the winner with his right foot.

"We mugged'em," confesses Ron Atkinson. "They did, too," agrees George Graham.

Saturday 20th November 1993 • Villa Park • 3.00pm

ASTON VILLA 1 SHEFFIELD UNITED 0

Half-time 0-0 • Attendance 24,686

Referee David FRAMPTON (Poole)

Linesmen M.K. BULLIVANT and R.J. HARRIS

Claret Shirts with Blue Stripes, White Shorts	Goals	Red and White Striped Shirts, Black Shorts	Goals
13 Mark BOSNICH		1 Alan KELLY	
2 Earl BARRETT		2 Kevin GAGE	
5 Paul McGRATH		14 David TUTTLE	
4 Shaun TEALE ❑		26 Jamie HOYLAND	
23 Bryan SMALL †		33 Roger NILSEN ❑	
6 Kevin RICHARDSON ‡		18 Dane WHITEHOUSE	
14 Andy TOWNSEND		8 Paul ROGERS †	
11 Tony DALEY		19 Willie FALCONER	
9 Dean SAUNDERS		10 Glyn HODGES ‡	
10 Dalian ATKINSON		17 Carl BRADSHAW	
22 Guy WHITTINGHAM	76	9 Adrian LITTLEJOHN	
Substitutes		*Substitutes*	
1 Nigel SPINK		13 Simon TRACEY	
8 Garry PARKER †73		11 Mitch WARD †25	
16 Ugo EHIOGU ‡87		21 Alan CORK ‡71	

BEFORE		P	W	D	L	F	A	pts	AFTER		P	W	D	L	F	A	pts
3	Villa	14	7	5	2	17	11	26	2	Villa	15	8	5	2	18	11	29
19	United	14	2	6	6	17	23	12	19	United	15	2	6	7	17	24	12

FACTFILE

Guy Whittingham scores for the second successive game, this one his first at Villa Park... It's now eleven league games without a win for Sheffield United... The Blades fail to score on a Villa Park visit for the first time since 1969/70... Last season's top three, Man Utd - Villa - Norwich, are leading the Premiership.

Sub Parker shows the way

It's been a black week on the international scene with only the Irish Republic of the British Isles nations reaching the World Cup finals.

Wales failed disappointingly despite Dean Saunders' goal against Romania in Cardiff though Paul McGrath, Ray Houghton, Andy Townsend and Steve Staunton were triumphant over Eire's draw in Belfast.

Staunton remains unfit though the trio who played against Northern Ireland all returned unscathed. "Let's hope they continue playing on a wave of adrenalin," is manager Ron Atkinson's view of the Irish contingent.

The effect on Deano is far more difficult to assess while, mercifully, the effect of England's sad demise is minimal at Villa Park.

Mark Bosnich is back in goal after intensive attention to the hip injury suffered at Arsenal two weeks earlier in saving Ian Wright's penalty and which kept jim out of Australia's World Cup qualifier in Argentina.

Sheffield United's visit, on a day when winter is closing in with a frozen chill in the air and the threat of snow, reduces the gate to below 25,000 for the first time in a league match since January 27... the last time the Blades visited!

Those who remained in the warm, anticipating a low-key affair, got it about right. If anything United are the better side in the poor-standard opening half and Villa begin to get a rough ride from fans looking for better things.

The quality of Villa's passing has deteriorated compared to the rhythm of last season and a set pattern

of play is difficult to define apart from the fact that it is 4-3-3 with Saunders, Dalian Atkinson and Guy Whittingham up front.

There is some booing around the ground as Villa leave the field at half-time though there is only a marginal improvement after the break. Both goalkeepers are blessed virtually with a spectating role as neither side succeed in conjuring meaningful scoring attempts.

The change arrives when Garry Parker is sent on as a tactical substitute, replacing Bryan Small with only 17 minutes remaining. His impact was immediate.

First he sends a dropping shot over the bar and then he releases Dalian Atkinson whose shot is blocked at the expense of a corner.

In a move they have practised in training, Atkinson takes Kevin Richardson's short corner and knocks it across goal.

Saunders cannot quite get a touch but Whittingham is there for his third goal in his last five starts, in the 76th minute. There is no way back for United now and Villa are left with the satisfaction of conjuring an emphatic winning goal from an otherwise indecisive display.

This is soured slightly a few minutes before the end when Kevin Richardson is helped off with a hamstring injury to end his astonishing 100% appearance record since he signed from Real Sociedad two and a half seasons ago.

Ron Atkinson, in a mood of scathing tongue-in-cheek humour, wise-cracked: "Parker confused us all by bringing the ball down and passing it." And he added: "At half-time we decided to change our tactics and tell them the game had started."

"We were awful at the start, and then we got worse..."

Although displays are less attractive, the record is better than at the same stage last season.

Guy Whittingham

Wednesday 24th November 1993 • Villa Park • 7.45pm

ASTON VILLA 0 SOUTHAMPTON 2

Half-time 0-0 • *Attendance* 16,180

Referee Kelvin MORTON (Bury St. Edmunds)

Linesmen R.D. FURNANDIZ and B. LOWE

Claret Shirts with Blue Stripes, White Shorts	Goals	Red and White Striped Shirts, Black Shorts	Goals
13 Mark BOSNICH		13 Ian ANDREWS	
2 Earl BARRETT		2 Jeff KENNA	
5 Paul McGRATH		6 Ken MONKOU	
4 Shaun TEALE		18 Steve WOOD	
24 Dariusz KUBICKI †		11 Francis BENALI ❏	
8 Garry PARKER		27 Paul ALLEN	
6 Kevin RICHARDSON		8 Glenn COCKERILL	
14 Andy TOWNSEND		10 Neil MADDISON	
11 Tony DALEY		14 Simon CHARLTON	
9 Dean SAUNDERS		9 Iain DOWIE ❏	
22 Guy WHITTINGHAM		7 Matthew LE TISSIER	50, 62
Substitutes		*Substitutes*	
1 Nigel SPINK		1 Dave BEASANT	
7 Ray HOUGHTON †53		3 Micky ADAMS	
16 Ugo EHIOGU		24 Frank BENNETT	

BEFORE	P	W	D	L	F	A	pts	AFTER	P	W	D	L	F	A	pts
3 Villa	15	8	5	2	18	11	29	3 Villa	16	8	5	3	18	13	29
20 Soton	15	3	2	10	16	26	11	19 Soton	16	4	2	10	18	26	14

FACTFILE

Despite a run of four straight Premiership wins, a combination of poor home performances and bad weather attracts Villa's lowest home league gate for 19 months... Dariusz Kubicki starts his first senior game since February 1992... Kevin Richardson makes his 100th league appearance for Villa.

Villa left out in the cold

The visit of Southampton, from the lower reaches of the Premiership and without an away league win in eight attempts this season, appears to offer the chance of a fifth successive victory in the Premiership.

In the event, on a chilly evening of light scattered snow showers, such expectations prove depressingly misplaced.

Garry Parker has retained the midfield place he secured as substitute last Saturday when his arrival lifted a drab team display and led to the winning goal.

The other changes are at full back where the Pole Dariusz Kubicki makes his first start of the season in place of Bryan Small, while Dalian Atkinson is ruled out with a groin strain.

Whatever the cause, be it the unpleasant weather, a reaction from Saturday's low-key display or the limited appeal of the opposition, the crowd 16,000 is the lowest in the league since Ron Atkinson became manager.

A fall of 8,000 from the 'low' 24,686 for Sheffield United, is a worrying trend indeed. Even more worrying, however, is the poor quality of Villa's performance.

Against fairly inept opposition a team plan never remotely begins to take shape while there appear to be no individual stars, either.

In the turgid opening 45 minutes Villa fail to muster a meaningful attack or even a scoring attempt on target. It is 43 minutes before they force their first corner!

Iain Dowie outjumps Ray Houghton

By now the supporters are showing their dissatisfaction with players who simply cannot get their act together.

It is 78 minutes before Saints' goalkeeper Ian Andrews is brought into the action and, by now, Southampton are in a winning position at 2-0 up.

Matthew Le Tissier, a talented enigma of a player, is the match winner, netting both Saints' goals in a 12 minute spell early in the second half.

Villa's defence, so easily pulled out of position, is powerless to intervene as Southampton claim their first away win in the league since last March.

Firstly a corner by Simon Charlton is not properly cleared and the ball bizarrly cannons off Iain Dowie's rear end and falls conveniently for Le Tissier to score in the six-yard area.

Goal No. 2 came from a Charlton free-kick which found Le Tissier unmarked six yards out of goal.

The Saints' striker's first header is blocked brilliantly by Mark Bosnich but he is able to follow up to knock in the rebound.

Ray Houghton has been sent on to replace Kubicki, whose form is a shade rusty, but there is no improvement in Villa's game as a sad displays sends thousands home to warm havens long before the final whistle.

Ron Atkinson holds a lengthy and one-sided inquest with his players afterwards and sends his No.2, Jim Barron, to the post-match press conference explaining that the manager 'is busy...'

Barron pulls no punches on Big Ron's behalf. "Rubbish," he said in summing up the performance. "We lacked commitment, lacked skill and Southampton were ahead of us in every department.

"The crowd was booing a team that was second in the league, and you couldn't blame them!"

Sunday 28th November 1993 • Anfield • 4.00pm

LIVERPOOL 2 ASTON VILLA 1

Half-time 1-0 • *Attendance* 38,484

Referee Alan WILKIE (Chester-le-Street)
Linesmen R. PEARSON and B.M. RICE

Red Shirts, Red Shorts	Goals		Green, Black and Red Striped Shirts, Black Shorts	Goals
1 Bruce GROBBELAAR			13 Mark BOSNICH	
4 Steve NICOL			17 Neil COX	
5 Mark WRIGHT			5 Paul McGRATH	
25 Neil RUDDOCK ❑			2 Earl BARRETT	
22 Steve HARKNESS			23 Bryan SMALL †	
15 Jamie REDKNAPP	62		7 Ray HOUGHTON	
14 Jan MOLBY †			6 Kevin RICHARDSON	
21 Dominic MATTEO			8 Garry PARKER	
10 John BARNES			14 Andy TOWNSEND	
23 Robbie FOWLER	44		9 Dean SAUNDERS	
9 Ian RUSH			10 Dalian ATKINSON	53
Substitutes			*Substitutes*	
13 David JAMES			1 Nigel SPINK	
11 Mark WALTERS †80			22 Guy WHITTINGHAM †80	
7 Nigel CLOUGH			16 Ugo EHIOGU	

BEFORE		P	W	D	L	F	A	pts	AFTER		P	W	D	L	F	A	pts
5	Villa	16	8	5	3	18	13	29	5	Villa	17	8	5	4	19	15	29
9	Liverpool	15	7	2	6	22	15	23	9	Liverpool	16	8	2	6	24	16	26

FACTFILE

Villa's unbeaten away record disappears in front of a live Sky TV audience...
A second successive defeat further undermines championship challenge... Shaun
Teale misses his first game of the season... Robbie Fowler takes his total to 11
goals in his first 11 senior games for Liverpool.

Liverpool steal the points

Villa have been on a bit of a 'downer' recently, what with a run of suspect form, the mid-week home defeat by Southampton and a £20,000 FA fine for irregularities relating to the signing of Mark Bosnich.

In such a mood Anfield is hardly the place to go looking for a pick-me-up, especially in a match switched to the Sunday afternoon spotlight of Sky TV cameras.

Pre-match team news doesn't help. Shaun Teale has had surgery on a nose injury while Dalian Atkinson has struggled to get over a groin problem which kept him out of the Saints game.

Ron Atkinson has made no secret of his disquiet over the Southampton display having had intense discussion with his players aimed at getting the old flowing form and confidence back.

Extensive changes have been made with Neil Cox, Ray Houghton and Atkinson replacing Dariusz Kubicki, Tony Daley and Guy Whittingham, while Earl Barrett partners Paul McGrath in the centre of the defence.

One of the oddities of the season so far has been the fact that Villa's away form and results have frequently been better than at home. This pattern emerges very clearly as Villa more than match Liverpool, who have won their previous five home games, with their amount of possession and the quality of their play.

Barrett is quite superb in the centre of the defence and a 0-0 half-time scoreline is on the cards until the dying seconds of the half. Then the prolific new young

Dalian Atkinson pounces on a Steve Nicol error to equalise

scorer Robbie Fowler is unmarked on the near-side as he backheads a right-wing corner past Bosnich.

Even so Villa are desperately close to going in at 1-1 as Bruce Grobbelaar gets the merest touch on a Dean Saunders drive, after a superb build-up, to deflect it against the crossbar.

In one of their best league displays of the season Villa keep up their momentum after the interval and equalise eight minutes into the new half. Dalian Atkinson, showing no signs of his injury, pounces on an indecisive header by Steve Nicol, skirts Grobbelaar and scores into an unguarded net.

Villa continue to play with style and conviction and though Liverpool are in good shape too, a 1-1 draw would adequately reflect a fine game. However, the lead survives only nine minutes. Fowler picks up a loose midfield ball and feeds Jamie Redknapp who catches the visiting defence unprepared to race clear and beat Bosnich.

Still there are close calls at either end with Villa striving hard to restore their ubeaten away record. Grobbelaar is in brilliant form as he keeps out an Atkinson volley but the Liverpool 'keeper looks relieved as Garry Parker's drive scrapes the wrong side of the bar.

In an entertaining 90 minutes Bosnich is in the thick of it, too, pulling off a double save from ex-Villa forward Mark Walters, on as substitute for Jan Molby.

Afterwards, the grim Villa boss of four days ago is replaced by the more-familiar relaxed version when, despite losing that away record, he declares: "I thought we played ever so well, actually. That's the level or performance I'm looking for. We looked a decent team today."

Tuesday 30th November 1993 • Highbury • 7.45pm

ARSENAL 0 ASTON VILLA 1

Half-time 0-1 • *Attendance* 26,453

Referee Rodger GIFFORD (Llanbradach)

Linesmen C.T. FINCH and J.F. MOORE

Red Shirts with White Sleeves, White Shorts	Goals	Green, Black and Red Striped Shirts, Black Shorts	Goals
1 David SEAMAN		13 Mark BOSNICH	
2 Lee DIXON †		17 Neil COX	
14 Martin KEOWN		5 Paul McGRATH	
12 Steve BOULD		2 Earl BARRETT	
3 Nigel WINTERBURN		4 Shaun TEALE	
11 Eddie McGOLDRICK		7 Ray HOUGHTON	
17 John JENSEN ‡		8 Garry PARKER	
21 Steve MORROW		6 Kevin RICHARDSON	
10 Paul MERSON		14 Andy TOWNSEND	
8 Ian WRIGHT		9 Dean SAUNDERS †	
9 Alan SMITH		10 Dalian ATKINSON	5
Substitutes		*Substitutes*	
13 Alan MILLER		1 Nigel SPINK	
4 Paul DAVIS †71		11 Tony DALEY †90	
7 Kevin CAMPBELL ‡71		22 Guy WHITTINGHAM	

Shaun Teale

FACTFILE

Villa win at Highbury for the third time this year and end Arsenal's run of 25 Cup games without defeat... Villa eliminate the League Cup holders for the second successive year having knocked out Manchester United last season... Shaun Teale plays in the infamiliar role of left-back... It is only the second time these clubs have been drawn together in the League Cup - Villa won a Highbury replay in the quarter-finals of 1985-86.

Aston Villa Review 1994

Early goal sees off the holders

The second major match in the space of forty-eight hours, and one Villa need to win, against all the odds, if the first half of the season is to stay alive.

New emphasis has been placed on the need to progress in the domestic cups by removal from Europe and Manchester United's increasing domination of the Premiership.

"Arsenal will look at it the same as ourselves," agrees Ron Atkinson before the start. "Realistically it will take a landslide to stop United in the league so they will be setting their stall out in the cups, just as they did last season."

Big Ron won't admit that there is extra pressure on him to win a cup. He doesn't have to. It speaks for itself... However Villa arrive at Highbury facing a monumental challenge against the side who pulled off a cup double last season.

Gunners have not been beaten in either competition since January 1992 (the Wrexham shocker), and they won't be surrendering this one after a run of 25 unbeaten cup-ties, including Europe.

In the event Villa are blessed with a dream start in the shape of a fifth minute strike by Dalian Atkinson and a lead they are never going to let go.

A Dean Saunders' feed unhinges Gunners' so-reliable defence allowing Atkinson to head off Nigel Winterburn's challenge before placing his shot under the diving David Seaman for his sixth goal in eight games.

There's 85 minutes still to go and, theoretically, Ian Wright to worry about but manager Atkinson has thought about that, and thought about it very well.

In a match-winning tactical move Shaun Teale has been recalled at left back with Earl Barrett given the job of stopping the England striker.

Villa's defence is so well-organised that Arsenal rarely so much as threaten to get the equaliser though this is much, much more than a defensive exercise.

The old Ron Atkinson-style midfield passing policy, evident at Anfield on Sunday, is there again as the Houghton-Parker-Richardson-Townsend quartet literally keep the ball rolling.

Remarkably it is Villa who dominate the forward play as Gunners' attack is kept totally at bay. Deano is close to making it 2-0 mid-way through the first half when he beats defender Bould but his finishing effort deflects off Seaman's heel.

Twice in the second half Villa are denied further goals by marginal off-side decisions, first when Saunders is assisted by Atkinson then the other way about in the 58th minute.

When Atkinson gets the ball in the net for the second time it is Saunders who is adjudged to be off-side, a very arguable decision.

However, 1-0 proves to be enough and the display prompts the manager to enthuse: "I thought we played smashing. After losing two on the bounce we are in the last eight of a major tournament and have given ourselves a kick start."

Big Ron is as delighted as the Villa fans' are with the part played by Barrett. "He stuck to

Earl Barrett

him (Wright) like a leech and was the best player on the park," adds the Villa boss.

The quarter-final draw brings another North-London trip in the shape of Spurs away. After this Highbury performance, no need to fret...

Saturday 4th December 1993 • Loftus Road • 3.00pm

QUEEN'S PARK RANGERS 2 ASTON VILLA 2

Half-time 2-1 • *Attendance* 14,915

Referee Keith HACKETT (Sheffield)

Linesmen G.M. LEE and M.L. SHORT

Blue and White Hooped Shirts, White Shorts		Goals	Claret Shirts with Blue Stripes, Blue Shorts		Goals
13	Jan STEJSKAL		13	Mark BOSNICH	
2	David BARDSLEY		17	Neil COX	
18	Karl READY		5	Paul McGRATH	(og 6)
6	Alan McDONALD †		2	Earl BARRETT	
3	Clive WILSON		4	Shaun TEALE	
7	Andrew IMPEY		7	Ray HOUGHTON	
14	Simon BARKER		8	Garry PARKER	48
4	Ray WILKINS		6	Kevin RICHARDSON	27
22	Michael MEAKER		14	Andy TOWNSEND †	
12	Gary PENRICE	41	9	Dean SAUNDERS	
10	Bradley ALLEN		10	Dalian ATKINSON	
	Substitutes			*Substitutes*	
1	Tony ROBERTS		1	Nigel SPINK	
8	Ian HOLLOWAY †74		11	Tony DALEY †45	
19	Devon WHITE		22	Guy WHITTINGHAM	

BEFORE		P	W	D	L	F	A	pts	AFTER		P	W	D	L	F	A	pts
5	Villa	17	8	5	4	19	15	29	5	Villa	18	8	6	4	21	17	30
8	QPR	17	8	3	6	29	23	27	8	QPR	18	8	4	6	31	25	28

FACTFILE

Paul McGrath and Kevin Richardson mark their birthdays with a goal - McGrath's an early gift for Rangers!... Garry Parker scores his first goal of the season... Andy Townsend faces surgery to have a bursa removed from his knee... Villa's record in London this season now reads P5 W2 D3 L0.

Super show after an early gift

Back to league action after the high drama of Highbury and the Coca Cola Cup and a chance for Villa to prove that their old fluency really is back to stay.

Ron Atkinson stays with the defensive line-up of Cox-McGrath-Barrett-Teale in an unchanged team charged with the duty of maintaining last Wednesday's high level of performance.

The worry and the enigma continues to be Dean Saunders. How could anybody try harder? How could anybody make so many daring, darting raids into enemy territory? How could anybody have so many shots on target...yet score so few goals?

In 39 games since February this year Deano has managed only six successful strikes, yet he has terrorised opposing defences and rattled a bombardment of shots and headers off woodwork around the league.

"He keeps making the runs, setting up chances doing the right things," stresses Ron Atkinson. The reward of a lovely hat-trick would be just the job, but it is not to be.

In fact Villa suffer the reverse experience to last Tuesday, when they were in the lead after only five minutes or so. This time Villa go a goal down in that brief opening spell.

Paul McGrath is deceived by a flick of Andy Impey's head and, in trying to intervene, deflects the ball past Mark Bosnich.

It is the Irishman's 34th birthday. What a way to celebrate!

Villa, whose game is instantly back on track, are not unduly perturbed by the deficit. Rolling their passes freely they go in search of the equaliser and find it after a further twenty-one minutes.

The scorer is skipper Kevin Richardson, with an accurately-placed low drive wide of Jan Stejskal for his fourth of the season. Today is Rico's 31st birthday. That's more like it.

By half-time, however, despite a good deal of attacking by Villa they are a goal down, ex-Villa Park forward Gary Penrice having made it 2-1 by forcing in a corner at the near post.

During the interval Andy Townsend is withdrawn and replaced by substitute Tony Daley. The Irish cap has been playing with injections for a knee injury for some time, now it is to prove that he needs minor surgery before he can play again. In another half-time change, Barrett is switched to left back to counter-act Impey's speed.

Villa's equaliser comes within a couple of minutes of the re-start. Appropriately it is scored by Garry Parker who has been outstanding with his midfield contribution.

Parker leaves Stejskal powerless to intervene with a rasping shot from the edge of the area, one of his specialities. Throughout the game Parker has been sharp and direct in midfield, passing with precision and repeatedly upsetting the opposition.

By then few would deny that Villa should have run out clear winners, Deano having failed with four chances of varying difficulty.

Ray Houghton, Dalian Atkinson and Daley should also have scored. "We did enough to have won," Atkinson insisted, with very good cause. The manager must know that, for Villa to be successful, more clinical finishing is required.

Garry Parker scores his first goal since April

Wednesday 8th December 1993 • Villa Park • 7.45pm

ASTON VILLA 2 SHEFFIELD WEDNESDAY 2

Half-time 1-1 • Attendance 20,304

Referee Peter FOAKES (Clacton)
Linesmen A.P. MONKS and P.M. ROBERTS

Claret Shirts with Blue Stripes, White Shorts		Goals	Blue and White Striped Shirts, Blue Shorts		Goals
13	Mark BOSNICH		13	Kevin PRESSMAN	
17	Neil COX	29	2	Roland NILLSON	
5	Paul McGRATH		4	Carlton PALMER	
4	Shaun TEALE	(og 69)	17	Des WALKER	
2	Earl BARRETT		3	Nigel WORTHINGTON	
7	Ray HOUGHTON		8	Chris WADDLE	
15	Gordon COWANS		16	Graham HYDE	
8	Garry PARKER		21	Ryan JONES	
19	Stefan BEINLICH		14	Chris BART-WILLIAMS †	24
9	Dean SAUNDERS	pen 53	10	Mark BRIGHT	
10	Dalian ATKINSON		19	Nigel JEMSON	
	Substitutes			*Substitutes*	
1	Nigel SPINK		23	Lance KEY	
16	Ugo EHIOGU		28	Simon COLEMAN †85	
22	Guy WHITTINGHAM		7	Adam PORIC	

BEFORE		P	W	D	L	F	A	pts	AFTER		P	W	D	L	F	A	pts
6	Villa	18	8	6	4	21	17	30	6	Villa	19	8	7	4	23	19	31
11	Wednesday	18	5	8	5	30	26	23	12	Wednesday	19	5	9	5	32	28	24

FACTFILE

Kevin Richardson's 128-match run of consecutive appearances ends after a back injury, suffered at home picking up his children's toys, keeps him out... Shaun Teale takes over as captain... Dean Saunders scores his first goal in nine games... Wednesday stretch unbeaten run to 13 league and cup games.

Costly errors in a windy draw

The urge to stage an exhilarating victory to delight the home fans is, unfortunately, not to be. Those who never travel have read with envy of the fabulous win at Highbury and the outstanding football played at Anfield and Loftus Road.

Can it all be repeated in a Villa Park spectacular of style, goals and points for which the public craves? Not this time, it seems, as two more points slip away and the gap behind leaders Manchester United becomes a daunting 17. As Leeds win at West Ham and Liverpool keep up their winning home form Villa's league position is put under strain.

Circumstances on the night do not help Villa's cause. With Andy Townsend recovering from his knee surgery, skipper Kevin Richardson is forced to end his 128-match run since he joined the club, because of a back injury.

Shaun Teale takes the captain's arm band, Stefan Beinlich comes in on the left of midfield and Gordon Cowans is in a central role, while Earl Barrett close marks Chris Waddle.

But the biggest influence on the pattern of the game is the swirling high wind which, even in the comparitive shelter of Villa Park, causes the ball to swerve and bounce unpredictably.

The dreadful weather, with rainfall mixed in with the wind, has kept the crowd down to just over 20,000 and, for both contingents, it proves a night of fluctuating feelings.

For Villa the opening spell is one to bring more pain than pleasure.

In the very first minute Ray Houghton is released with only Kevin Pressman to beat but hits his shot straight at the Wednesday 'keeper.

Soon afterwards Dean Saunders has a similarly inviting chance but, under the pressure of not having scored in the previous eight matches, slices his shot wide.

Worse is to come. In the 23rd minute Waddle escapes Barrett's attentions out on the Wednesday right and pumps a ball in to Nigel Jemson. Villa defenders are caught in a momentary confusion of who-marks-whom and Chris Bart-Williams is left unattended with a dolly of a chance.

To Villa's credit they apply themselves wholeheartedly to the task of getting back on terms and take only five minutes to square it. Garry Parker accepts a short corner on the left, attacking the Holte End, and though his ball in is wind-affected, Neil Cox bends and stretches in order to muster enough power to head in the equaliser.

By half time Villa are relieved to have held on to the 1-1 scoreline, Jemson having headed against the post and Mark Bright turned a Waddle free kick wide.

That mood changes eight minutes into the second half as Nilsson clearly fouls the dashing Dalian Atkinson to concede an obvious penalty. Here Deano's exuberant attitude, despite his catalogue of missed chances, bubbles to the surface. Relishing the chance of ending that bleak spell he places the ball firmly and whacks it with power and confidence past Pressman to set up a 2-1 lead.

On target Deano

This survives until the last 20 minutes when Teale, racing back towards his own goal as Nilsson drives in a hard low centre from the right, slides in to intercept but directs the ball for an own goal instead of the corner he intended.

"Not a bad old game considering the conditions," said Ron Atkinson. But only two points have been gained out of the last twelve, with five out of six dropped at home.

Saturday 11th December 1993 • Villa Park • 3.00pm

ASTON VILLA 0 WIMBLEDON 1

Half-time 0-0 • *Attendance* 17,940

Referee Allan GUNN (Sussex)

Linesmen K.J. HAWKES and A. SCHNEIDER

Claret Shirts with Blue Stripes, White Shorts	Goals	Dark Blue Shirts, Dark Blue Shorts	Goals
13 Mark BOSNICH ❑		1 Hans SEGERS	
17 Neil COX		2 Warren BARTON	
5 Paul McGRATH		15 John SCALES	
4 Shaun TEALE		6 Scott FITZGERALD	
2 Earl BARRETT		3 Brian McALLISTER	
7 Ray HOUGHTON ‡		24 Peter FEAR	
15 Gordon COWANS		4 Vinnie JONES	
8 Garry PARKER		8 Robbie EARLE	
19 Stefan BEINLICH		26 Neil ARDLEY	
9 Dean SAUNDERS		10 Dean HOLDSWORTH	77
10 Dalian ATKINSON †		9 John FASHANU	
Substitutes		*Substitutes*	
1 Nigel SPINK		23 Neil SULLIVAN	
22 Guy WHITTINGHAM †45		18 Steve TALBOYS	
16 Ugo EHIOGU ‡85		7 Andy CLARKE	

BEFORE		P	W	D	L	F	A	pts	AFTER		P	W	D	L	F	A	pts
6	Villa	19	8	7	4	23	19	31	7	Villa	20	8	7	5	23	20	31
16	Wimbledon	18	5	7	6	20	26	22	14	Wimbledon	19	6	7	6	21	26	25

FACTFILE

Fifth home defeat of season and fifth goalless display at Villa Park... Dean Saunders is captain for the day... Shaun Teale's 100th league game for Villa is also his 200th league game overall... The Dons record their fourth league win in seven Villa Park visits and become the first London club to beat Villa this season.

Poor home form continues

This is Villa's second home game in four days, a situation described by Ron Atkinson as 'barmy', bearing in mind that Villa recently played two away games, at Anfield and Highbury in the space of 48 hours.

After three Premiership games without a win, two at Villa Park, the visit of Wimbledon is not the most eagerly-awaited occasion of a surprisingly mixed season.

Andy Townsend and Kevin Richardson are still unfit, so the line-up remains the same. On a raw, damp day, the attendance is restricted to 17,000, many fans having switched their attention to Christmas Shopping.

Expectations of an attractive game are not high as Wimbledon arrive amid debate about their direct robust style of play.

The John Fashanu incident when Spurs' Gary Mabbutt was elbowed in the face and seriously injured is still in people's mind and Atkinson preludes the kick-off with a a brief hint of it in his programme notes.

"How Wimbledon play is up to them," he wrote. "As long as they stay within the framework of the laws."

Reports leak through from the dressing area that Wimbledon have, as usual, had their ghetto-blaster switched on full volume while Villa have responded by 'entertaining' Dons with a spot of Nigel Kennedy violin music.

When the match starts it is, on balance, less entertaining. Villa are unable to find any rhythm and Wimbledon as uncompromising as ever though to be fair, 'within the framework of the laws'.

There are early indications of uncertainty in the Villa defence as Paul McGrath makes a bad back pass to present Peter Fear with a free shot which he knocks wide of Mark Bosnich.

Mercifully from Villa's point of view Fashanu had already been adjudged offside earlier in the build-up and there is cause to thank referee Alan Gunn again when he rules out a Vinnie Jones header for a pushing offence against Neil Cox.

The attacking story is no less encouraging. Since the four goals against QPR on opening day, only six home league goals have been scored in eight matches and there is little sign of the situation improving here.

"The lads certainly don't have a phobia about playing at home," Ron Atkinson insists, though facts and figures suggest otherwise.

At half-time Dalian Atkinson remains in the dressing room because of a calf strain and Guy Whittingham is sent out as substitute. The former Portsmouth striker shows a pugnacious attitude towards getting the goals Villa need, but to no avail.

With 13 minutes to go it is the Dons who break the deadlock. From a Neil Ardley corner another Jones header flies goalwards. Ray Houghton blocks the effort on the goalline but Dean Holdsworth follows up to put Villa 0-1 down.

In a last desperate throw of the dice Ugo Ehiogu is sent on as an extra attacker and in this spell Hans Segers pulls off a spectacular save from a 20-yard drive by McGrath.

"I can't remember a season when I've lost so many home games," said the downcast Villa boss. Supporters are beginning to applaud the fact that next month's cup-ties are not at Villa Park...

Paul McGrath

Sunday 19th December 1993 • Old Trafford • 4.00pm

MANCHESTER UNITED 3 ASTON VILLA 1

Half-time 1-0 • *Attendance* 44,499

Referee Joe WORRALL (Warrington)

Linesmen J.F. COPELAND and J. McGRATH

Red Shirts, White Shorts	Goals	Green, Black and Red Striped Shirts, Black Shorts	Goals
1 Peter SCHMEICHEL		13 Mark BOSNICH	
2 Paul PARKER		17 Neil COX ❑	90
4 Steve BRUCE		5 Paul McGRATH	
6 Gary PALLISTER		4 Shaun TEALE ❑	
3 Denis IRWIN		23 Bryan SMALL	
14 Andrei KANCHELSKIS		10 Dalian ATKINSON	
8 Paul INCE	89	6 Kevin RICHARDSON	
16 Roy KEANE		2 Earl BARRETT	
5 Lee SHARPE †		8 Garry PARKER	
7 Eric CANTONA	21, 88	9 Dean SAUNDERS †	
10 Mark HUGHES		22 Guy WHITTINGHAM	
Substitutes		*Substitutes*	
13 Les SEALEY		1 Nigel SPINK	
11 Ryan GIGGS †81		11 Tony DALEY †63	
9 Brian McCLAIR		15 Gordon COWANS	

BEFORE	P	W	D	L	F	A	pts	AFTER	P	W	D	L	F	A	pts
1 United	20	15	4	1	40	16	49	1 United	21	16	4	1	43	17	52
9 Villa	20	8	7	5	23	20	31	9 Villa	21	8	7	6	24	24	31

FACTFILE

Villa's three subs have played a combined total of 1232 league and cup games for the club... United increase their lead over Leeds at the top of the Premiership to 13 points... Eric Cantona nets his 12th and 13th goals of the season... It is the third successive Villa-United game to be shown 'live' on Sky.

Champions do a double over Villa

Villa go to Old Trafford for the Sunday fixture on Sky TV knowing that only a performance outstripping anything under Ron Atkinson's reign will deliver the three points.

Compared to the corresponding fixture last March, when Villa were in head-to-head conflict as joint leaders on points, and earned a 1-1 draw, the advantage has swung heavily United's way.

Recent form guides are not good. Villa have, in recent matches, added defensive lapses to their obvious goalscoring deficiences lowering confidence by a crucial fraction.

In contrast, Alex Ferguson now has such a powerful squad that he can leave Ryan Giggs on the subs bench, while record signing Roy Keane has not yet established an automatic place.

Villa, sadly, are still without Steve Staunton who is such an influential character when fully fit. They arrive at the home of the Champions having taken only two points from their previous five League games.

Ron Atkinson, understandably, decides that special tactics are required if his team are to conjure a result which would breathe new life into a championship race which is rapidly becoming a formality. In a five-man defence Earl Barrett is given the job of close-marking Eric Cantona with Bryan Small called up to complete the line.

Sky viewers are served up an entertaining game with a remarkable kick in its tail.

Bryan Small

Villa quickly demonstrate that their attitude is right by attacking from the start. Garry Parker fires a warning shot in the shape of a half-volley which just clears its target.

Another indication that Villa are charged up for the challenge immediately follows as Neil Cox is too aggressive in a tackle on Lee Sharpe and is shown a yellow card.

Small's task is to watch the speedy Russian Andrei Kanchelskis and copes well in a high-speed game of compulsive action, in which Villa mostly give as good as they get.

Barrett dutifully sticks to Cantona but the Frenchman shrewdly moves around, dragging his marker with him and creating problems for the defence.

Fortunately Paul McGrath is in towering form back at his former ground but even this show of defiance by Villa cannot prevent Cantona giving his side a 21st minute lead.

Just beforehand there is the fleeting chance of Villa getting their noses in front as Dean Saunders gets possession just inside the area but Peter Schmeichel is as alert as ever in stopping the Welsh international's shot. Punishment for the failure to accept the half-chance is instant and as far as the outcome is concerned, terminal. Keane beats Atkinson and drills a low centre across the face of the goal. Defenders fail to cut it out and Cantona is not one to miss from close range.

United are then pushed back by a determined Villa seeking an equaliser. "If the score was to change I could only see 1-1," said Big Ron who was staggered by a three goal finale.

As injury time looms Cantona strikes with his second goal and before Villa can regroup Paul Ince has made it a misleading 3-0. Still a few seconds of injury time remain when Cox arrives just on time at the far post to get on the end of Parker's precise cross.

"United have progressed since winning the title," concedes Ron Atkinson. "They have a squad of 16 very good players."

Wednesday 29th December 1993 • Carrow Road • 7.45pm

NORWICH CITY 1   ASTON VILLA 2

Half-time 1-0 • *Attendance* 20,650

Referee David ELLERAY (Harrow)

Linesmen R.J. HARRIS and P.A. VOSPER

Yellow Shirts, Green Shorts		Goals	Claret Shirts with Blue Stripes, White Shorts		Goals
1	Bryan GUNN		13	Mark BOSNICH	
3	Rob NEWMAN		17	Neil COX ❑	
5	Ian CULVERHOUSE		5	Paul McGRATH	
17	Ian BUTTERWORTH †		2	Earl BARRETT	
8	Colin WOODTHORPE		4	Shaun TEALE	
2	Mark BOWEN		3	Steve STAUNTON	
14	Ruel FOX		7	Ray HOUGHTON	56
4	Ian CROOK		6	Kevin RICHARDSON	
21	David SMITH ‡		14	Andy TOWNSEND	
22	Chris SUTTON	27	9	Dean SAUNDERS	59
7	Efan EKOKU		22	Guy WHITTINGHAM †	
	Substitutes			*Substitutes*	
13	Scott HOWIE		1	Nigel SPINK	
19	Andy JOHNSON †76		18	Dwight YORKE †74	
18	Robert ULLATHORNE ‡83		21	Dave FARRELL	

BEFORE		P	W	D	L	F	A	pts	AFTER		P	W	D	L	F	A	pts
7	Norwich	20	9	7	4	32	22	34	7	Norwich	21	9	7	5	33	24	34
9	Villa	21	8	7	6	24	23	31	8	Villa	22	9	7	6	26	24	34

FACTFILE

Ray Houghton scores his first league goal of the season... Dwight Yorke makes his first appearance of the season... Villa win at Carrow Road for the first time since the championship season of 1980/81... It's Norwich's biggest gate so far this season.

Deano serves up a stylish winner

This is to prove the match when Dean Saunders' goalless frustration is purged with a Carrow Road winner fit for a leading place among his personal favourites.

Deano hadn't scored in open play in eleven starts dating back to October, including the more recent spell of six games without a win.

"I had forgotten how to celebrate a goal," jokes the Welsh international afterwards, though the ear-to-ear grin tells a contradictory story.

The stunning 59th minute strike gives him his seventh goal of the season and must surely lift a huge burden of creeping self-doubt off his shoulders.

For all Villa devotees the lead-up to the half-way stage in the Premiership programme had been increasingly disappointing. A slide down the table to a place among the also-rans had cast a cloud over Villa Park.

This culminated in a feeling of shock among fans when the scheduled Boxing Day match against Manchester City was postponed due to a frostbound pitch when other games in the region survived.

Consequently spirits urgently need a lift at Norwich and the early portents are good. Although Garry Parker and Dalian Atkinson are unfit Ron Atkinson is able to recall both Steve Staunton and Andy Townsend.

Another of the long-term injured, Dwight Yorke, is on the bench along with the young winger Dave Farrell, an indication of the Villa manager's attacking intentions.

The young West Indian is to reappear, after his lengthy absence through injury, as a second-half substitute for Whittingham who has been suffering from a cold.

Also, Norwich's home record, especially in the goalscoring department, is a poor one so Villa's confidence is high. Although there has been wintery weather conditions around the country the Carrow Road pitch is in its usual fine condition.

Villa play five at the back with Kevin Richardson, Ray Houghton and Townsend in midfield and both sides settle into a pattern of smooth passing football.

Despite their numbers there are tremors in Villa's defence, however, and in the 26th minutes Chris Sutton takes advantage of one of these by intercepting an intended pass from Shaun Teale to Earl Barrett before beating Mark Bosnich.

At the other end Villa are denied when Bryan Gunn saves brilliantly from Guy Whittingham while Townsend misses the target from a good position.

The equaliser in a match which never ceases its restless concentration on controlled attacking play arrives eleven minutes into the second half. This time it is Norwich's turn to make a poor pass in front of goal, Houghton pouncing on Ian Culverhouse's mistake to force the ball home.

The home defence is left in disarray, some claiming the goal should have been disallowed others blaming each other for it when Saunders conjures his winner. After a neat build-up he is in possession 25 yards out on Villa's left when he spots Gunn off his line and swivels to beat him with a superb cross shot.

Right to the end Norwich then battle to get back on terms in an enthralling finale. Bosnich is again in superb form throughout and the Canaries are never going to be allowed to prevent Villa's return to winning ways.

"People who have watched us regularly know we haven't had a lucky break for a month," said manager Atkinson. "We have not been able to win a game for love nor money but we had the courage to go out and get the lead and then to hold on to it."

Saturday 1st January 1994 • Villa Park • 3.00pm

ASTON VILLA 0 BLACKBURN ROVERS 1

Half-time 0-1 • *Attendance* 40,903

Referee Lawrence DILKES (Mossley)

Linesmen D.S. BRAMMER and A.N. BUTLER

Claret Shirts with Blue Stripes, White Shorts		Goals	Blue and White Halved Shirts, Blue Shorts		Goals
13	Mark BOSNICH		26	Tim FLOWERS	
17	Neil COX		20	Henning BERG	
5	Paul McGRATH		2	David MAY	
2	Earl BARRETT		5	Colin HENDRY	
3	Steve STAUNTON ‡		6	Graeme LE SAUX	
7	Ray HOUGHTON		7	Stuart RIPLEY	
6	Kevin RICHARDSON		4	Tim SHERWOOD	
14	Andy TOWNSEND		23	David BATTY	
21	Dave FARRELL †		11	Jason WILCOX	
9	Dean SAUNDERS		9	Alan SHEARER	37
22	Guy WHITTINGHAM		8	Kevin GALLACHER	
	Substitutes			*Substitutes*	
1	Nigel SPINK		1	Bobby MIMMS	
18	Dwight YORKE †61		3	Alan WRIGHT	
4	Shaun TEALE ‡70		12	Nick MARKER	

BEFORE		P	W	D	L	F	A	pts	AFTER		P	W	D	L	F	A	pts
2	Blackburn	22	12	6	4	31	18	42	2	Blackburn	23	13	6	4	32	18	45
8	Villa	22	9	7	6	26	24	34	8	Villa	23	9	7	7	26	25	34

FACTFILE

It's Villa Park's biggest gate for four years as the top deck of the new Witton Lane Stand is opened (delayed by the postponement of the Boxing Day game with Man City)... Dave Farrell starts his first game of the season... Sub Dwight Yorke makes his 100th Villa appearance in league and cup.

Big let down for holiday crowd

The first home game of the festive season, due to the Boxing Day postponement, attracts a gate of 40,000 as capacity is enhanced by the opening of the Witton Lane upper tier.

Blackburn Rovers arrive as the team now most favoured to apply pressure to Manchester United as the Old Trafford giants defend their title from a runaway lead.

Expectations are high after the mid-week win at Norwich with fans well aware that, if Villa are to pursue runners-up place again, home performances have to improve quickly.

Ron Atkinson sounds the unnecessary pre-match warning that Alan Shearer is the big threat and forecasts that this jewel in Blackburn's £22m crown will become Europe's No.1 striker.

Despite the Carrow Road victory the Villa manager makes changes, bringing in Dave Farrell for width in attack and demoting Shaun Teale to substitute. This is clearly a tactical move aimed at handing Earl Barrett the task of marking Shearer.

With Steve Staunton and Andy Townsend making their first home appearances for a considerable time and Dwight Yorke on the bench yearning to join them, the pre-match atmosphere is one of optimism.

Sadly, this mood proves to be mis-placed. Frustration sets in quickly as the strange claret-and-blue home phobia persists and Blackburn are able to dominate the shape of a game Villa are never going to win.

Drive and confidence are absent from Villa's game

and in the 37th minute Shearer justifies Ron Atkinson's fears by conjuring the lead from his first scoring opportunity.

Goalkeeper Mark Bosnich's first meaningful touch of the ball is to pluck it from the back of the net after a centre from left back Graeme Le Saux is rifled in by the England striker. This is to prove the only goal of a game which leaves the Villa manager almost speechless with anger.

Atkinson's fury is well-founded. His players seem to have less passion than Kenny Dalglish's who, from Villa's viewpoint, win possession far too often and use the ball better.

There is no marked improvement in the second half, though Yorke is brought on in place of Farrell, who has done his best in difficult circumstances, while Teale replaces Staunton who has not seemed fully match fit.

Villa's only significant chance of an equaliser comes when Ray Houghton's centre reaches the far post but Dean Saunders' header is collected easily by Tim Flowers.

By this time hopes of that runners-up place behind United look feeble, indeed, as home form heads towards crisis proportions.

Atkinson confesses to being as puzzled and concerned by it as everyone else though sympathy with some of his players appears to have run out. "It is beyond me to explain how they could perform like that," he confessed. "We aren't talking about kids here but 50-cap internationals with loads of experience.

"People paid good money to come and watch that. I'll take nothing away from Blackburn because I think they are the next best team after United but the disappointing feature was that they showed more passion and belief than we did."

Rovers' Jason Wilcox avoids a Neil Cox tackle

Saturday 8th January 1994 • St. James' Park • 3.00pm

EXETER CITY 0 ASTON VILLA 1

Half-time 0-0 • Attendance 10,570

Referee Keith COOPER (Pontypridd)
Linesmen G. BEALE and D. RICHARDS

Red and White Striped Shirts, Black Shorts		Goals	Claret Shirts with Blue Stripes, White Shorts		Goals
1	Peter FOX		13	Mark BOSNICH	
2	Jason MINETT		17	Neil COX	
5	Scott DANIELS		4	Shaun TEALE	
6	Peter WHISTON		2	Earl BARRETT	
3	Jon BROWN		3	Steve STAUNTON	
11	Danny BAILEY		7	Ray HOUGHTON	
8	Russell COUGHLIN		6	Kevin RICHARDSON	
4	Simon DAVIES		14	Andy TOWNSEND ❑	
7	Stuart STORER		8	Garry PARKER	
10	Mickey ROSS ❑		9	Dean SAUNDERS	pen 59
9	Steve WIGLEY †		10	Dalian ATKINSON	
	Substitutes			*Substitutes*	
13	Kenny VEYSEY		1	Nigel SPINK	
12	Martin PHILLIPS †66		23	Bryan SMALL	
14	Toby REDWOOD		22	Guy WHITTINGHAM	

Villa win with a penalty, having missed spot kicks in both of last season's third round games with Bristol Rovers and then being eliminated on penalties by Wimbledon in round four... A capacity crowd generates record gate receipts of around £80,000, double the previous St. James' Park record... Exeter, who have not got past the third round since 1951, have beaten Farnborough Town 3-1 in the first round and Leyton Orient on penalties in round 2... The Grecians have not won in the league since beating Fulham 6-4 two months ago... They are currently 18th in the Second Division and are eventually relegated.

A cupful of controversy

Although the third round tie in Devon is not regarded as one of the round's highlights, Villa make Saturday morning national paper head-lines of the sort they could do without.

The name in the news in 'Paul McGrath' for another of the AWOL episodes which have cropped up too often previously in his career.

Macca, it seems, was missing when the coach left for the West Country on Friday afternoon, despite his having been in for training during the morning. Ron Atkinson is making no com-ment about Macca's absence, but is said to be 'furious'.

The player's story differs slightly. He says his knees were 'too sore' to play at Exeter and that the manager was aware of this and knew of his intended absence.

Against this controversial backdrop and faced by a 'hiding-to-nothing' situation against Alan Ball's team, Villa attempt to make their superior class tell.

Earl Barrett and Shaun Teale are in the cen-tre of the defence for a tie which was always going to be a difficult ride but is made even more so by the muddy surface.

Exeter, no doubt sensing Villa's discomfort,

go for the big prize of a fourth round place and by half-time it is Villa who give the impression of hanging on for a replay.

The feeling persists in the second half with the Second Division team producing the more dangerous attacks in what is mainly an untidy midfield stalemate.

Villa badly need a touch of inspiration and it is provided by Dean Saunders after 58 minutes.

Fed by a cunning pass from Ray Houghton, who earlier had almost scored with a volley, the Welshman is closing in dangerously when he is tripped by defender Peter Whiston.

For Deano, hungry for elusive goal chances, the penalty opportunity is too appetising to miss and his shot is blasted in as goalkeeper Peter Fox dives the wrong way.

Once ahead, a relieved Villa have no inten-tion of letting go especially as Exeter, for all their heart, are short of true guile and fire power. In the last ten minutes or so both Garry Parker and Dalian Atkinson are close to increas-ing Villa's lead, though that would have given a misleading scoreline.

"If Villa go all the way to Wembley they won't have a harder game than this one," declares Ball afterwards, clearly forgetting what it can be like at Old Trafford.

Ron Atkinson, still irritated that the McGrath problem should blow up at such a time declines his normal press conference and says a state-ment will be made on Monday.

Andy Townsend expresses the mood, how-ever, when he declares: "We are just glad to be in the next round."

The following day a Sunday newspaper prints details of McGrath's private life in which he is quoted as saying he has problems. The article and others also quote him as saying that because he was not playing the next day he had consumed 'five pints of lager'.

Monday's papers claim that he has been fined two week's wages, a figure estimated as high as £10,000 though this is not official.

Ray Houghton is challenged by Steve Wigley

Wednesday 12th January 1994 • White Hart Lane • 7.45pm

TOTTENHAM HOTSPUR 1 ASTON VILLA 2

Half-time 0-0 • *Attendance* 31,408

Referee Terry HOLBROOK (Wolverhampton)

Linesmen L.E. CABLE and M. STOBBART

White Shirts, Navy Blue Shorts	Goals	Claret Shirts with Blue Stripes, White Shorts	Goals
1 Erik THORSTVEDT		13 Mark BOSNICH	
22 David KERSLAKE		2 Earl BARRETT	69
5 Colin CALDERWOOD		5 Paul McGRATH	
14 Steve SEDGLEY		4 Shaun TEALE	
3 Justin EDINBURGH		3 Steve STAUNTON	
4 Vinny SAMWAYS		7 Ray HOUGHTON	57
9 Darren ANDERTON		6 Kevin RICHARDSON	
20 Darren CASKEY	64	8 Garry PARKER	
12 Jason DOZZELL		14 Andy TOWNSEND	
23 Sol CAMPBELL †		9 Dean SAUNDERS	
7 Nick BARMBY		10 Dalian ATKINSON	
Substitutes		*Substitutes*	
13 Ian WALKER		1 Nigel SPINK	
25 John HENDRY †52		11 Tony DALEY	
2 Dean AUSTIN		17 Neil COX	

FACTFILE

Villa reach the League Cup semi-finals for a record ninth time, and are drawn against Forest or Tranmere... It's an 8th unbeaten visit to Spurs and Arsenal under Ron Atkinson's reign... Earl Barrett's goal is his first of the season and only his second in 92 appearances for the club... Around 5,500 Villa fans make the trip to London.

Match-winner Earl Barrett

Earl is the king of the night

With Paul McGrath restored to the heart of the defence, his latest AWOL controversy now behind him, Ron Atkinson is able to field what looks his strongest team at White Hart Lane.

The travelling fans are out in force, on a wretched night when yet more downpours swell the floods around the country, as Villa go for a semi-final place.

North London has been a happy hunting ground for Villa during Atkinson's reign and Spurs' home record, with no White Hart Lane win since October, augers well for the visitors.

The stadium is packed with rival fans all with a possible Wembley visit on their minds. Sheffield Wednesday have already won one semi-final place, the Forest-Tranmere tie has been postponed while Manchester United-Portsmouth is to emerge as a 2-2 draw.

There's everything to go for... and Villa go for it with a confidence and resolve missing too often from Villa Park performances.

From the foundation of well-organised defence, with Steve Staunton back at his best after his lengthy injury lay-off, the attacks snake forward threateningly, though their forward play is spasmodic rather than sustained.

There is much work for Villa in defence and Mark Bosnich deals safely with the flak which pierces the McGrath inspired back four though Jason Dozzell and Vinny Samways cause plenty of problems.

The most menacing moment, on a skidding pitch flecked white with sleet, is a Darren Anderton shot which rattles an upright plus a Dozzell shot which the Wizard of Oz saves superbly.

This is matched by a Dean Saunders free-kick which Spurs 'keeper Eric Thorstvedt finger-tips for a corner with a thrilling dive to his left.

"What DO I have to do...?" wonders the Welsh international, victim so often of hairline saves like that.

By half-time of a riveting tie Spurs have the edge but Villa are unbowed and the torrents have eased a little.

Dalian Atkinson, a fairly anonymous figure in the first half, begins to make an impact.

In the 58th minute he dispossesses Samways to start a 12-minute spell of goalscoring excitement. The enigmatical Dalian, anonymous one second inspirational the next, surges forward, and slides a pass to Ray Houghton whose low cross-shot is out of Thorstvedt's reach.

Only seven minutes later Spurs are level though they have lost striker Sol Campbell, stretchered off after twisting a knee. The scorer is Darren Caskey with a low shot through a packed defence which, unluckily for the diving Bosnich, deflects off Shaun Teale's foot.

Now Villa's winner is only five minutes away. Earl Barrett, excellent in defence throughout, decides to try his hand or rather his head, as an attacker and is unmarked as Garry Parker's left wing corner floats in.

Barrett's downward header deceives the Norwegian goalkeeper by bouncing under his floundering body in a treacherous goalmouth and Villa are through to the semi-finals.

It is a tribute to their tactical awareness that they rarely allow Tottenham to so much as threaten a second equaliser other than a first-time volley by substitute John Hendry which bounces off the top of the crossbar.

Even then Villa might have gone 3-1 up when Deano rounds the Spurs' 'keeper but loses his footing when he's about to shoot and misses the inviting target.

Villa are through on sheer merit, though Spurs are left lamenting over two defensive mistakes. "I would think that is as well as Spurs have played for some time," said Ron Atkinson "But we defended well and, in the second half, came to life and frightened them a little."

Saturday 15th January 1994 • Villa Park • 3.00pm

ASTON VILLA 3 WEST HAM UNITED 1

Half-time 2-1 • *Attendance* 28,869

Referee Stephen LODGE (Barnsley)

Linesmen J. LEECH and A. STREETS

Claret Shirts with Blue Stripes, White Shorts		Goals	Light Blue Shirts with 2 Claret Hoops, Light Blue Shorts		Goals
13	Mark BOSNICH		1	Ludek MIKLOSKO	
2	Earl BARRETT		2	Tim BREACKER	
5	Paul McGRATH		4	Steve POTTS	
4	Shaun TEALE		12	Tony GALE	
3	Steve STAUNTON †		23	Keith ROWLAND	
7	Ray HOUGHTON		9	Trevor MORLEY †	
6	Kevin RICHARDSON	15	6	Martin ALLEN	30
14	Andy TOWNSEND		14	Ian BISHOP	
11	Tony DALEY		16	Matt HOLMES	
9	Dean SAUNDERS		34	Mike MARSH	
10	Dalian ATKINSON	43, 68	25	Lee CHAPMAN	
	Substitutes			*Substitutes*	
1	Nigel SPINK		13	Gerry PEYTON	
17	Neil COX †87		17	Steve JONES †76	
22	Guy WHITTINGHAM		15	Kenny BROWN	

BEFORE	P	W	D	L	F	A	pts	AFTER	P	W	D	L	F	A	pts
10 Villa	23	9	7	7	26	25	34	9 Villa	24	10	7	7	29	26	37
11 West Ham	25	9	7	9	21	29	34	11 West Ham	26	9	7	10	22	32	34

FACTFILE

It's Villa's first home win since mid-November (five games)...
Dalian Atkinson takes his goal tally to 12 with his third brace of the season...
The score is a repeat of the Hammers' last visit to Villa Park in 1991/92.

Dalian's double ends home jinx

Ron Atkinson's programme notes clearly set out his attitude to the recent cup progress... FORGET IT AND START CLIMBING THE LEAGUE.

'It's high time we blew that poor recent home record sky high and started giving the home fans something to shout about,' is the theme of Ron's message.

Villa's manager describes the run of four home games without a win and only one point from 12 as a 'total mystery'.

Big Ron realises that another home slip would be hard for those supporters to take but this proves never to be on the cards as Villa eagerly put together their best Villa Park display in months. This time, with England winger Tony Daley recalled in place of Garry Parker, they go for it right from the start against a visiting side who play a similar passing game to Villa's.

A number of previous Villa home games have been disapointing in both result and performance but here at least is the kind of match the home crowd relishes.

All it needs is a goal to sharpen Villa's attacking claws and the required breakthrough arrives after only 15 minutes.

An attack initiated by Earl Barrett sees Dalian Atkinson feed Kevin Richardson who blasts a 30-yard drive well out of Czech 'keeper Ludek Miklosko's reach.

The roar of welcome from around the ground is fuelled as much by relief as celebration but there proves to be a worrying moment or two

Dalian Atkinson robs Keith Rowland for Villa's second goal

before the three points are stored away.

Both sides are attacking with controlled menace and Daley, assisted by Atkinson, cuts in with pace to bury a shot into the netting just the wrong side of the post. Ray Houghton is also close to increasing the lead.

A 2-0 scoreline could have seriously demoralised the visitors but after half-an-hour they are all-square as Martin Allen's bullet header beats Bosnich. That feeling of 'Oh no, not again...' filters through to the crowd for a while but, a couple of minutes before half-time, Villa are ahead again.

A long forward pass by Andy Townsend, near the half-way line, like sends Atkinson away hungrily in search of a shooting chance. Keith Rowland appears to have the danger covered but the Villa man surges past him, side-tracks Miklosko, and knocks in goal No.2.

The re-start features shots at each end with Ian Bishop forcing Bosnich to go down to smother and Miklosko making a more difficult save from Dean Saunders.

Before Villa's third goal Hammers are close to equalising again as Lee Chapman heads wide of an unguarded goal after Bosnich has been lured out by a tempting Rowland centre.

This proves the last real scare for Villa fans. In the 68th minute Houghton cleverly sets up another shooting chance for Atkinson who raps it into the roof of the net for his 12th goal of the season.

"I should have had three," confessed Atkinson afterwards, referring to a header from a Steve Staunton centre which he had steered over the bar from a good position.

Two fine goals is enough, however, to send supporters home feeling far more happy about Villa's ability to climb back into the top three.

Saturday 22nd January 1994 • Stamford Bridge • 3.00pm

CHELSEA 1 ASTON VILLA 1

Half-time 0-1 • *Attendance* 18,341

Referee Graham POLL (Birkhamstead)

Linesmen D.C. RICHARDS and M.R. SIMS

Blue Shirts, Blue Shorts	Goals	Claret Shirts with Blue Stripes, White Shorts	Goals
1 Dmitri KHARINE		13 Mark BOSNICH	
12 Steve CLARKE		2 Earl BARRETT	
6 Frank SINCLAIR		5 Paul McGRATH	
5 Erland JOHNSEN ❏		4 Shaun TEALE	
26 Andy DOW ‡		3 Steve STAUNTON	
17 Nigel SPACKMAN		7 Ray HOUGHTON	
24 Craig BURLEY		6 Kevin RICHARDSON	
27 David HOPKIN		14 Andy TOWNSEND	
10 Gavin PEACOCK		11 Tony DALEY	
21 Mark STEIN	67	9 Dean SAUNDERS	39
19 Neil SHIPPERLEY †		10 Dalian ATKINSON	
Substitutes		*Substitutes*	
13 Kevin HITCHCOCK		1 Nigel SPINK	
7 John SPENCER †76		17 Neil COX	
15 Mal DONAGHY ‡82		18 Dwight YORKE	

BEFORE		P	W	D	L	F	A	pts	AFTER		P	W	D	L	F	A	pts
9	Villa	24	10	7	7	29	26	37	10	Villa	25	10	8	7	30	27	38
17	Chelsea	24	6	7	11	22	39	25	17	Chelsea	25	6	8	11	23	40	26

Mark Stein takes his Chelsea goals tally to eight in the last eight games... It is the 94th league meeting between these clubs - Villa have won 41, Chelsea 32 and this is the 21st draw. Villa have scored 160 goals to Chelsea's 139.

Boo boys fail to rattle Townsend

Andy Townsend's first return to Stamford Bridge since the Irish international's £2.1m close season move ought to have been a routine affair but the mindless minority choose to cast a shadow.

Townsend is even dubbed a 'Judas' by some of the Chelsea morons who add to their infamy by failing to observe the nationwide one-minute silence for Sir Matt Busby who died during the week.

After three successive victories Villa's mood is a positive one as they pursue a league place back among the chasing pack.

Yet the atmosphere in the ground remains unpleasant. Townsend is not the only player subjected to verbal abuse. Dean Saunders is also singled out because of the incident involving Paul Elliott more than a year earlier.

The main culprits are, surprisingly, not the occupants of the ground's notorious 'Shed' but spectators in the West Stand.

Such unwarranted behaviour deserves to be punished by footballing means on the field of play and the early signs are positive.

The game is 39 minutes old when Tony Daley robs Craig Burley down the left side and supplies Deano with a precisely judged cross. The home defence is thrown by the speed and accuracy of the thrust as Saunders hits the net with an explosive volley.

Once the floodgates have been opened Villa, with their command of the attacking play, appear to have the route open to pour in more for a resounding victory.

A one-goal half-time lead is less than Villa's domination justifies and early in the second half the chance to put the scoreline beyond Chelsea's reach arrives. Again Daley is the provider and again Saunders is on the receiving end of a well-judged pass. This time, however, the Welshman has time and space to manoeuvre himself into position, delays too long, and the defence has time to re-group.

It proves an expensive lapse for Villa as second-best Chelsea keep plugging away at a defence which, with Shaun Teale outstanding, seems unlikely to crack.

So little threat has been offered by Chelsea, and so many openings created by Villa, that an away win looks a formality with the game three-quarters over.

An attack of no particular merit then changes the outlook. A couple of shots rebound off Teale in a well-guarded goalmouth but the second of them falls to the lethal Mark Stein and a 1-1 scoreline is posted. "It is a sign of a good striker when he can score on a day when the team is not functioning effectively," said Chelsea boss Glenn Hoddle.

Ron Atkinson is frustrated that two points have been allowed to drift. "We had the game under control, but we took our foot off the pedal." Mixing his metaphors in colourful fashion, he adds: "With all the experienced players we have we should have put the game to bed...

Prior to kick-off there was a minute's silence for Sir Matt Busby

Saturday 29th January 1994 • Blundell Park • 3.00pm

GRIMSBY TOWN 1 ASTON VILLA 2

Half-time 0-1 • Attendance 15,771

Referee Ian HEMLEY (Bedfordshire)
Linesmen J. BARLOW and W.J. NATTRASS

White Shirts with Black Stripes, Black Shorts	Goals		Claret Shirts with Blue Stripes, White Shorts	Goals
1 Paul CHRICHTON		13	Mark BOSNICH	
2 Tony FORD		2	Earl BARRETT	
5 Peter HANDYSIDE †		5	Paul McGRATH	
4 Paul FUTCHER		4	Shaun TEALE ■	
3 Gary CROFT		3	Steve STAUNTON	
7 Gary CHILDS		7	Ray HOUGHTON	13
6 Jim DOBBIN ‡		6	Kevin RICHARDSON	
10 Paul GROVES	58	14	Andy TOWNSEND	
11 Dave GILBERT ❑		11	Tony DALEY †	
8 Clive MENDONCA		9	Dean SAUNDERS ‡	
9 Steve LIVINGSTONE ■		10	Dalian ATKINSON	
Substitutes			*Substitutes*	
13 Mark CLOHESSY		1	Nigel SPINK	
12 Mark LEVER †80		17	Neil COX †24	
14 Craig SHAKESPEARE ‡80		18	Dwight YORKE ‡34	78

FACTFILE

Shaun Teale becomes the first Villa player to be sent off since Ron Atkinson took over... Villa go in at half-time minus three of the players they started with... Dwight Yorke's winner is his first goal of the season... Villa face another away tie in round five, against the winners of Monday's Bolton-Arsenal tie... This is the first ever meeting between these sides in the FA Cup, although they did meet in the League Cup two seasons ago when the Mariners put Villa out on the away goals rule... Grimsby are currently 18th in Division One and put Wigan out in the last round of the FA Cup with a 1-0 home win... Highlights of the game are shown on BBC 'Match of the Day'.

Sub Yorke sinks the Mariners

Build-up to FA Cup fourth round day has been over-shadowed all around the country by major events, as the morning banner headlines illustrate. In a news-packed Friday, Terry Venables was yesterday confirmed as Graham Taylor's successor as England team coach while Graeme Souness left his job as boss at Anfield after a stormy reign.

The second of these items does, however, have relevance to today's events with Souness's departure having been escalated by FA Cup defeat by Bristol City at home. "If it can happen to Liverpool, it can happen to anybody," warns Ron Atkinson in his pre-match briefing.

This danger is quickly confirmed as 'Match of the Day' cameras record a bright and dangerous start by Grimsby in typical Alan Buckley 'passing' mode.

Clive Mendonca and Paul Groves threaten Bosnich's goal in the opening 13 minutes yet Villa, who have not previously mounted a meaningful attack hit Grimsby on the break to take the lead. And what a break..!

Kevin Richardson feeds a ball forward and Peter Handysides, a Scottish Under-21 defender looks to have time to clear but he totally under-estimates Dalian Atkinson's explosive pace. The Villa man powers the ball away into inviting space ahead of him and places it so accurately into the Grimsby goalmouth that defenders unprepared for such speedy attacks allow Ray Houghton to tap it in unchallenged.

Villa instantly have to guard their lead and as Shaun Teale defends tigerishly he finds himself heading for an early bath for the first time in his career. The rugged centre back is going full-throttle for an intended headed clearance when former Coventry City striker Steve Livingstone comes at him, elbow raised dangerously.

An ugly maul flares as the two players wrestle briefly and when peace is restored both men are shown the red card. Big Ron has no alternative but to re-group and, with Earl Barrett switched to partner Paul McGrath in the middle Neil Cox is sent on at right back and Tony Daley is withdrawn.

Yet more trauma lies ahead. Dean Saunders, who has twice promised to increase Villa's lead, suddenly pulls up painfully with a back problem and limps out of the game. Dwight Yorke, back after injury, goes on to fill the gap and Villa's lead survives safely to half-time.

Grimsby start the second-half as they did the first but Villa are still dangerous, notably when an Atkinson drive almost knocks goalkeeper Paul Crichton off his feet.

The home team are worthy of a goal and Villa hearts miss a beat when Barrett pushes Mendonca in the back. It looks a clear penalty but the referee thinks otherwise and Grimsby push on to finally earn a 58th miute reward.

Despite Grimsby's attacking aggression Bosnich has not been seriously troubled until Groves drives a scoring shot under his dive.

A replay looks on the cards until 12 minutes from time when Atkinson's searing pace again wrecks the home defence and Yorke is presented with just the opportunity he's been waiting for. Controlling the ball nimbly he beats two defenders as he veers in on goal to beat Crichton and mark his return with a fifth round ticket.

Substitute Dwight Yorke fires Villa into the last sixteen

Sunday 6th February 1994 • Villa Park • 4.00pm

ASTON VILLA 1 LEEDS UNITED 0

Half-time 0-0 • Attendance 26,919

Referee Jim BORRETT (Great Yarmouth)
Linesmen S. R. BRAND and P.A. ROBERTS

Claret Shirts with Blue Stripes, White Shorts		Goals	White Shirts with 2 Blue & 1 Yellow Hoop, Blue Shorts		Goals
13	Mark BOSNICH		13	Mark BEENEY	
2	Earl BARRETT		22	Gary KELLY	
5	Paul McGRATH		5	Chris FAIRCLOUGH	
4	Shaun TEALE		16	Jon NEWSOME	
3	Steve STAUNTON †		3	Tony DORIGO	
7	Ray HOUGHTON ‡		7	Gordon STRACHAN	
6	Kevin RICHARDSON		11	Gary SPEED ❏	
14	Andy TOWNSEND	68	10	Gary McALLISTER	
11	Tony DALEY		14	Steve HODGE	
9	Dean SAUNDERS		9	Brian DEANE	
10	Dalian ATKINSON		4	David WHITE †	

	Substitutes			*Substitutes*	
1	Nigel SPINK		1	John LUKIC	
17	Neil COX †58 ❏		25	Noel WHELAN †71	
18	Dwight YORKE ‡73		12	John PEMBERTON	

BEFORE	P	W	D	L	F	A	pts	AFTER	P	W	D	L	F	A	pts
7 Leeds	26	11	10	5	39	28	43	7 Leeds	27	11	10	6	39	29	43
10 Villa	25	10	8	7	30	27	38	8 Villa	26	11	8	7	31	27	41

Villa win in front of a live TV audience for the first time in six games this season, this one on Sky... Leeds have now gone six games without a league win... This is the 59th league meeting between these clubs - it is Villa's 20th win, equalling Leeds' total, with 19 games drawn. The goals total is 91-83 in Leeds' favour.

Last laugh for strong arm Andy

The demands of Sky TV dictate a four o'clock kick-off, disrupting the traditional English Sunday afternoon and, at three o'clock, the heavens open. An anticipated 30,000 crowd is reduced by around 3,000 but bedraggled arrivals are greeted by the welcoming sight of covers being removed to reveal a well-nigh perfect pitch.

The Villa players are refreshed by a few days training on the sunshine island of Tenerife since the FA Cup win at Grimsby.

There is just one hiccup in the air of stability, namely that Dalian Atkinson is reported to have asked for a move following 'a bust-up' with the manager. Ron Atkinson confirms the newspaper stories in essence but reports that calm has been restored and that any differences with Dalian will be put on hold to the end of the season.

With so many talented players on view, especially in the midfields, expectations of an entertaining 90 minutes are high but these expectations go unrealised in a disappointing first half. Play is untidy and uninspired with neither side able to keep their football flowing. This is largely because both sides tend to play in a tight, compact unit, denying each other the time and space to spread their distribution around.

Intercepted passes and bodily collisions are more in evidence than creative play and Andy Townsend proves to be a consistent victim.

In the 17th minute Jon Newsome's elbow gives him a bloody nose while in double that time the aggressive and slightly clumsy Brian Deane steps on his forearm. Although the scoreline is blank at half-time it is not for the want of close calls, largely as a result of errors.

Shaun Teale sends a header rebounding off the underside of his own crossbar, Paul McGrath almost back-heels an own goal. In the midst of all this confusion Mark Bosnich runs off his line for a centre-half style clearance and almost misses the ball, connecting only with the faintest of slices.

What happens next..?

The ball spins agonisingly towards his own net but Steve Staunton clears up at the post. The operative words is... PHEW! Atkinson's ability to flit in and out of the action sees him put his foot down to go turbo-charged past defenders but his feet outstrip his brain.

Faced with Mark Beeney coming off his line and Ray Houghton and Dean Saunders motoring into unmarked positions on the centre-right of the goal, Atkinson frustratingly opts to pass the ball weakly to the Leeds 'keeper.

The second half sees a general improvement, with Villa seizing the initiative. Townsend, arm heavily strapped, ignores his discomfort to drive forward whenever possible.

Atkinson, foot on the pedal again, sends in a sizzler which Beeney just turns away. The Leeds 'keeper also saves a super cross-shot from Deano.

Two substitutions have to be made due to injuries, Neil Cox for the limping Staunton and Dwight Yorke for Houghton.

Happily, Cox's arrival on the right of defence, with Earl Barrett switching flanks, leads to the Villa breakthough. His raking 70th minute pass finds Townsend who bears down on goal from the right and fires a swerving shot across Beeney with the outside of his left foot. Nicely done...

"I was that knackered when I got to the ball I hardly had the strength to hit it," said the 30-year-old World Cup-bound Irishman. He could have fooled us.

Andy Townsend

Saturday 12th February 1994 • Villa Park • 3.00pm

ASTON VILLA 5 SWINDON TOWN 0

Half-time 1-0 • *Attendance* 27,637

Referee Robert HART (Darlington)
Linesmen R.H. ANDREWS and E.G. HANNAH

Claret Shirts with Blue Stripes, White Shorts	Goals	Yellow Shirts, Light Blue Shorts	Goals
13 Mark BOSNICH		40 Jon SHEFFIELD	
17 Neil COX		14 Adrian WHITBREAD †	
2 Earl BARRETT		31 Brian KILCLINE	
5 Paul McGRATH ‡		6 Shaun TAYLOR	
12 Steve FROGGATT	55	16 Kevin HORLOCK	
7 Ray HOUGHTON		2 Nicky SUMMERBEE ❏	
6 Kevin RICHARDSON	73	5 Luc NIJHOLT	
14 Andy TOWNSEND †		7 John MONCUR	
11 Tony DALEY		10 Martin LING	
9 Dean SAUNDERS 31, pens 66 & 84		9 Jan Aage FJORTOFT ‡	
10 Dalian ATKINSON		27 Keith SCOTT	
Substitutes		*Substitutes*	
1 Nigel SPINK		23 Nicky HAMMOND	
18 Dwight YORKE †73		3 Paul BODIN †66	
16 Ugo EHIOGU ‡78		26 Terry FENWICK ‡84	

BEFORE	P	W	D	L	F	A	pts	AFTER	P	W	D	L	F	A	pts
8 Villa	26	11	8	7	31	27	41	6 Villa	27	12	8	7	36	27	44
22 Swindon	28	4	10	14	31	62	22	22 Swindon	29	4	10	15	31	67	22

FACTFILE

Villa score five for the first time in 13 months... Deano nets his first hat-trick for the club... Steve Froggatt scores on his first appearance for four months... Shaun Teale is suspended... Swindon 'keeper Jon Sheffield, on loan from Cambridge, has a nightmare debut wearing the Premiership's highest shirt number!

In tune Villa hammer Swindon

The visit of struggling Swindon provides Villa with the opportunity to win three home games on the trot for the first time this season and it proves a chance not to be wasted.

In a surprise selection move Ron Atkinson recalls Steve Froggatt for his first senior game since he played at Swindon on October 30.

Froggatt replaces the injured Steve Staunton at left back while, to replace the suspended Shaun Teale at centre back, Earl Barrett moves over to accommodate Neil Cox.

The manager has instilled in his players the need to push thoughts of the two forthcoming cup-ties out of their minds to concentrate on a climb back up the table.

Early play gives no hint of the goal-rush which lies ahead with Swindon, who have improved a shade recently, playing extremely well.

When Dean Saunders scores in the 31st minute the scoreline seems a slight injustice to the visitors. In-form Kevin Richardson's forward pass pierces the defence and Andy Townsend nods the bouncing ball into the Welshman's path. Deano, near the edge of the box, connects with a screamer which swerves away from goal-keeper Jon Sheffield, who is on loan from Cambridge United and making his Premiership debut.

Within minutes Swindon are close to equalising as Ray Houghton, covering well behind his defence, clears a Shaun Taylor header off the line.

Villa fans are quite relieved to reach half-time with a slender lead but any fears of a return to those home day blues are quickly dispersed.

Ten minutes into the second half Villa go two up with a goal which marks the end of an unhappy period for Froggatt.

Tony Daley skins his defender with one of his electrifying spurts down the left wing and Froggy is perfectly positioned, like a seasoned target man steaming through the middle, to get on the end of it with a perfect header.

Afterwards both managers agree that this was the goal which effectively pushed the scoreline Villa's way and ensured a home victory.

Villa go three up in 66 minutes when 'keeper Sheffield bundles Saunders to floor for an undisputed penalty. Deano gets to his feet to take the kick for his second goal, though it's a close call as Sheffield gets to the ball and all but turns it away.

From now on it is a question of 'how many?' and only seven minutes elapse before the answer is 'four... at least'. This time Richardson is the marksman as he confidently puts away a chance provided by Dalian Atkinson.

Six minutes from time the fifth arrives, via a second Saunders penalty after Dwight Yorke, on as sub for Townsend, is floored by Luc Nijholt.

Deano is naturally well pleased with his first Villa hat-trick though he has to concede that a couple of other chances have been sprayed off-target.

"In the second half we would have taken many teams to the cleaners," said Ron Atkinson, satisfied that the 'home jinx' talk has been put to sleep.

Deano is sent tumbling for the first penalty

Wednesday 16th February 1994 • Prenton Park • 7.30pm

TRANMERE ROVERS 3 ASTON VILLA 1

Half-time 2-0 • Attendance 17,148

Referee Roger MILFORD (Bristol)
Linesmen A.N. BUTLER and P.R. RICHARDS

White Shirts, White Shorts		Goals	Claret Shirts with Blue Stripes, Black Shorts		Goals
1	Eric NIXON		13	Mark BOSNICH	
2	John McGREAL		17	Neil COX	
5	Mark HUGHES	24	2	Earl BARRETT	
11	Shaun GARNETT		5	Paul McGRATH	
3	Ian NOLAN	5	3	Steve STAUNTON †	
4	Ged BRANNAN		7	Ray HOUGHTON	
7	Kenny IRONS		6	Kevin RICHARDSON	
6	Liam O'BRIEN ❑		14	Andy TOWNSEND	
10	Pat NEVIN		11	Tony DALEY	
8	John ALDRIDGE	78	9	Dean SAUNDERS	
9	Chris MALKIN		10	Dalian ATKINSON	90
	Substitutes			*Substitutes*	
13	Danny COYNE		1	Nigel SPINK	
12	John MORRISSEY		12	Steve FROGGATT †74	
14	Steve MUNGALL		16	Ugo EHIOGU	

FACTFILE

Villa are appearing in the semi-finals for a record ninth time... John Aldridge, then with Oxford, killed off Villa's hopes the last time they reached the last four... Shaun Teale misses his second game through suspension... Steve Staunton is withdrawn and requires groin surgery... Ticket restrictions keep Villa's travelling support down to 4,220 in the sell-out crowd... Tranmere, currently 6th in Division One, reached the semi-finals by beating Oxford 6-2 on aggregate, Grimsby 4-1 and Premiership Oldham 3-0 at home and Nottingham Forest 2-0 in a Prenton Park replay after a 1-1 draw at The City Ground... Manchester United beat Sheffield Wednesday 1-0 at Old Trafford in the first leg of the other semi-final.

Cup catastrophe on Merseyside

With only two-legs against a lower division side now barring the path to Wembley Villa kick off at Prenton Park as long-odds favourites to meet either Manchester United or Sheffield Wednesday in the Final.

By the final whistle, however, that situation has swung dramatically and alarmingly with Tranmere now holding a clear initiative.

In the 24 hours leading up the the kick-off the weather threatens to play a leading part as two to three inches of snow blanket the Villa training ground.

However, conditions are okay, though a shade heavy, on Merseyside as Villa, with Shaun Teale out through suspension, gamble a little on Staunton's fitness at left back though before the end he is replaced by Steve Froggatt.

It could not have been a much worse start. The talented and effective Pat Nevin works an opening to feed Ian Nolan who blasts in an unstoppable cross-shot which Mark Bosnich can only palm into the net.

Tranmere's passing football is creating problems for Villa whose main object now is to hold fast and soak up the pressure with the second leg in mind.

What they could have done without was the decisive slice of luck which favoured Tranmere in the 24th minute. Defender Mark Hughes is backing up his forwards on the right flank and floats over a right-footed volley towards the far post while struggling to keep his feet.

It looks nothing more than a hopeful punt into the pack but this is Tranmere's night, not Villa's, and the ball finds the net for a 2-0 scoreline which produces near-frenzy around the ground.

The onus is now on Villa to force the attacking pace in search of a less daunting target for the second leg on Sunday week.

Now, however, Tranmere are as determined in midfield and defence as they had been going forward and there are few routes left open with both Dean Saunders and Dalian Atkinson kept quiet. So intent are Villa going forward from half-time that what seems the killer blow arrives in the 78th minute. John Aldridge is released from near the half-way line as Villa claim off-side, but the trusty Aldridge, whom Ron Atkinson attempted to sign last season, ignores it all.

Single-mindedly racing forward he whacks a shot against the post but follows up with his famed predatory instincts to beat Bosnich on the rebound.

On the line, assistant manager Jim Barron is ticked off for the intensity of his protests.

A 3-0 scorline brings Wembley hopes crashing into ruins but, in injury time, Kevin Richardson's long free kick into the goalmouth is headed across by Daley for Dalian Atkinson to volley a precious away goal.

"It will take a superhuman effort at Villa Park, but the lads feel they can do it," says manager Atkinson. "At 3-0 down you feel you are dead but that has thrown us a lifeline.

"If you were given a one-off chance to get to Wembley by beating Tranmere 2-0 after extra time, you would maybe fancy your chances."

Dalian Atkinson puts Tranmere 'keeper Eric Nixon under pressure

Sunday 20th February 1994 • Burnden Park • 3.05pm

BOLTON WANDERERS 1 ASTON VILLA 0

Half-time 0-0 • *Attendance* 18,817

Referee Brian HILL (Kettering)

Linesmen P.J. JOSLIN and G.M. LEE

White Shirts, Dark Blue Shorts		Goals	Claret Shirts with Blue Stripes, White Shorts		Goals
1	Aidan DAVISON		13	Mark BOSNICH	
2	Phil BROWN		17	Neil COX	
8	Alan STUBBS	82	2	Earl BARRETT	
6	Mark SEAGRAVES		5	Paul McGRATH	
3	Jimmy PHILLIPS		12	Steve FROGGATT	
7	David LEE		7	Ray HOUGHTON	
4	Tony KELLY		6	Kevin RICHARDSON	
5	Jason McATEER		14	Andy TOWNSEND	
11	Mark PATTERSON		11	Tony DALEY ‡	
10	John McGINLAY		9	Dean SAUNDERS	
9	Owen COYLE		10	Dalian ATKINSON †	
	Substitutes			*Substitutes*	
13	Martyn MARGETSON		1	Nigel SPINK	
12	Andy WALKER		18	Dwight YORKE †45	
14	David BURKE		16	Ugo EHIOGU ‡83	

It's Villa's fourth away defeat of the season and they've all been in the North-west. Three of them have been on live TV - this one on BBC... First Division Bolton who have already eliminated Premiership sides in Everton and Arsenal are drawn at home to Oldham in the quarter-final (they lose 1-0)... In a disastrous campaign for Premiership clubs, Villa, Arsenal, Blackburn (Charlton), Everton, Ipswich (Wolves), Leeds (Oxford), Liverpool (Bristol City), Newcastle and West Ham (both Luton) are all knocked out by First Division clubs whilst Man City (Cardiff), QPR (Stockport) and Southampton (Port Vale) fall to teams from the Second Division.

FA Cup misery at Bolton

The scoreline tells the sad story of five unhappy days for the club with removal from the FA Cup following closely in the footsteps of a Coca Cola Cup campaign which lost its fizz at Tranmere.

Two uninspired away performances at First Division grounds, when no-one could complain about the defeats, has put the season on 'hold'.

There has been much talk of the 'Year of the Underdog' with the Premiership having taken a battering from Endsleigh League clubs and pride is at stake at Burnden Park.

Bolton have already disposed of Everton and Arsenal having eliminated Liverpool at Anfield last season while Villa are not exactly bubbling with confidence.

Ron Atkinson, tongue only slightly in cheek, expresses satisfaction at Villa having become the 'underdogs' themselves at 15/2 outsiders for the trophy but he knows that this is the toughest of hurdles.

Screened live on BBC TV the match never reaches any great heights apart from being fiercely competitive in midfield.

Drier weather has resulted in the pitch being a shade firmer than in recent months but it is still slightly soft on the surface.

The football from both sides is fragmented with little creativity from either midfield and few genuine scoring chances. Defences are basically in command with Villa falling foul of Bolton's well-marshalled offside trap.

Earl Barrett covers well for the absence of the suspended

Shaun Teale, likewise Steve Froggatt who is at left back in place of the injured Steve Staunton.

Townsend and Richardson work hard in midfield but achieve little, Dalian Atkinson has one shot off target and by half-time Dean Saunders has been anonymous.

The closest call of the first half is a power drive by Jimmy Phillips which smashes against the underside of Villa's bar before being cleared by Kevin Richardson.

Dalian Atkinson apparently suffering from a hamstring injury, is replaced by Dwight Yorke at half-time and this adds a touch more aggression up front.

Eight minutes into the second half comes Villa's best chance of the match as Saunders meets a near-post cross from Tony Daley but turns it a fraction off-target.

Yorke immediately appears to have a better opening, having sprinted ahead of defenders, but he is distracted by Phillips moving in forcefully at him from an angle and, thrown off balance slightly, the West Indian hooks the bouncing ball well wide.

A Villa Park replay looks on the cards until eight minutes from time when Bolton's defensive hero, Alan Stubbs, fires a long free kick which swerves wide of the wall to the right.

Mark Bosnich would normally have the space covered but he is more centre goal and cannot reach with his dive as the ball finds the corner of the net.

There is no way Villa will pull back now and dejection descends. Looking ahead to Tuesday night's Premiership match against Manchester City, Ron Atkinson observes grimly: "I will have to take stock..."

Kevin Richardson

Tuesday 22nd February 1994 • Villa Park • 7.45pm

ASTON VILLA 0 MANCHESTER CITY 0

Half-time 0-0 • Attendance 19,254

Referee Martin BODENHAM

Linesmen M.R. SIMS and S.R. BRAND

Claret Shirts with Blue Stripes, White Shorts	Goals	Light Blue Shirts, White Shorts	Goals
13 Mark BOSNICH		1 Tony COTON	
2 Earl BARRETT		22 Richard EDGHILL	
4 Shaun TEALE		15 Alan KERNAGHAN	
16 Ugo EHIOGU		5 Michel VONK	
23 Bryan SMALL		3 Terry PHELAN †	
8 Garry PARKER		7 David ROCASTLE	
6 Kevin RICHARDSON		4 Steve McMAHON	
14 Andy TOWNSEND		21 Steve LOMAS	
18 Dwight YORKE		19 Fitzroy SIMPSON	
22 Guy WHITTINGHAM †		8 Mike SHERON	
25 Graham FENTON ❑		28 Carl SHUTT	
Substitutes		*Substitutes*	
1 Nigel SPINK		25 Andy DIBBLE	
9 Dean SAUNDERS †72		2 Andy HILL †68	
17 Neil COX		11 Carl GRIFFITHS	

BEFORE	P	W	D	L	F	A	pts	AFTER	P	W	D	L	F	A	pts
6 Villa	27	12	8	7	36	27	44	6 Villa	28	12	9	7	36	27	45
20 City	28	5	10	13	23	37	25	19 City	29	5	11	13	23	37	26

FACTFILE *Substitute Dean Saunders misses an 82nd minute penalty... Graham Fenton is booked on his first team debut... The game is played with an orange ball in snowy conditions... This fixture was originally scheduled for Boxing Day but was postponed on the morning due to a frozen pitch.*

Sub Saunders is the Villain

The return to Premiership action after the disappointment of FA Cup exit coincides with the most sweeping team changes since Ron Atkinson took charge but another disappointment at the end of an unproductive seven days.

Nineteen-year-old Graham Fenton is recalled from his loan period at The Hawthorns to share the attacking duties with Guy Whittingham, who still badly needs to prove himself.

A combination of injuries and the need to give players a rest sees Paul McGrath, Steve Staunton, Tony Daley, Steve Froggatt, Ray Houghton and Dalian Atkinson all missing and Dean Saunders on the bench.

City, whose political unrest was calmed four matches earlier by the arrival of Francis Lee as chairman, were defeated 4-0 at Coventry on Saturday when their defence collapsed.

After their three home wins on the trot Villa have the chance to raise spirits in the camp by adding a fourth in pursuit of a possible return to the UEFA Cup on league position.

Ron Atkinson saw the Highfield Road game and clearly hopes that his side will rub in City's misery by taking the three points required to claim fourth place in the table.

The attendance is kept below 20,000 by the arrival of falling snow to add to the wind-chill factor on a thoroughly unpleasant evening.

As the match unfolds it proves a familiar story of Villa dictating the pattern of the game but producing too little genuine threat.

Guy Whittingham and Richard Edghill perform ballet on ice

Fenton, who had scored three goals in four games for West Bromwich Albion, responds to his call with great gusto, 'putting himself about' and 'giving us some exuberance' as the manager had suggested.

Early on Kevin Richardson sends him storming down the wing but, in his youthful enthusiasm, he shoots into the side-netting when a centre might have been more favourable. Later he tries a powerful run through the middle but Tony Coton deals comfortably with his shot.

Surface conditions are treacherous adding to the general discomfort of the players who rarely succeed in raising the standard above the mediocre.

Largely because of the difficult conditions there are some defensive errors, too, and the occasional but fleeting threat of a City goal.

Whittingham has not been able to make any impact and is replaced by Saunders with eighteen minutes left. Ten minutes after his arrival on the field the Welshman gets the one clear chance to win the game as he is brought down inside the penalty area by Richard Edghill.

Their are lengthy disputes against the penalty decision by City players but, when calm is restored, Deano disappointingly fails to hit the target as his poorly-struck shot passes two yards wide of an upright.

By now many spectators are hurrying away to the warmth of their homes or the local, depressed by three important matches in a week which have yielded two away cup defeats and a home league draw.

"We played some quality football despite the conditions and deserved to win," said manager Atkinson. "Fenton was bright, strong and never over-awed. He has given us another option."

Sunday 27th February 1994 • Villa Park • 3.00pm

ASTON VILLA 3 TRANMERE ROVERS 1

After extra time • Aggregate 4-4 • Villa win 5-4 on penalties
Half-time 2-1 • Attendance 40,593
Referee Allan GUNN (Sussex)
Linesmen D.C. MADGWICK and B.A. WIGGINTON

Claret Shirts with Blue Stripes, White Shorts	Goals	White Shirts, Blue Shorts	Goals
13 Mark BOSNICH		1 Eric NIXON	
17 Neil COX †		11 John McGREAL	
5 Paul McGRATH		5 Mark HUGHES †	
4 Shaun TEALE	23	2 Dave HIGGINS	
2 Earl BARRETT		3 Ian NOLAN	
7 Ray HOUGHTON ‡		10 Pat NEVIN ‡	
6 Kevin RICHARDSON		6 Liam O'BRIEN	
14 Andy TOWNSEND		7 Kenny IRONS	
11 Tony DALEY		4 Ged BRANNAN	
9 Dean SAUNDERS	19	8 John ALDRIDGE	pen 29
10 Dalian ATKINSON	88	9 Chris MALKIN	
Substitutes		*Substitutes*	
1 Nigel SPINK		13 Danny COYNE	
25 Graham FENTON †77		14 Tony THOMAS †90	
16 Ugo EHIOGU ‡90		12 John MORRISSEY ‡98	

PENALTY SHOOT-OUT

1	Dean SAUNDERS	✔		1-0
2	Shaun TEALE	✔		2-1
3	Graham FENTON	✔		3-2
4	Dalian ATKINSON	✔		4-2
5	Ugo EHIOGU	✘	*Hit bar*	4-3
6	Kevin RICHARDSON	✘	*Over bar*	4-4
7	Tony DALEY	✔		5-4

PENALTY SHOOT-OUT

1	Kenny IRONS	✔		1-1
2	Tony THOMAS	✔		2-2
3	Ged BRANNAN	✘	*Saved*	3-2
4	Dave HIGGINS	✔		4-3
5	John ALDRIDGE	✔		4-4
6	Liam O'BRIEN	✘	*Saved*	4-4
7	Ian NOLAN	✘	*Saved*	5-4

Villa become the first club in League Cup history to overturn a first-leg two-goal deficit in the semi-final thanks to another late Dalian Atkinson goal.

Bozzie's the hero in penalty drama

Villa Park has staged some magnificent fixtures during its eventful history but this one is to rank very high on the role of honour as Mark Bosnich's penalty-saving miracles supply a breathtaking finale.

With the prize of the club's first Wembley Cup Final in seventeen years on offer and the threat of a season of hope turning sour, as the punishment for failure, the ground hums with high-octane expectation.

Starting at 3-1 down and encouraged to thoughts of success only on the back of the away goal at Prenton Park, Ron Atkinson's side have no alternative but to go for it. Two-nil after extra time would do it, but it is not to be.

Fans are in a positive lather of mixed emotions as, by mid-way through the first-half, the foundations of a cliff-hanger have been put down.

Villa are pushing foward incessantly as Andy Townsend and Tony Daley exchange passes down the left flank after 19 minutes. The Irish skipper, in search of a first Wembley final at his sixth attempt, makes a surging run to accept Daley's return pass and motors on to near the corner flag before crossing low and hard.

Defenders are caught back-pedalling when Dean Saunders hares in to meet the cross for a 'sniffer dog' type close-in strike at the near post.

Only four minutes later it's 2-0 with Kevin Richardson knocking over a free-kick from the right for Shaun Teale to complete a lung-bursting charge before diving to head a stunner.

That moment typifies Villa's mood of this special Sunday afternoon. "We're getting there. And nobody is going to stop us..."

Along the way, though, there are more heart-stopping moments than any doctor would recommend, one of them but six minutes away.

As Villa's taste for 'blood' turns their head they are caught too far forward and John Aldridge is released on a forward run.

Mark Bosnich dives and misses the ball taking Aldridge's back foot to send him sprawling. A penalty, no doubt about that. Some even claim Bozzie should be sent off.

The referee sees no such offence, however, and the Australian remains to make an unsuccessful attempt to stop the score being dragged back to 3-4 on aggregate.

A very long hour's play follows and dejection is setting in. That Wembley dream is now seconds from disappearing when Dalian Atkinson gets on the end of Tony Daley's cross from the right to triumphantly plonk an equaliser at the feet of the ecstatic Holte Enders.

Extra-time is unproductive. So now, the dreaded penalty shoot-out is to offer life or death in terms of Cup Final expectations.

Neither the millions watching on TV, nor the 40,000 live audience has experienced anything to match the emotional roller-coaster which follows.

Seven penalties for each side, three fabulous saves by Bosnich, two misses by Villa, the advantage moving this way and that and a pitch invasion of pure adrenalin-fuelled relief at the end.

We're on our way to Wembley. But shed a tear for Tranmere. They didn't deserve to go out. Not like that...

Fenton and Nolan - the Dambusters

Wednesday 2nd March 1994 • White Hart Lane • 7.45pm

TOTTENHAM HOTSPUR 1 ASTON VILLA 1

Half-time 0-1 • *Attendance* 17,452

Referee Kelvin MORTON (Suffolk)

Linesmen A.P. MONKS and J.A. ELWIN

White Shirts, Navy Blue Shorts		Goals	Claret Shirts with Blue Stripes, White Shorts		Goals
13	Ian WALKER		13	Mark BOSNICH	
2	Dean AUSTIN		17	Neil COX †	
8	Kevin SCOTT		5	Paul McGRATH	
6	Gary MABBUTT		4	Shaun TEALE	
23	Sol CAMPBELL		2	Earl BARRETT	
7	Nick BARMBY		11	Tony DALEY	
4	Vinny SAMWAYS		8	Garry PARKER	8
12	Jason DOZZELL		6	Kevin RICHARDSON	
14	Steve SEDGLEY		12	Steve FROGGATT	
9	Darren ANDERTON		9	Dean SAUNDERS	
11	Ronnie ROSENTHAL	73	10	Dalian ATKINSON	
	Substitutes			*Substitutes*	
30	Chris DAY		1	Nigel SPINK	
20	Darren CASKEY		19	Stefan BEINLICH †55	
33	Andy GRAY		18	Dwight YORKE	

BEFORE	P	W	D	L	F	A	pts	AFTER	P	W	D	L	F	A	pts
7 Villa	28	12	9	7	36	27	45	7 Villa	29	12	10	7	37	28	46
16 Spurs	30	7	9	14	39	43	30	16 Spurs	31	7	10	14	40	44	31

FACTFILE

After saving three on Sunday Mark Bosnich stops two more penalties to take his total to eight this season. He keeps out Darren Anderton (44 mins) and Nick Barmby (52)... Spurs have lost the last seven league games and have not won at home since October 3rd... This is the lowest White Hart Lane gate of the season.

Two more Bozzie penalty saves

So it's back to North London again, a happy hunting ground for Villa under Ron Atkinson's reign with White Lane a venue which apparently holds no fears.

This one is potentially a searching test of Villa's character with so little time to recover physically, mentally and emotionally from the heady stuff of last Sunday.

In the event they hold out narrowly helped, amazingly, by two more penalty saves from the remarkable Mark Bosnich, now known nationwide as a phenomenon of the spot kick.

Ron Atkinson has made it clear that he is considering using his squad strength more widely and, in any event, changes are inevitable due to the injuries suffered by Andy Townsend and Ray Houghton against Tranmere.

Garry Parker returns to midfield while Steve Froggatt is also back with the German Stefan Beinlich on the bench and used as a second half substitute for Neil Cox.

Spurs are going through a dreadful time with manager Ossie Ardiles striving to keep his side away from the dreaded prospect of relegation after a traumatic seven defeats on the trot. The long-term absence of Teddy Sheringham has been a terrible blow to them but, as Atkinson puts it 'in these situations you can only think about yourself'.

Parker quickly 'signs in' with a neatly-taken cross-shot from the right of the Spurs goal which flies across Ian Walker to give Villa a welcome 1-0 lead past a static home defence after Dalian Atkinson had hit the Spurs bar a few seconds earlier.

Piling in on top of all their recent failures it is a stunner for Spurs and at this stage Villa look well able to see it through to victory and a useful leg up the table.

But as half-time approaches Villa's lead is placed in danger by the first of the penalty decisions as Cox fells Nick Barmby.

Surely the Wizard of Oz can't do it again? Or can he?

There is a deathly hush as Darren Anderton, named in Terry Venables' first England squad, strides up to strike the ball to Bosnich's right side. Once again that instant reflex-action save works the oracle and Bosnich's almost unbelievable penalty-saving record goes on. And on.

Six minutes into the second half another Villa defensive tangle sees Cox miss the ball with his challenge once again and Anderton goes down. Over to Barmby...

This time the shot is placed to Bosnich's left, but with a similar result as he goes for it, gets it, and puts another 'saved' entry into his superlative record.

From here onward Villa allow a good victory chance to slip away as Spurs, to their credit, absorb the three blows already suffered and pull the game around.

The equaliser arrives in the 74th minute when Barmby's centre is headed past the stranded Bosnich by Ronnie Rosenthal.

Penalty king Bosnich

There is just a fleeting opportunity for Villa to get back into the lead when Daley cuts through the home defence with a dazzling run but his finish is just off-target.

An away draw's not bad so soon after the rigors of the Coca Cola Cup semi-final success but the debt to Bozzie the Flying Aussie is growing.

Sunday 6th March 1994 • Highfield Road • 4.00pm

COVENTRY CITY 0 ASTON VILLA 1

Half-time 0-1 • *Attendance* 14,325

Referee Keith HACKETT (Sheffield)

Linesmen R.D. FURNANDIZ and B. LOWE

Sky Blue Shirts, Sky Blue Shorts		Goals	Claret Shirts with Blue Stripes, White Shorts		Goals
1	Steve OGRIZOVIC		13	Mark BOSNICH	
2	Brian BORROWS		17	Neil COX	
4	Peter ATHERTON		16	Ugo EHIOGU	
20	Phil BABB		4	Shaun TEALE	
3	Steve MORGAN		2	Earl BARRETT	
6	David RENNIE		8	Garry PARKER	
18	Sean FLYNN		6	Kevin RICHARDSON	
25	Julain DARBY		14	Andy TOWNSEND	
12	Peter NDLOVU		11	Tony DALEY	19
10	Mick QUINN		9	Dean SAUNDERS	
7	John WILLIAMS		25	Graham FENTON	
	Substitutes			*Substitutes*	
23	Jonathan GOULD		1	Nigel SPINK	
16	Willie BOLAND		23	Bryan SMALL	
22	Leigh JENKINSON		18	Dwight YORKE	

BEFORE	P	W	D	L	F	A	pts	AFTER	P	W	D	L	F	A	pts
7 Villa	29	12	10	7	37	28	46	5 Villa	30	13	10	7	38	28	49
12 Coventry	31	9	11	11	32	37	38	12 Coventry	32	9	11	12	32	38	38

FACTFILE

Tony Daley scores his first goal since the final game of last season... Villa halt a run of six successive Highfield Road defeats... Paul McGrath misses the game following the death of his sister in Ireland... The match is screened live on Sky Sports.

Daley ends the Sky Blue jinx

It's high time Villa put an end to the goalles run against Sky Blues who have been something of a jinx team in recent meetings.

The switch to Sunday afternoon for the convenience of Sky TV is not to everyone's liking but there is still a fair claret-and-blue following in the 14,325 crowd.

This is never going to be a high-profile occasion with Coventry striving to keep away from the relegation area and Villa's attention inevitably focussed on Wembley.

Paul McGrath is missing from the centre of the defence after news of a family bereavement giving a chance for Ugo Ehiogu to keep up his challenge for a Wembley squad place.

The atmosphere at Highfield Road is distinctly low-key with Coventry in an extremely mediocre mode and Villa supplying the West Midland derby's most entertaining moments.

This much is positively confirmed in the 19th minute with the goal which is to prove a three-pointer and which ends that Coventry unbeaten run against Villa.

Appropriately it is scored by Tony Daley who is, at last, building an encouraging plateau of form after all his inconsistencies.

The build-up is started by the ever-creative Garry Parker, another of the recent 'fringe' players anxious to establish a regular place.

Parker's delivery into the penalty area sees Andy Townsend 'dummy' over the ball and after a Dean Saunders effort rebounds

off defender Peter Atherton, Daley whacks a cross-shot past Steve Ogrizovic.

"I said to him (Daley) before the start that he was due a goal," said Ron Atkinson. "Since he's been back in the team his attitude and commitment have been excellent.

"I'm satisfied now that he wants his future to be with Villa so it is up to him to keep up the good work."

Villa's slender lead survives to the final whistle, though only just, as Coventry launch a late revival and are particularly unlucky with refereeing decisions.

In the 74th minute the talented Peter Ndlovu is scythed down by Neil Cox when the Zimabwean would have threatened Mark Bosnich's goal but referee Keith Hackett sees no offence.

Only two minutes later Shaun Teale's arm shoots up to make contact with an intended centre by Mick Quinn but once again the decision goes in Villa's favour.

"I wouldn't have argued if either had been a penalty," added a relieved Villa boss. "The second one shook me rigid," said a disbelieving Coventry boss Phil Neal.

The 'rub of the green' has certainly gone Villa's way this afternoon but, once again, the cause is helped by a significant contribution by Mark Bosnich.

In the last ten minutes the acrobatic Aussie cartwheels to keep out a Dave Rennie header and on the stroke of time he dives to deny Ndlovu.

The result enables Villa to climb to fifth in the Premiership, five points behind third-placed Arsenal... a welcome three points and a fixture Villa are glad to have behind them.

Earl Barrett holds of Peter Ndlovu

Saturday 12th March 1994 • Villa Park • 3.00pm

ASTON VILLA 0 IPSWICH TOWN 1

Half-time 0-1 • Attendance 23,732

Referee Alan WILKIE (Chester-le-Street)
Linesmen A.N. BUTLER and P.J. JOSLIN

Claret Shirts with Blue Stripes, White Shorts	Goals	Blue Shirts with White Sleeves, Blue Shorts	Goals
13 Mark BOSNICH		13 Clive BAKER	
17 Neil COX		2 Mick STOCKWELL	
16 Ugo EHIOGU		5 John WARK	
4 Shaun TEALE		15 Phil WHELAN	
2 Earl BARRETT		8 Gavin JOHNSON	8
8 Garry PARKER ‡		4 Paul MASON	
6 Kevin RICHARDSON		18 Steve PALMER	
14 Andy TOWNSEND †		21 Stuart SLATER	
11 Tony DALEY		22 Lee DURRANT	
9 Dean SAUNDERS		10 Ian MARSHALL	
10 Dalian ATKINSON		11 Chris KIWOMYA	
Substitutes		*Substitutes*	
1 Nigel SPINK		23 Phil MORGAN	
25 Graham FENTON †45		3 Neil THOMPSON	
18 Dwight YORKE ‡62		9 Bontcho GUENTCHEV	

BEFORE		P	W	D	L	F	A	pts	AFTER		P	W	D	L	F	A	pts
5	Villa	30	13	10	7	38	28	49	5	Villa	31	13	10	8	38	29	49
15	Ipswich	30	8	12	10	27	37	36	12	Ipswich	31	9	12	10	28	37	39

FACTFILE

After seven unbeaten games Villa fall to a first Premiership defeat since New Year's Day... Ipswich win at Villa Park for the first time since October 1981 and record their first league success anywhere over Villa in nine attempts... The Suffolk side have won only one of their last nine league games.

Shocking Villa are booed off

Many teams experience a dip in form between the semi-final and final of cup competitions. This is Aston Villa's. And it's a shocker.

Any possibility of the club competing for a UEFA Cup place on league position will be blown away by the March winds if there are any repetitions of this dreadful display.

Perhaps it's too late to go for it already.

A home fixture against a lowly-placed Ipswich side looks an ideal opportunity to move back into the top five or six on a weekend when the Premiership programme is decimated by FA Cup quarter-final demands.

It is also an obvious occasion to show to fans that a forthcoming Wembley appearance is not intefering with Premiership progress by entertaining them with a proud performance.

In the event, as a depressingly poor show unfolds, and a comparitively small crowd remains almost silent in disappointment, it is Ipswich who are allowed to climb the table.

Any pride on show is theirs.

The end of the game is marked by booing from a section of the crowd, a surprising scenario only a couple of weeks from the Coca Cola Cup Final against Manchester United at Wembley, but no-one says it isn't justified, least of all Ron Atkinson whose grim countenance says it all.

One cause of the poor quality of the game is Ipswich's style of play which, because of their precarious league position at the start of the game, demands that they avoid defeat.

Ugo Ehiogu

To say that they are 'not adventurous' is putting it mildly. On a better day Villa would unhinge them with the enthusiasm and drive of their own performance but this is, distinctly, not a 'better' day.

There are two even worse aspects for Villa, firstly in Ipswich taking an eighth minute lead through Gavin Johnson and secondly in that Mark Bosnich appears to have plenty of time to prevent it.

The speculative 20-yard shot seems to take an age to reach its target during which time the brilliant Aussie would normally be waiting to gobble it up. This time, it seems, he is unsighted until too late to make the necesssry save and Villa go one down.

Eighty-two minutes to go and plenty of time to equalise, or so the fans think. However, as Andy Colquhoun puts it later in the Birmingham Post, Ipswich 'pulled up the drawbridge and began preparing the boiling oil'.

Whatever the defensive formula it is too formidable for Villa on this day of lukewarm footballing passions. The 'boiling oil' isn't necessary because a feeble home attack never even begins to scale the ramparts.

Garry Parker is replaced by Dwight Yorke after 62 minutes and though some of the fans disapprove, the manager explains afterwards it was for being 'lippy' with the bench.

Kevin Richardson and Dean Saunders are somewhere near their normal application but Villa's plus-points are in defence where Ugo Ehiogu continues to display his blossoming capabilities and Shaun Teale is as defiant as ever. Otherwise it is not a day when reputations are enhanced, more one to ask how players capable of the Tranmere fightback can slide to such a defeat with so little defiance.

Wednesday 16th March 1994 • Elland Road • 7.45pm

LEEDS UNITED 2 ASTON VILLA 0

Half-time 1-0 • *Attendance* 33,120

Referee David ALLISON (Lancaster)

Linesmen J. BARLOW and N.E. GREEN

White Shirts with 2 Blue & 1 Yellow Hoop, White Shorts		Goals
1	John LUKIC	
22	Gary KELLY	
18	David WETHERALL	
6	David O'LEARY †	
3	Tony DORIGO	
7	Gordon STRACHAN	
5	Chris FAIRCLOUGH	
10	Gary McALLISTER	
11	Gary SPEED	
8	Rod WALLACE	27
9	Brian DEANE	51
	Substitutes	
13	Mark BEENEY	
16	Jon NEWSOME †41	
25	Noel WHELAN	

Claret Shirts with Blue Stripes, Blue Shorts		Goals
13	Mark BOSNICH	
2	Earl BARRETT	
5	Paul McGRATH	
4	Shaun TEALE	
23	Bryan SMALL †	
17	Neil COX	
8	Garry PARKER	
6	Kevin RICHARDSON	
11	Steve FROGGATT	
9	Dean SAUNDERS	
10	Dalian ATKINSON ‡	
	Substitutes	
1	Nigel SPINK	
18	Dwight YORKE †56	
25	Graham FENTON ‡72	

BEFORE		P	W	D	L	F	A	pts
6	Leeds	31	12	13	6	44	32	49
7	Villa	31	13	10	8	38	29	49

AFTER		P	W	D	L	F	A	pts
5	Leeds	32	13	13	6	46	32	52
7	Villa	32	13	10	9	38	31	49

FACTFILE

Bryan Small comes in at left-back, Earl Barrett reverts to right-back and Neil Cox pushes into midfield... Only two wins in the last eight matches... Pre-Wembley injury for Dalian Atkinson... This game was originally postponed on Monday 3rd January due to a waterlogged pitch when it was to be televised live on Sky Sports.

A cold blast for Villa's prospects

Away games at Elland Road are never an appetizing prospect and this trip is made worse by surprisingly poor weather conditions for March which see the game end in a near-blizzard and a cold blast, indeed, for Villa prospects.

Although Paul McGrath is restored to the heart of the defence Ray Houghton, Andy Townsend and Tony Daley are all out injured, precariously close to the Wembley Final on Sunday week.

This gives Steve Froggatt a chance to play wide on the left of midfield with Bryan Small in Steve Staunton's berth at left back.

In the pre-match build up Ron Atkinson lays his feelings on the line about last Saturday's home defeat by Ipswich which prompted a wave of criticism. "It left a nasty taste in the mouth," he said bluntly. "We'd have put some distance between ourselves and Leeds and Liverpool if we had won that. I'm looking for two hundred per cent improvement in all aspects our game... that's enthusiasm, quality and professional pride.

"If you don't perform at Elland Road, you get found out..."

Unhappily, Villa are to 'get found out' as, in difficult conditions, the record and reputation they had built up in away games is to take another blow following the Cup defeats at Bolton and Tranmere.

By the end of the night they are five points behind fourth place with a game more played. Thus the league route back into the UEFA Cup is virtually sealed off, pouring more emphasis on the Coca Cola Cup Final. Basically Leeds get well on top and stay there as, once again, Villa offer very little in the shape of any attacking menace.

Mark Bosnich's first contribution arrives after only five minutes when he dives to pull-off a one-handed save from a bicycle kick by Brian Deane.

The rescue act gives Villa a brief respite and there is the fleeting promise of a goal lead in the 11th minute when Garry Parker's free kick finds Dalian Atkinson whose header is tipped over by John Lukic.

Come the 28th minute, however, and Villa are as good as beaten. Gary Speed's through ball catches them on the break and Rod Wallace races through a spreadeagled defence to arrow his shot out of the 'keeper's reach.

Once ahead Leeds assume complete control apart from a quick break by Atkinson whose attempt to equalise, after beating Tony Dorigo, scrapes the wrong side of the bar.

Six minutes into the second half Deane gets a second for Leeds with a goal which Villa's defence, and maybe Bosnich, ought to have cleared. Wallace is in the picture again, this time measuring over a low centre which the striker heads in from around knee height.

Bryan Small - given an uneasy time

Travelling fans who brave the poor conditions look for signs of a fight-back but few are to be found. Soon after the goal Dwight Yorke replaces Small, who has had an uneasy time then, after 72 minutes Dalian Atkinson limps off with a hamstring injury.

Another below-par performance with more questions raised for Ron Atkinson than answered. The road to Wembley is not proving to be a carefree one.

Saturday 19th March 1994 • Villa Park • 3.00pm

ASTON VILLA 1   OLDHAM ATHLETIC 2

Half-time 0-0 • Attendance 21,214

Referee Joe WORRALL (Warrington)

Linesmen J. McGRATH and B.M. RICE

Claret Shirts with Blue Stripes, White Shorts		Goals	Blue Shirts, White Shorts		Goals
13	Mark BOSNICH		13	Jon HALLWORTH	
2	Earl BARRETT		22	Chris MAKIN	
5	Paul McGRATH		6	Steve REDMOND	(og 58)
4	Shaun TEALE		23	Richard GRAHAM	
3	Steve STAUNTON		3	Neil POINTON	
7	Ray HOUGHTON		4	Nick HENRY	
6	Kevin RICHARDSON		8	Andy RITCHIE †	
8	Garry PARKER		10	Mike MILLIGAN	
12	Steve FROGGATT		25	Rick HOLDEN	73
9	Dean SAUNDERS †		17	Darren BECKFORD	67
25	Graham FENTON		21	Sean McCARTHY	
Substitutes			*Substitutes*		
1	Nigel SPINK		1	Paul GERRARD	
18	Dwight YORKE †76		19	Roger PALMER †84	
16	Ugo EHIOGU		18	Neil McDONALD	

BEFORE		P	W	D	L	F	A	pts	AFTER		P	W	D	L	F	A	pts
7	Villa	32	13	10	9	38	31	49	7	Villa	33	13	10	10	39	33	49
20	Oldham	30	6	9	15	26	50	27	20	Oldham	31	7	9	15	28	51	30

FACTFILE

A third successive defeat inside eight days as Villa prepare for Wembley...
Oldham also have a Wembley meeting with Manchester United to look forward
to, in the FA Cup semi-final... Strikers again fail to deliver... Steve Staunton
returns after missing seven games through injury.

Fans jeer a miserable show

Anyone looking for a massive pre-Wembley boost after two successive defeats is left in a state of severe shock after yet another home defeat. With the Coca Cola Cup Final against Manchester United only eight days away the players, once again, fail miserably to provide supporters with a measure of confidence for the big day.

Long before the final whistle it is Villa, not Oldham, who look like relegation material as Joe Royle's struggling side repeat last season's Villa Park victory.

Villa have now lost as many league games at Villa Park as they have won and, sadly, with the exception of the Coca Cola Cup semi-final, have looked no more than an average side at home for much of the season.

Wembley places are said to be 'up for grabs' depending on performance yet, surprisingly, the individual and collective effort level is disappointingly below par.

The two brightest features of a forlorn occasion is that Steve Staunton is back after his groin surgery looking fully recovered while Graham Fenton gives a gutsy display in place of the injured Dalian Atkinson.

Otherwise Villa slip to that seventh home league defeat with barely an attacking whimper in reply despite having been gifted a 58th minute lead.

But for an early shot by Fenton which was narrowly off-target and a Garry Parker effort which forced Jon Hallworth into a nimble save Villa have offered little of a positive nature when the lead arrives in the shape of an own goal. Steve Froggatt's corner is cleared only weakly by the defence to Ray Houghton who returns it to the Villa winger. This time Froggy's cross is turned in by Steve Redmond.

Fans naturally now expect Villa to forcefully drive home their advantage but the reverse is the case. Oldham's equaliser arrives after nine minutes of visitors' pressure. Earl Barrett is dispossessed by Rick Holden and this leads to Darren Beckford making it 1-1.

Another six minutes and Kevin Richardson concedes a free-kick for Holden to drive a superbly-placed winner out of Mark Bosnich's reach.

Villa's lack of goal threat is now a positive worry for Ron Atkinson who sends on Dwight Yorke to replace Dean Saunders, with no appreciable improvement.

Not surprisingly, Ron Atkinson is simmering with unsuppressed rage when he meets the media an hour after the final whistle. His condemnation reflects the feelings of fans, many of whom had booed the team off the pitch at the end.

"I don't blame them booing," he said. "I started it. The performance was an insult to themselves, the fans and to professional football. It was terrible and, at the moment, I am just disgusted.

Graham Fenton

"What really galls me is that I have got players up for new contracts who have turned down increases that are more than Joe Royle's players are being paid."

Few sets of players can have gone into a Wembley Final with such a scathing criticism from their manager ringing in their ears. Needless to say, Manchester United are clear favourites for tomorrow week.

Sunday 27th March 1994 • Wembley Stadium • 5.00pm

ASTON VILLA 3 MANCHESTER UNITED 1

Half-time 1-0 • *Attendance* 77,231

Referee Keith COOPER (Pontypridd)

Linesmen J. ELWIN and R. HARRIS

Claret Shirts with Blue Stripes, White Shorts		Goals	Yellow and Green Halved Shirts, Black Shorts		Goals
13	Mark BOSNICH		13	Les SEALEY	
2	Earl BARRETT		2	Paul PARKER	
5	Paul McGRATH		4	Steve BRUCE ‡	
4	Shaun TEALE		6	Gary PALLISTER	
3	Steve STAUNTON †		3	Denis IRWIN	
10	Dalian ATKINSON	25	14	Andrei KANCHELSKIS ■	
14	Andy TOWNSEND		16	Roy KEANE	
6	Kevin RICHARDSON		8	Paul INCE	
25	Graham FENTON		11	Ryan GIGGS †	
11	Tony DALEY		7	Eric CANTONA	
9	Dean SAUNDERS	75, pen 89	10	Mark HUGHES	83
	Substitutes			*Substitutes*	
1	Nigel SPINK		25	Gary WALSH	
17	Neil COX †78		14	Lee SHARPE †61	
7	Ray HOUGHTON		12	Brian McCLAIR ‡84	

It's glory, glory Aston Villa

Although previous signs have not been good, Wembley Day dawns with a new wave of optimism sweeping through claret-and-blue ranks.

Villa have been seen nationally as cannon fodder for the start of a unique treble, but cracks have begun to appear in Manchester United's make-up. Goalkeeper Peter Schmeichel is suspended while Eric Cantona, though available for the Final is then banned for five games for being sent off twice in successive matches.

Tensions have certainly arrived in Alex Ferguson's camp while, in contrast, Ron Atkinson has gone for a more relaxed approach. The manager's recent scathing criticism has long been forgotten with players now encouraged to enjoy their spell in the national limelight.

All are fit for the big day leaving Atkinson with the kind of selection problem he likes best, namely whom to leave out. This allows him to hatch a cunning game plan which proves to be his Wembley masterpiece.

On the eve of the match Graham Fenton is told that he is in at Ray Houghton's expense. The 19-year-old is deployed in a five-man midfield, featuring the electrifying pace of Dalian Atkinson and Tony Daley on the flanks with Dean Saunders a lone ranger up front.

Early on United seem likely to make their class tell though Villa have started brightly, too, revealing all the hunger they have recently lacked.

Shaun Teale is phenomenal in the heart of defence, winning all the air balls, tackling tigerishly, supervising positional play and setting an inspiring standard of pugnacious defiance.

Kevin Richardson and Andy Townsend have similar qualities in midfield while Fenton's young legs add a new dimension in terms of aggressive mobility.

Cantona is left to roam his own territory and clearly no-one has been briefed to close-mark him. The Frenchman can be as ineffectual as he so often is inspirational and this is to be one of those days.

The Ukranian Andrei Kanchelskis, however, does trouble Villa fleetingly but he is usually swamped by back-tracking opponents. Likewise Ryan Giggs on the other side though he makes one chance with a touch of magic from which Mark Hughes could have scored.

After absorbing United's early pressure Villa's intention to hit them on the break works perfectly. Earl Barrett quickly takes a free kick deep on Villa's right touchline, the ball is whipped neatly from Fenton to Townsend and on to Saunders who flicks it over Steve Bruce to Atkinson, a predator going for his prey. Atkinson steers it away from Les Sealey and sends it successfully on his way with his right shin.

Goal No.2 arrives in the 75th minute as Richardson quickly knocks in an acutely-angled free kick from the left at an awkward height for defenders to cut out and Deano's outflung toe diverts it home.

United go forward with increasing desperation and a touch of class conjures Hughes a heart-stopping goal and the Welsh international threatens an equaliser until Mark Bosnich swoops into one of his full-stretch, one-handed saves.

What a Cup run, what a Final and, glory be, what a finale. As the last coronary-inducing moments tick away, Daley's cross-shot hits the post, Atkinson smacks in the rebound and Kanchelskis stops it, an otherwise certain goal, on the line, with his hand. The stadium is deathly silent... Kanchelskis gets his red card... and Saunders steps boldly forward to complete a 3-1 victory from the penalty spot.

"I've always felt that our name was on the trophy," said Ron Atkinson who later, and appropriately, sings "My Way" to guests at the celebration banquet.

Wednesday 30th March 1994 • Villa Park • 7.45pm

ASTON VILLA 0 EVERTON 0

Half-time 0-0 • *Attendance 36,044*

Referee Rodger GIFFORD (Mid Glamorgan)

Linesmen D.S. BRAMMER and D.M. HORLICK

Claret Shirts with Blue Stripes, White Shorts	Goals	White Shirts with Dark Blue Stripes, Dark Blue Shorts	Goals
13 Mark BOSNICH		1 Neville SOUTHALL	
2 Earl BARRETT		2 Matthew JACKSON	
16 Ugo EHIOGU		4 Ian SNODIN	
4 Shaun TEALE		5 Dave WATSON	
3 Steve STAUNTON		26 David UNSWORTH	
7 Ray HOUGHTON		3 Andy HINCHCLIFFE	
6 Kevin RICHARDSON		8 Graham STUART	
8 Garry PARKER		10 Barry HORNE	
12 Steve FROGGATT		14 John EBBRELL	
9 Dean SAUNDERS		17 Anders LIMPAR	
18 Dwight YORKE †		22 Brett ANGELL	
Substitutes		*Substitutes*	
1 Nigel SPINK		13 Jason KEARTON	
25 Graham FENTON †74		21 Gary ROWETT	
17 Neil COX		9 Tony COTTEE	

BEFORE		P	W	D	L	F	A	pts	AFTER		P	W	D	L	F	A	pts
8	Villa	33	13	10	10	39	33	49	8	Villa	34	13	11	10	39	33	50
17	Everton	34	10	6	18	36	48	36	16	Everton	35	10	7	18	36	48	37

As in 1975, when Bolton spoilt the party, Villa's Cup celebrations are dampened by a goalless mid-week home fixture... Villa and Everton have met in the league more than any other clubs (this is the 158th meeting) but until 1985-86 there had never been a goalless draw in Birmingham, now it's three in the last eight.

FACTFILE

Celebration party goes flat

This one ought to be on the theme of 'After the Lord Mayor's Show' but the City Council have, strangely, been 'unable' to arrange the traditional civic reception for the Cup winners.

Tetchy words are exchanged between the club and the council but there is nothing 'tetchy' about the pre-match reception for the players parading their trophy before the fans.

A crowd of 36,000, whole batteries of cameras and popping flashbulbs and a general air of excitable anticipation gives Villa Park a carnival atmosphere. That's before the kick-off.

Once the 'action' starts the entertainment virtually ends as relegation-threatened Everton present a point-seeking formation and Villa struggle to find inspiration.

As anticipated there are changes from the Wembley-winning team. Ugo Ehiogu is in Paul McGrath's place while Ray Houghton, Garry Parker, Steve Froggatt and Dwight Yorke are also in. Ron Atkinson clearly hopes that fresh legs and a chance for some of the fringe players to compete for a regular call will give the performance a lift, but it is not to be.

To add to the atmosphere of low-key anticlimax which now prevails the wind-chill weather is awful with rain cascading down and supporters huddling under cover.

Winning the Coca Cola Cup has proved to be an oasis in a desert of barren results with the only plus point being that the previous run of three successive league defeats is ended.

Everton boss Mike Walker's selection could not have made his aims more clear... strike pair Tony Cottee and ex-Villa man Paul Rideout have been dropped leaving Brett Angell as a lone striker.

A Matt Jackson effort hits Mark Bosnich on the legs and Anders Limpar tries a hopeful but inaccurate long-shot from the centre circle. Otherwise it is left to Villa to attempt unsuccessfully, to 'force the pace'.

It takes 41 minutes to muster the first scoring attempt, a long-range shot by Kevin Richardson which Neville Southall tips to safety.

Houghton misses a second half half-chance, Froggatt makes occasional runs down the left and in the 74th minute there is a rousing reception for Graham Fenton.

Like the rest he fails to make an impression as Everton guard their point and the final whistle is blessed relief for supporters.

The Coca-Cola Cup is brought back to Villa Park, and a heroes welcome

Saturday 2nd April 1994 • Maine Road • 3.00pm

MANCHESTER CITY 3   ASTON VILLA 0

Half-time 2-0 • Attendance 26,075

Referee Paul DURKIN (Dorset)
Linesmen A.R. LEAKE and A. STREETS

Sky Blue Shirts, White Shorts		Goals	Claret Shirts with Blue Stripes, White Shorts		Goals
25	Andy DIBBLE		13	Mark BOSNICH	
2	Andy HILL		2	Earl BARRETT	
5	Keith CURLE		16	Ugo EHIOGU	
6	Michel VONK		4	Shaun TEALE	
18	David BRIGHTWELL		3	Steve STAUNTON	
7	David ROCASTLE		11	Tony DALEY	
4	Steve McMAHON		6	Kevin RICHARDSON	
12	Ian BRIGHTWELL		14	Andy TOWNSEND	
32	Peter BEAGRIE	39	8	Garry PARKER †	
28	Uwe RÖSLER †	53	9	Dean SAUNDERS	
31	Paul WALSH	44	25	Graham FENTON	
	Substitutes			*Substitutes*	
13	Martyn MARGETSON		1	Nigel SPINK	
8	Mike SHERON †84		18	Dwight YORKE †77	
31	Stefen KARL		17	Neil COX	

BEFORE	P	W	D	L	F	A	pts	AFTER	P	W	D	L	F	A	pts
8 Villa	34	13	11	10	39	33	50	10 Villa	35	13	11	11	39	36	50
20 City	35	6	15	14	28	42	33	19 City	36	7	15	14	31	42	36

FACTFILE

City end a run of five games without a win and climb out of bottom three for the first time since February 5th... Peter Beagrie scores his first goal for City since signing from Everton... Like Villa, City have two Germans on their books - Uwe Rösler and Stefen Karl are both in the 14 for this game.

Daley is mugged in heavy defeat

With only one Premiership victory recorded in the previous seven starts, over Coventry City at Highfield Road, Villa badly need to put Wembley to the back of the mind and finish the season with a healthy run.

Dalian Atkinson is still out injured but Tony Daley and Andy Townsend are back, while Graham Fenton partners Dean Saunders up front.

Tony Daley

Early indications are promising against a City side battling to get away from the bottom three relegation places.

The opening 39 minutes see Villa threatening to add to the Maine Road problems with encouraging signs of the old flowing football.

Any suggestions of Wembley 'hangover' appear to have been dispelled and with Ugo Ehiogu deputising confidently again for McGrath the likelihood of a City breakthrough looks remote.

Fenton is powerfully mobile, the spring is back in everyone's step and a goal now would surely set Villa well on their way to the Premiership win needed to end the slump.

Suddenly, catastrophe as City hit two goals in the final six minutes before the interval, one of them right on the stroke of half-time, and Villa are entitled to feel aggrieved.

First of all a free kick by Peter Beagrie takes a deflection off Kevin Richardson to beat Mark Bosnich for a classic against-the-run-of-play lead.

Villa swallow hard at the opposition's good fortune, Tony Daley is going full-throttle for

goal and Keith Curle crashes him to the ground. Professional foul? A red card ?

Unbelievably, neither.

Afterwards Ron Atkinson is asked if he thought Daley had been fouled. "You mean after he had been mugged?" replies the manager with black humour.

So, in moments the possibility of 1-1 is to be replaced by an irretrievable 0-2. The lively if diminutive Paul Walsh is allowed to head in to leave Big Ron fretting over defensive ineptitude.

Worse is to follow. A previously poor-looking City side, whose manager Brian Horton is under severe pressure, make it 3-0 with a strike by Uwe Rösler to complete their best win since last September.

All, or most of Villa's early sparkle has been dimmed and there is certainly no way back. "If we had gone in at half-time just one goal behind we could have swung it," says Atkinson.

"Their first took a fortunate deflection but I certainly wasn't happy about the other two we conceded."

Ugo Ehiogu

Monday 4th April 1994 • Villa Park • 3.00pm

ASTON VILLA 0 NORWICH CITY 0

Half-time 0-0 • Attendance 25,416

Referee Martin BODENHAM (Looe)

Linesmen R.H. ANDREWS and J. HILDITCH

Claret Shirts with Blue Stripes, White Shorts	Goals	Yellow Shirts, Green Shorts	Goals
13 Mark BOSNICH		1 Bryan GUNN	
2 Earl BARRETT		2 Mark BOWEN	
16 Ugo EHIOGU		27 Spencer PRIOR	
4 Shaun TEALE		5 Ian CULVERHOUSE	
3 Steve STAUNTON		8 Colin WOODTHORPE	
10 Dalian ATKINSON		18 Robert ULLATHORNE	
6 Kevin RICHARDSON		9 Gary MEGSON †	
14 Andy TOWNSEND		11 Jeremy GOSS	
11 Tony DALEY		4 Ian CROOK	
9 Dean SAUNDERS		22 Chris SUTTON	
25 Graham FENTON †		20 Darren EADIE ‡	
Substitutes		*Substitutes*	
1 Nigel SPINK		13 Scott HOWIE	
18 Dwight YORKE †45		21 David SMITH †53	
17 Neil COX		6 Neil ADAMS ‡78	

BEFORE		P	W	D	L	F	A	pts	AFTER		P	W	D	L	F	A	pts
10	Villa	35	13	11	11	39	36	50	10	Villa	36	13	12	11	39	36	51
11	Norwich	36	11	14	21	58	63	47	11	Norwich	37	11	15	21	58	63	48

FACTFILE

Dalian Atkinson is back but the goal drought goes on... A second successive goalless home draw and Villa have failed to score in 10 out of 23 home games... This is the first ever goalless draw between Villa and Norwich in 51 league and cup meetings.

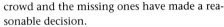

It's a frustrating blank holiday

Wembley triumph now seems a long, long way back as the Premiership problems drag on and fans yearn for a re-run of those spectacular Coca Cola Cup Final strikes.

The visit of Norwich has often, in the past, inspired high-scoring games though the Carrow Road club had the winning edge in a five-goal thriller last season.

Now, however, managed by ex-Villa favourite John Deehan, who took charge when Mike Walker moved to Everton, they are having a bad time and need at least a point to stabilise.

Norwich have lost five of their last six games and soon it is apparent that Deehan's system is designed, like Walker's in the previous home game, for safety-first purposes rather than glory.

The intelligence has clearly spread that Villa can be closed down by appropriate tactics and a remarkably sterile recent record confirms the view. In the last six league matches, either side of the League Cup triumph no Villa player has scored, the only goal being an own goal in the 2-1 defeat by Oldham.

Dalian Atkinson is now back after injury, though even he has scored in only one league game this year, his double against West Ham.

Again the weather is dreadful on a typical British Bank Holiday as rain, sleet and even snow add to teeth-chattering temperatures.

In the circumstances, considering the team's recent disappointments, there is no bumper Easter

Steve Staunton - tested Bryan Gunn from 30 yards

crowd and the missing ones have made a reasonable decision.

Yet this time, as in the opening spell at Maine Road, there is much to admire about Villa's approach play as they find their way through Canaries' five-man midfield.

With Atkinson playing his wide Wembley role and Daley on the other side there are four front men backed by attacking full-backs in a determined attempt to end the goal drought.

Many of the scoring attempts launched at Bryan Gunn's goal are from some distance out and fail to bring the required breakthrough.

Fenton almost makes it with a fierce drive from the edge of the area, Kevin Richardson fails to control the ball as Atkinson steps over Dean Saunders' centre from the left and Fenton is close again, this time with a diving header.

Steve Staunton joins the assault with a thunderous 30-yarder but Gunn intercepts with a safe pair of hands.

So it goes on with Norwich attacking rarely and Villa dominating the pattern but without the end-product. To change the shape a little Fenton is replaced by Dwight Yorke who almost gets the necessary touch on a Daley delivery.

Once again the home fans are to be denied goals and, as against Everton, they have to settle disappointingly for a point.

The mystery remains of how Villa can have performed so well at Wembley, and away from home in the league for much of the season, yet have scored so few goals at Villa Park.

"We had more shots on goal than we've had for a long time," says Ron Atkinson with justification. "The performance was good and on another day we might have got two or three goals and gone away saying how good it all was."

Monday 11th April 1994 • Ewood Park • 8.00pm

BLACKBURN ROVERS 1 ASTON VILLA 0

Half-time 1-0 • *Attendance* 19,287

Referee David ALLISON (Lancaster)

Linesmen T.A. ATKINSON and R. PEARSON

Blue and White Halved Shirts, White Shorts	Goals	Claret Shirts with Blue Stripes, White Shorts	Goals
26 Tim FLOWERS		13 Mark BOSNICH	
20 Henning BERG		2 Earl BARRETT	
2 David MAY		16 Ugo EHIOGU	
5 Colin HENDRY		4 Shaun TEALE	
6 Graeme LE SAUX		3 Steve STAUNTON	
7 Stuart RIPLEY †		10 Dalian ATKINSON	
4 Tim SHERWOOD		6 Kevin RICHARDSON	
23 David BATTY ‡		14 Andy TOWNSEND	
11 Jason WILCOX		25 Graham FENTON	
9 Alan SHEARER	10	11 Tony DALEY	
10 Mike NEWELL		9 Dean SAUNDERS †	
Substitutes		*Substitutes*	
1 Bobby MIMMS		1 Nigel SPINK	
3 Alan WRIGHT †71		7 Ray HOUGHTON †45	
24 Paul WARHURST ‡79		17 Neil COX	

BEFORE		P	W	D	L	F	A	pts	AFTER		P	W	D	L	F	A	pts
2	Blackburn	36	23	7	6	57	29	76	2	Blackburn	37	24	7	6	58	29	79
10	Villa	36	13	12	11	39	36	51	10	Villa	37	13	12	12	39	37	51

FACTFILE

Six of Villa's seven away defeats this season have been in Lancashire and four of them have been on live TV... Only one Villa goal in seven league games, an own goal... Villa have failed to score against Blackburn in any of the last four meetings... Kevin Richardson plays his 400th league game.

Luckless Villa as Shearer strikes

The sobering thought as Villa arrive at Ewood Park is that they have yet to score against Blackburn in three Premiership fixtures and this thought persists as they complete their fourth.

Kenny Dalglish's team need the three points to catch the ailing Manchester United at the top of the table while mid-table Villa have little more than pride on the line.

Paul McGrath is out again with his neck injury but otherwise it is a full-strength line-up and Ron Atkinson opts for the Wembley-style 4-5-1 formation with Dean Saunders a lone raider but well-supported from midfield.

Villa's biggest hope is that Blackburn will be affected by the sense of occasion whipped up by the Monday night Sky cameras and the nationwide focus on whether pressure will be applied on United.

Not only has the Old Trafford club been robbed, by Villa, of their 'treble' chance, but at the weekend Oldham took them to an FA Cup semi-final replay.

So, from being low-odds bets to win all three domestic competitions there is now a distinct possibility of Alex Ferguson's team ending up with nothing.

If Villa hope that Rovers, burdened with such a responsibility, will start slowly they are soon to learn better. In reality the home team opens up looking composed and confident, finding their men smoothly and with style.

It takes only ten minutes for the remarkable Alan Shearer to conjure a goal lead with his 30th goal in 35 Premiership appearances, six of them as substitute. It is the England striker's 55th goal for Blackburn in less than two years since leaving Southampton and for a large slice of that time he was out injured.

The chance is fed in by Jason Wilcox, recently named in Terry Venables' latest England party and nodded down by Mike Newell. The ball spins off Shaun Teale's knee and Shearer finds the merest gap to direct the ball away from Mark Bosnich.

To Villa's credit they are not deflated by going behind so soon and, as the game progresses, there is growing promise that an equaliser, at least, is on the cards.

The first significant Villa attack, mid-way through the first half, sees Andy Townsend arrive a touch too late to get on the end of Steve Staunton's centre. Dalian Atkinson, operating from a right wing base, gives a whiff of danger to the home defence each time he cuts in but half-time arrives without an equaliser.

Now, with Saunders suffering from a recurrence of his back problem he stays behind in the second half, Ray Houghton taking over in a return to 4-4-2 with Atkinson and Graham Fenton up front.

The change in formation, and Blackburn's apparent preparedness to settle for their narrow scoreline, brings a marked change in the pattern of play.

The Irish World Cup player initiates some promising attacks but the goal Villa need so badly to end their depressing run in the league continues to elude them.

A right-footed drive by Fenton is saved brilliantly by another Ewood Park England man, Tim Flowers who later deals comfortably with a shot by Tony Daley.

By the final whistle Villa have had more than their share of the attacking play and have in no way been 'outplayed'. The difference could be summed up in a name: Shearer.

Ray Houghton

Saturday 16th April 1994 • Bramall Lane • 3.00pm

SHEFFIELD UNITED 1 ASTON VILLA 2

Half-time 1-2 • Attendance 18,402

Referee Graham POLL (Hertfordshire)
Linesmen J.F. COPELAND and J. McGRATH

Red and White Striped Shirts, White Shorts	Goals	Claret Shirts with Blue Stripes, White Shorts	Goals
13 Simon TRACEY		1 Nigel SPINK	
17 Carl BRADSHAW		2 Earl BARRETT	
5 Brian GAYLE		16 Ugo EHIOGU ❏	
14 David TUTTLE		4 Shaun TEALE ❏	
33 Roger NILSEN		3 Steve STAUNTON	
7 Franz CARR		7 Ray HOUGHTON	
8 Paul ROGERS ❏		6 Kevin RICHARDSON	23
4 John GANNON ‡		14 Andy TOWNSEND	
18 Dane WHITEHOUSE ❏		21 Dave FARRELL †	
12 Jostein FLO		25 Graham FENTON	24
9 Adrian LITTLEJOHN †	17	19 Stefan BEINLICH	
Substitutes		*Substitutes*	
31 Salvatore BIBBO		30 Michael OAKES	
30 Nathan BLAKE †65		11 Tony DALEY †79	
10 Glyn HODGES ‡65		17 Neil COX	

BEFORE	P	W	D	L	F	A	pts	AFTER	P	W	D	L	F	A	pts
9 Villa	37	13	12	12	39	37	51	8 Villa	38	14	12	12	41	38	54
21 United	37	6	7	14	35	54	35	21 United	38	6	7	15	36	56	35

FACTFILE *Villa's first league win in eight games... Kevin Richardson's goal ends a run of 415 minutes since Villa's last league goal (an own goal against Oldham) and 724 Premiership minutes since a Villa player last scored (Tony Daley at Coventry)... Graham Fenton scores his first senior goal for the club.*

Fenton's first is a match winner

This one looks a potential minefield in view of Sheffield United's precarious position in the bottom three and their reputation for great escapes.

Villa arrive at Bramall Lane without a win in their last seven league games and with several big guns missing. Consequently there is a 'new' look in attack and a large question mark over how things will turn out.

Dean Saunders and Dalian Atkinson are both out injured along with Paul McGrath while Mark Bosnich fails a late fitness test on a shoulder injury.

Yet, in the circumstances, there are no complaints about the situation from Ron Atkinson who has repeatedly expressed his desire to give younger players a chance. With little but prestige now at stake in the Premiership, apart from extra revenue based on league position, what better opportunity could there be?

Graham Fenton and the German Stefan Beinlich, who netted a hat-trick against the Blades' reserves three days ago, are the front two with winger Dave Farrell forcing Tony Daley onto the bench.

Although United take a 17th minute lead through Littlejohn it quickly becomes clear that the changes have introduced a new freshness to Villa's game with Farrell seeking to get down the flanks to supply crosses and Fenton and Beinlich full of eager running.

United's defence is constantly stretched by the width of Villa's attacking game and the mobility of the young front men.

Dave Bassett's side had not lost in their previous eight fixtures but afterwards the United manager is forced to suggest, tongue-in-cheek: "Probably a pity for us Saunders and Atkinson were not playing. The two lads up front got through a lot of work..."

In fact United contribute to their own downfall with some untidy defending that allow 'the two lads' a stream of scoring chances which, with one exception, they fail to put away.

More experienced calm in this area and Villa could have secured their highest away league win of the season. Beinlich, for instance, could have scored his first senior goal, had he been more prepared for a well-driven Farrell cross which he heads wide from only four or five yards out.

United, in desperation, have a cutting edge to their tackles, and this tends to prod Villa into an increased determination which brings the equaliser and the lead in a crushing two-minute blitz.

Andy Townsend is full of driving aggression but it is his central midfield partner, Richardson, who makes it 1-1. One of Farrell's crosses rebounds out to the Villa skipper who drives in from 20 yards.

With the attacking momentum still in full swing Fenton helps a long forward ball to loop over Simon Tracey's head before celebrating his first goal for the club. After this Villa rarely look like letting go, with Richardson an inspirational leader and the younger players seizing their chance to stake a claim.

Fenton's enthusiasm sees him in position often enough to score at least a hat-trick but no-one is complaining when inexperience sees him narrowly fail.

Dave Farrell skips a Brian Gayle challenge

Saturday 23rd April 1994 • Villa Park • 3.00pm

ASTON VILLA 1 ARSENAL 2

Half-time 0-1 • *Attendance* 31,580

Referee Keith COOPER (Pontypridd)

Linesmen D.C. MADGWICK and A.P. MONKS

Claret Shirts with Blue Stripes, White Shorts		Goals	Yellow Shirts, Blue Shorts		Goals
1	Nigel SPINK		1	David SEAMAN	
17	Neil COX		2	Lee DIXON	
16	Ugo EHIOGU		5	Andy LINIGHAN	
4	Shaun TEALE		12	Steve BOULD	
2	Earl BARRETT		14	Martin KEOWN	
7	Ray HOUGHTON	57	24	Mark FLATTS	
6	Kevin RICHARDSON		21	Steve MORROW	
14	Andy TOWNSEND		4	Paul DAVIS ❏ †	
21	Dave FARRELL		7	Kevin CAMPBELL	
10	Dalian ATKINSON		9	Alan SMITH	
25	Graham FENTON		8	Ian WRIGHT	pen 30, 89
Substitutes			*Substitutes*		
30	Michael OAKES		13	Alan MILLER	
9	Dean SAUNDERS		23	Ray PARLOUR †77	
19	Stefan BEINLICH		11	Eddie McGOLDRICK	

BEFORE		P	W	D	L	F	A	pts	AFTER		P	W	D	L	F	A	pts
4	Arsenal	38	17	16	5	50	22	67	4	Arsenal	39	18	16	5	52	23	70
9	Villa	38	14	12	12	41	38	54	10	Villa	39	14	12	13	42	40	54

FACTFILE

European Cup-winners' Cup finalists Arsenal extend their unbeaten run to 18 Premiership games, gaining revenge for four successive league and cup defeats by Villa... Ian Wright remains the only Gunners player to have scored against Villa in the last six meetings.

Arsenal gain some revenge

Arsenal arrive at Villa Park as European Cup Winners' Cup finalists and seeking revenge for two Villa wins at Highbury earlier in the season.

Their credentials are impressive, with no defeat in the league since before Christmas and an aura of confidence spreading through their ranks.

Ron Atkinson, with little to aim for in the Premiership and keen to give young players an extended run, keeps Dave Farrell and Graham Fenton in his line-up while Neil Cox is in defence along with Ugo Ehiogu. Mark Bosnich is still on the injured list enabling Michael Oakes to take a 'subtitute' role.

Arsenal are in their most professional mood, playing a tightly-controlled game and restricting Villa to a subdued opening half in which any scoring attempts are from a distance.

In contrast there are moments, early on, when Gunners threaten to take the lead, one of them in the 15th minute when a Shaun Teale tackle on Kevin Campbell is perilously near to being a penalty.

Oddly that incident had looked more likely to be penalised than a Cox tackle on Ian Wright on the half-hour but this time the referee points to the spot and the England striker smacks it past Nigel Spink with relish.

Half-time arrives with Villa a goal down and Gunners seemingly taking control but the second half sees an impressive improvement in Villa's standard of play.

There is more accuracy and movement about their forward play and though Andy Townsend gets the ball into the net a goal is ruled out by Dalian Atkinson's foul on David Seaman.

Then Fenton is only narrowly wide of the target and Atkinson is denied by Arsenal's England 'keeper after gliding past three defenders.

An equaliser arrives in just under the hour as home fans begin to warm to an entertaining game. As Kevin Richardson's through ball pierces the Arsenal back line Ray Houghton cruises on to it and spots his chance to chip his scoring shot over the advancing 'keeper.

Now there is the distinct possibility of George Graham's unbeaten league run coming to an end, with Farrell and Fenton showing up well.

The young pair prise another opening for Atkinson whose shot cannons off Seaman's shins. By now hopes of that first home league win in ten weeks are fading fast but at least defeat has been avoided. Or has it?

Seconds before the final whistle the lethal Wright accepts a return pass from Campbell to sweep in a low left footer from close range for an Arsenal victory which, on the 90 minutes, they barely deserve.

A section of supporters had taunted the controversial front man because suspension was to deny him his Cup Winners' Cup Final place. On the final whistle his salute to the Holte End confirms that this time the last laugh was his.

The Villa manager is philosophical about the frustrating outcome of the promising second half. "I thought it was a smashing game and it was a bonus for us to see our young players coming through it so well."

Andy Townsend barges his way past Steve Bould

Wednesday 27th April 1994 • St. James' Park • 7.45pm

NEWCASTLE UNITED 5 ASTON VILLA 1

Half-time 3-1 • *Attendance 32,216*

Referee John LLOYD (Wrexham)
Linesmen A.J. HILL and A. STREETS

Black and White Striped Shirts, Black Shorts	Goals	Claret Shirts with Blue Stripes, White Shorts	Goals
1 Pavel SRNICEK		1 Nigel SPINK	
2 Barry VENISON		2 Earl BARRETT	
20 Alan NEILSEN		16 Ugo EHIOGU	
15 Darren PEACOCK		4 Shaun TEALE †	
3 John BERESFORD		3 Steve STAUNTON	
4 Paul BRACEWELL †	15	7 Ray HOUGHTON	
7 Robert LEE		6 Kevin RICHARDSON	
5 Ruel FOX		14 Andy TOWNSEND	
11 Scott SELLARS	79	21 Dave FARRELL ‡	
9 Andy COLE ‡	41	25 Graham FENTON	
8 Peter BEARDSLEY pen 23, 66		19 Stefan BEINLICH	10
Substitutes		*Substitutes*	
30 Mike HOOPER		30 Michael OAKES	
19 Steve WATSON †69		11 Tony DALEY †50	
14 Alex MATTHIE ‡87		20 Matthias BREITKREUTZ ‡69	

BEFORE		P	W	D	L	F	A	pts	AFTER		P	W	D	L	F	A	pts
3	Newcastle	39	21	8	10	75	38	71	3	Newcastle	40	22	8	10	80	39	74
10	Villa	39	14	12	13	42	40	54	10	Villa	40	14	12	14	43	45	54

FACTFILE

Villa's heaviest defeat under Ron Atkinson... Stefan Beinlich opens his first team goal account... Andy Cole breaks Newcastle's club scoring record with his 40th league and cup goal of the season... Peter Beardsley makes his 600th appearance in league and cups and takes his goals tally to 203.

A long journey to disaster

This has become the league season that can't end too soon, a series of mystifying contrasts to the glory of Wembley success in the Coca Cola Cup Final.

Visits to St James' Park during the reign of 'king' Kevin Keegan are never going to be an easy ride. This proves to be a journey to disaster. Advance signs have not been good. Injuries to key players have meant that Mark Bosnich, Paul McGrath, Dalian Atkinson and Dean Saunders are all missing.

To add to the unsettled air another chapter has been written in the McGrath saga or, more correctly, an entire book. Coinciding with the publication of his life story, serialised in *The Sun*, the Irish international has been 'missing' again, in Dublin for its launch.

Specialist appointments for his neck injury have not been kept, nor has his routine daily training commitments. This time Ron Atkinson appears to be losing his patience.

Forced to play youngsters again, Atkinson gets the early reward of an enthusiastic opening spell and first league goal for Stefan Beinlich in the 10th minute.

A little earlier Andy Townsend has been close to scoring but the Czech goalkeeper Pavel Srnicek recovers to push the ball for a corner after almost allowing it to loop over his head.

Appropriately, having been so narrowly denied, it is Townsend who supplies the nodded down 'assist' for the young German to volley home from 20 yards.

The fanatical Geordie fans, ready to celebrate a club record 40th goal of the season in cup and league by the prolific Andy Cole, have to wait only five minutes for the equaliser, though Paul Bracewell is the provider.

Ugo Ehiogu's clearance drops fortuitously for him and it's 1-1. By half-time another two have gone in and Cole has arrived at his landmark.

Peter Beardsley marks his 600th league and cup appearance by posting the lead from the penalty spot after being fouled by Steve Staunton. Cole's big moment arrives after Spink has twice intervened to keep him waiting.

Chasing a long ball from Scott Sellars he rounds the Villa 'keeper to make it 3-1 after 42 minutes and earn the well-deserved acclaim of the Tyneside worshippers.

Villa's defence is now visibly in trouble and even a partially-fit McGrath's experience and expertise would be invaluable. The latest AWOL offence is looking more significant than ever.

But worse news is around the corner. Shaun Teale is carried off four minutes into the second half after a tackle from behind by Cole and Tony Daley arrives as hardly the ideal replacement for the defensive rock.

Daley goes to right back with Earl Barrett moving inside but Beardsley adds a fourth and Sellars a fifth as the decimated visiting defence is unable to cope.

On a depressed journey home, with a stern-faced manager keeping his innermost thoughts to himself, Wembley seems a long, long time ago. Tenth position in the Premiership, thirty-one points adrift of Manchester United, is a depressing fall from the second place finish of last season.

Stefan Beinlich put Villa ahead with a 20 yard volley

Saturday 30th April 1994 • The Dell • 3.00pm

SOUTHAMPTON 4 ASTON VILLA 1

Half-time 2-0 • *Attendance* 19,003

Referee Steve LODGE (Barnsley)

Linesmen S.G. CLINGO and M.R. SIMS

Red and White Striped Shirts, Black Shorts		Goals	Claret Shirts with Blue Stripes, White Shorts		Goals
1	Dave BEASANT		1	Nigel SPINK ∎	
2	Jeff KENNA		2	Earl BARRETT	
6	Ken MONKOU	39	16	Ugo EHIOGU	
11	Francis BENALI		5	Paul McGRATH †	
21	Tommy WIDDRINGTON		3	Steve STAUNTON	
14	Simon CHARLTON		7	Ray HOUGHTON	
27	Paul ALLEN †		6	Kevin RICHARDSON	
4	Jim MAGILTON		14	Andy TOWNSEND ❑	
10	Neil MADDISON ❑	88	20	Matthias BREITKREUTZ ‡	
9	Iain DOWIE ❑		9	Dean SAUNDERS	58
7	Matthew LE TISSIER	19, 77	19	Stefan BEINLICH	
	Substitutes			*Substitutes*	
13	Ian ANDREWS		30	Michael OAKES	
15	Jason DODD †83		17	Neil COX †45	
8	Craig MASKELL		11	Tony DALEY ‡70	

BEFORE		P	W	D	L	F	A	pts	AFTER		P	W	D	L	F	A	pts
10	Villa	40	14	12	14	43	45	54	10	Villa	41	14	12	15	44	49	54
19	Soton	39	11	6	22	42	60	39	17	Soton	40	12	6	22	46	61	42

Nigel Spink is sent off for the first time in his career... Neil Cox plays the last 12 minutes in goal, conceding one... Matthias Breitkreutz starts his first senior game of the season... The final away game of 93/94 sees a proud record falls - it is the first time Villa have lost in a game played south of Birmingham this season.

A story of Saints and sinners...

There was a time, throughout most of the season, when away games inspired confidence of another likely victory. Not anymore, unhappily.

With four defeats from the last five away games in the Premiership and five goals conceded three days ago, there is bound to be apprehension at The Dell against relegation-threatened Saints.

Paul McGrath has been disciplined for his most recent absence and, despite his neck injury, is recalled to the heart of the defence.

With injured Mark Bosnich, Dalian Atkinson and Shaun Teale missing and the Germans Matthias Breitkreutz and Stefan Beinlich in the side, Ron Atkinson sends out a 4-5-1 formation.

The idea is obviously a 'containing' one, with damage limitation the prime objective but once again things to do not work out for the dispirited Villa side who are trailing by two goals at the break.

Southampton are the attacking aggressors more or less from the start, perked no doubt by the knowledge of Villa's recent vulnerability at St. James' Park.

In 19 minutes the highly talented Matthew Le Tissier, back after suspension, puts Southampton one up after Jeff Kenna breaks from the half-way line.

Villa show little sign of immediate recovery and 20 minutes later there is no-one marking Ken Monkou as he heads in Le Tissier's corner.

It is early in the second-half, after the struggling McGrath is replaced by Neil Cox, before Villa begin to show some of their true

Nigel Spink - sent off

capabilities and are rewarded by a 58th minute Dean Saunders strike.

Deano's shot for his 16th goal of the season flies past goalkeeper Dave Beasant, helped by a deflection off defender Simon Charlton's boot.

Now, with Ray Houghton and ex-Saint Andy Townsend beginning to take a measure of midfield control, a 2-1 deficit looks far from insurmountable as the home goal is put under a 20-minute Villa siege.

An equaliser now would bring the boost which has largely been needed since Wembley but the reverse proves to be the case as Le Tissier pounces for his 77th minute second goal and a 3-1 Southampton lead.

The last 13 minutes - and beyond - prove disastrous for Villa as Nigel Spink is shown a red card after a collision with Ian Dowie and Neil Maddison heads a fourth goal past Spink's deputy, Cox.

Ron Atkinson is adamant, after watching a video of the incident, that Spink was not guilty of any offence, merely going hard for a ball which he believed to be his.

But the manager did add ruefully: "We are doing something we have not done since I became manager. We are shipping goals."

After the final whistle a small group of Villa followers invade the pitch and break one of the goals in an unwarranted act of vandalism.

Chairman Doug Ellis apologises for the affair, agrees to pay for the damage, and condemns the behaviour as unacceptable. "If we could find the right people I would ban them forever and a day," he said.

It is an embarrassing ending to another disappointing performance.

Saturday 7th May 1994 • Villa Park • 3.00pm

ASTON VILLA 2 LIVERPOOL 1

Half-time 0-1 • Attendance 45,347

Referee Keith BURGE (Tonypandy)
Linesmen G.M. LEE and M. STOBBART

Claret Shirts with Blue Stripes, White Shorts		Goals	White Shirts with Green Sleeves, Black Shorts		Goals
13	Mark BOSNICH		13	David JAMES	
2	Earl BARRETT		2	Rob JONES	
5	Paul McGRATH		4	Steve NICOL	
16	Ugo EHIOGU		25	Neil RUDDOCK	
3	Steve STAUNTON		3	Julian DICKS	
7	Ray HOUGHTON		15	Jamie REDKNAPP	
6	Kevin RICHARDSON		6	Don HUTCHISON	
14	Andy TOWNSEND		12	Ronnie WHELAN †	
11	Tony DALEY †		10	John BARNES	
19	Stefan BEINLICH ‡		9	Ian RUSH	
9	Dean SAUNDERS		23	Robbie FOWLER	17
	Substitutes			*Substitutes*	
30	Michael OAKES		1	Bruce GROBBELAAR	
23	Bryan SMALL †45		22	Steve HARKNESS †77	
18	Dwight YORKE ‡45	65, 81	7	Nigel CLOUGH	

BEFORE		P	W	D	L	F	A	pts	AFTER		P	W	D	L	F	A	pts
8	Liverpool	41	17	9	15	58	53	60	8	Liverpool	42	17	9	16	59	55	60
11	Villa	41	14	12	15	44	49	54	10	Villa	42	15	12	15	46	50	57

Dwight Yorke scores the final goals in front of the Holte End terracing...
The attendance is the largest anywhere in the two seasons of the Premier League...
The result means Villa avoid equalling their worst ever home figures of 7 wins
and 22 goals in a season as the totals are pushed to 8 and 23 respectively.

A rousing finale to the season

A day of unashamed nostalgia arrives, a day for the history books. The Holte End is to be used for the last time as a standing enclosure and, amazingly the Premiership's biggest crowd, of 45,347, flocks in.

Everyone, all 19,210, using soccer's biggest bank of terracing before it becomes a two-tier all-seater showpiece receives a signed commemorative certificate, on the way in, to mark the occasion.

Legendry players from the past are paraded to help revive treasured memories, some a shade greyer or wider but all the more warmly received for that.

The biggest terrace in football is a singing, swaying, colourful mass as the League Cup winning season ends in party-time. But, don't forget, there's a match to be played.

There's an extra dash of pressure, too, with the huge crowd yearning for a winning sign-off after all those home defeats. The players want it, too, but it's not going to be easy.

Mark Bosnich is back in goal and though Shaun Teale is out injured, Paul McGrath is in there, too, his latest indiscretions behind him now.

Early signs are not too hopeful as Liverpool, according to their manager Roy Evans, reel off their best football since he took over from Graeme Souness.

Bosnich makes three saves, Liverpool appeal unsuccessfuly for a couple of penalties and in the midst of it all Robbie Fowler gives the Merseysiders a 17th minute lead.

It's a little gem, too, as he inter-passes with Ian Rush, draws away from Andy Townsend and Ugo Ehiogu, escapes the attentions of Earl Barrett and slides the ball wide of Bosnich.

As half-time arrives it seems that the air of celebration off the field is not to be rewarded by an end-of-an-era result and performance to cherish.

Happily this it to prove an entirely inaccurate impression, thanks to an inspired substitution and a touch of Carribean flair.

During the interval Bryan Small takes over from Tony Daley (unwell) and, more significantly it proves, Dwight Yorke replaces Stefan Beinlich, who received a blow in the face.

What a difference now... Villa take charge of the attacking pattern and it is the visiting goal suddenly and decisively under seige.

Twenty minutes into the half a Dean Saunders cross-shot presents Yorke with a simple tap-in goal, just what he needed to give his disappointing, injury-hit season a glow.

And there's more. Excellent work by Ray Houghton supplies the West Indian with a second chance after 81 minutes and this he puts away, once again, with ease.

Down the road at Edgbaston, Dwight's best pal, Brian Lara, the World-record breaking West Indian Test batsman has been scoring centuries for Warwickshire. There's no way the player Ron Atkinson has described as his 'little Yorkie bar' is going to be left out of the headlines.

As a finale to the season and a 'bye, bye' to the Holte it couldn't have been better... especially as the Coca Cola Cup is paraded at the end.

Forget those baffling inconsistencies at home. A new page in the history of Aston Villa has been written and, come December, a £6m construction matching the majestic traditions of the Trinity Road Stand will have appeared on the Aston sky-line.

Dwight Yorke

COCA-COLA CUP 93

Monday 19th July 1993 • in Tokyo • 7.00pm

YOMIURI NIPPON 1   ASTON VILLA 2

Green Shirts, White Shorts	Goals	Claret Shirts with Blue Stripes, White Shorts	Goals
1 Shinkichi KIKUCHI		1 Mark BOSNICH	
2 Tadashi NAKAMURA		2 Earl BARRETT	
3 Luiz Carlos PEREIRA		3 Steve FROGGATT	
4 Gene HANSSEN		4 Ugo EHIOGU	
5 Tetsuji HASHIRATANI		5 Neil COX	
6 Ko ISHIKAWA		6 Kevin RICHARDSON	
8 Tsuyoshi KITAZAWA		7 Tony DALEY	
9 Nobuhiro TAKEDA		8 Garry PARKER	
11 Kazuyoshi MIURA		9 Dean SAUNDERS	
13 Eric Van ROSSUM		10 Dalian ATKINSON	2 goals
14 Tetsuya TOTSUKA		11 Gordon COWANS	
Substitutes		*Substitutes*	
7 Hideki NAGAI		15 Nigel SPINK	
10 Ruy RAMOS		12 Dwight YORKE	
12 Shinji FUJIYOSHI		14 Stefan BEINLICH	
15 Kazuo OZAKI		16 Chris BODEN	
16 Takayuki FUJIKAWA			
17 Shiro KIKUHARA			
18 Mitsuhiro KAWAMOTO			

FACTFILE

First game of the season, first win, first trophy... Villa win the Coca-Cola Cup in Japan - an omen perhaps for the season ahead!... The game is played in Tokyo's highly impressive 'Big Egg' stadium, a totally covered arena not unlike Detroit's Pontiac Silverdome used in the World Cup.

Tuesday 27th July 1993 • Boothferry Park • 7.30pm

HULL CITY 0 ASTON VILLA 2

Half-time 0-0 • Attendance 5,699

Referee G. GRANDIDGE
Linesmen D. SPARKE and R. GRAHAM

Amber and Black Shirts, Black Shorts	Goals	Claret Shirts with Blue Stripes, White Shorts	Goals
1 Alan FERRIS †		1 Nigel SPINK	
2 David NORTON		2 Neil COX ##	
3 Gary HOBSON		3 Steve STAUNTON ≠	
4 Neil ALLISON #		4 Shaun TEALE	
5 Russ WILCOX		5 Paul McGRATH †	
6 Greg ABBOTT		6 Kevin RICHARDSON ‡	
7 Steve BROWN ‡		8 Garry PARKER §	
8 Steve MORAN		10 Dalian ATKINSON §§	
9 Chris HARGREAVES		11 Tony DALEY ‡‡ §§62	82
10 Dean WINDASS §		17 Stefan BEINLICH #	
11 Graeme ATKINSON		18 Matthias BREITKREUTZ ††	
Substitutes		*Substitutes*	
13 Steve WILSON †45		13 Mark BOSNICH	
12 Lee WARREN		7 Ray HOUGHTON #45	
14 Neil MANN ‡62		9 Andy TOWNSEND ‡45	
15 Robert MILLER #62		12 Steve FROGGATT ‡‡ 45	46
16 Matthew HOPKINS §77		14 Gordon COWANS §45	
		16 Ugo EHIOGU †45	
		19 Dave FARRELL ≠72	
		20 Graham FENTON ††45	
		21 Dariusz KUBICKI ##62	

FACTFILE

Andy Townsend makes his first appearance on Villa colours... Hull include former Villa utility player David Norton in their line-up... Garry Parker returns to one of his former clubs.

Monday 2nd August 1993 • Vale Park • 7.30pm

PORT VALE 2 ASTON VILLA 3

Half-time 0-2 • Attendance 7,117

Referee John HILDITCH (Stoke-on-Trent)

White Shirts, Black Shorts	Goals	Claret Shirts with Blue Stripes, White Shorts	Goals
1 Paul MUSSELWHITE		1 Nigel SPINK	
2 Kevin KENT ‡		2 Earl BARRETT	
3 Allen TANKARD		3 Steve STAUNTON §	
4 Neil ASPIN		4 Shaun TEALE	
5 Peter BILLING		5 Paul McGRATH ††	6
6 Dean GLOVER		6 Gordon COWANS ‡	
7 Bernie SLAVEN		7 Ray HOUGHTON	
8 Andy PORTER	86	8 Andy TOWNSEND #	32
9 Martin FOYLE		9 Dean SAUNDERS †	
10 Paul KERR	52	10 Dwight YORKE	
11 Ian TAYLOR †		11 Steve FROGGATT	
Substitutes		*Substitutes*	
12 Robin VAN DER LAAN †45		13 Michael OAKES	
14 Bradley SANDEMAN ‡45		12 Kevin RICHARDSON ‡45	
		14 Tony DALEY †38	73
		15 Garry PARKER #45	
		17 Neil COX §62	
		19 Ugo EHIOGU ††62	

FACTFILE

The match is a benefit for Vale manager John Rudge who will celebrate ten years in charge of the Potteries club in December and by the end of the season becomes Vale's longest serving manager of all time... Andy Townsend scores his first goal for the club... Former Villa team-mates Gordon Cowans and Dean Glover are the two captains... Steve Froggatt moves to left back when Neil Cox comes on.

Wednesday 4th August 1993 • Bescot Stadium • 8.00pm (delayed from 7.45)

WALSALL 0 ASTON VILLA 4

Half-time 0-2 • Attendance 5,937

Referee Jim RUSHTON (Stoke -on-Trent)
Linesmen P. REJER and A. SHEFFIELD

Red Shirts, White Shorts	Goals	Green, Black and Red Striped Shirts, Black Shorts	Goals
1 Mark GAYLE †		1 Nigel SPINK §	
2 Chris MARSH		2 Earl BARRETT	
3 Bernard GALLACHER ‡		3 Steve STAUNTON	
4 Stuart WATKISS #	(og 53)	4 Shaun TEALE	
5 Stuart RYDER		5 Paul McGRATH	
6 Dean SMITH		6 Kevin RICHARDSON #	
7 Charlie NTAMARK		7 Tony DALEY †	
8 John TINKLER		8 Andy TOWNSEND ††	
9 Mike CECERE		9 Guy WHITTINGHAM	84
10 Kyle LIGHTBORNE		10 Dalian ATKINSON	9, 39
11 Rod McDONALD		11 Garry PARKER ‡	
Substitutes		*Substitutes*	
12 James WALKER †53		13 Michael OAKES §53	
14 Richard KNIGHT ‡84		12 Steve FROGGATT †45	
15 Martin BUTLER		14 Gordon COWANS #45	
16 Stephen O'HARA		15 Ray HOUGHTON ‡45	
Wayne EVANS #86		16 Ugo EHIOGU	
		17 Dariusz KUBICKI	
		18 Dave FARRELL ††84	

FACTFILE

Guy Whittingham makes his Villa debut just 24 hours after signing from Portsmouth and nets a fine goal... Former Villa full-back Bernie Gallacher is the Saddlers left-back, on trial... The game is arranged as part of the agreement which saw Villa play reserve fixtures at Bescot last season.

Saturday 7th August 1993 • Springfield Park • 3.00pm

WIGAN ATHLETIC 0 ASTON VILLA 1

Half-time 0-1 • Attendance 1,634

Referee John ROBERTSON
Linesmen J. ATHERTON and M. STEPHENS

Blue and Black Striped Shirts, Black Shorts	Goals	Claret Shirts with Blue Stripes, White Shorts	Goals
1 Simon FARNWORTH		1 Nigel SPINK	
2 Chris DUFFY		2 Earl BARRETT	
3 Paul WEST †		3 Steve STAUNTON	
4 John ROBERTSON		4 Shaun TEALE	
5 Peter SKIPPER		5 Paul McGRATH ††	
6 Alan JOHNSON		6 Kevin RICHARDSON †	
7 Greg STRONG ‡		7 Ray HOUGHTON §	
8 David McKEARNEY		8 Andy TOWNSEND #	
9 Pat GAVIN		9 Guy WHITTINGHAM	22
10 Neil MORTON		10 Dalian ATKINSON	
11 Kevin LANGLEY		11 Steve FROGGATT ‡	
Substitutes		*Substitutes*	
13 Anthony PEACOCK		13 Michael OAKES	
12 Neil OGDEN ‡85		12 Gordon COWANS †45	
14 Steve HOLLIS †62		14 Tony DALEY ‡45	
15 Julian DOWE		15 Garry PARKER #45	
		16 Neil COX ††74	
		17 Dave FARRELL §62	

> **FACTFILE**
>
> *Villa make it five wins out of five as the series of warm-up games for the new season is completed... Guy Whittingham scores his second goal in two games for the club... Shaun Teale takes the captain's arm band in the second half... Wigan are managed by Villa's European Cup final full-back Kenny Swain.*

Monday 9th May 1994 • The Hawthorns • 7.20pm

WEST BROMWICH ALBION 1 ASTON VILLA 2

Half-time 0-1 • *Attendance* 9,000

Referee Terry HOLBROOK (Wolverhampton)

Linesmen P. REJER and A. SHEFFIELD

Blue and White Striped Shirts, White Shorts	Goals	Claret Shirts with Blue Stripes, Blue Shorts	
1 Neil CUTLER ††		1 Mark BOSNICH § ##76	
2 Bernard McNALLY		2 Earl BARRETT	
3 Derek STATHAM ‡		3 Steve STAUNTON ‡‡	
4 Justin ROBSON §		4 Bryan SMALL †	
5 Gary STRODDER		5 Ugo EHIOGU	
6 Paul RAVEN		6 Kevin RICHARDSON ##	
7 Bryan ROBSON #		7 Ray HOUGHTON #	
8 Gary ROBSON		8 Andy TOWNSEND ‡	
9 Bob TAYLOR		9 Dean SAUNDERS ††	17
10 Cyrille REGIS †		10 Dwight YORKE	
11 John TREWICK		19 Steve FROGGATT	
Substitutes		*Substitutes*	
19 Gary GERMAINE ††80		13 Michael OAKES §45	
12 Andy HUNT †45	78	11 Tony DALEY #45	
Scott DARTON ‡45		14 Stefan BEINLICH †31	
Ian HAMILTON #45		16 Guy WHITTINGHAM ††45	59
17 Kevin DONOVAN §55		17 Dave FARRELL ‡‡45	
		20 Matthias BREITKREUTZ ‡33	

Around 4,000 fans are reported to be locked out with The Hawthorns' capacity severely reduced by groundwork... Albion fans have turned up not only to pay tribute to Gary Robson's 12 years service for the club but also to celebrate the Baggies' First Division survival after yesterday's win at Portsmouth... Villa win comfortably, finishing with Mark Bosnich in attack wearing the number 7 shirt!

PAUL DAVIES TESTIMONIAL MATCH

Monday 16th May 1994 • Aggborough Stadium • 7.30pm

KIDDERMINSTER HARRIERS 2 ASTON VILLA 3

Half-time 1-1 • Attendance 3,550

Referee Vic CALLOW (Solihull)
Linesmen N. GREEN and G. PEARSON

Red and White Halved Shirts, Red Shorts	Goals	Green, Black and Red Striped Shirts, Black Shorts	Goals
1 Kevin ROSE †		13 Mark BOSNICH ‡	
2 Simeon HODSON		2 Earl BARRETT †	
3 Paul BANCROFT		3 Steve FROGGATT #	
4 Martin WOODALL ‡		4 Dennis PEARCE	
5 Chris BRINDLEY		5 Ugo EHIOGU	89
6 Richard FORSYTH		6 Darren EVANS	
7 Neil CARTWRIGHT		7 Scott MURRAY	75
8 Mark WOOLSEY		8 Stefan BEINLICH	
9 Delwyn HUMPHREYS	56	9 Guy WHITTINGHAM	
10 Paul DAVIES §	38	10 Matthias BREITKREUTZ	
11 John DEAKIN #		11 Dave FARRELL	44
Substitutes		*Substitutes*	
13 Darren STEADMAN †45		13 Michael OAKES ‡45	
12 Craig GILLETT §88		12 Paul BROWNE †45	
16 Micky TOUHY #77		14 Steven COWE #82	
17 Craig LANGFORD ‡45			

Sunday 22nd May 1994 • Ellis Park, Johannesburg • 3.15pm

LIVERPOOL 2 ASTON VILLA 1

Half-time 1-1 • *Attendance* 25,000

Referee Petras MATHABELA

Red Shirts, Red Shorts		Goals	Green, Black and Red Striped Shirts, Black Shorts		
13	David JAMES ‡		13	Mark BOSNICH	
22	Steve HARKNESS		6	Neil COX	25
25	Neil RUDDOCK		4	Shaun TEALE	
4	Steve NICOL		5	Ugo EHIOGU	
21	Dominic MATTEO		3	Steve FROGGATT	
15	Jamie REDKNAPP		11	Dwight YORKE	
10	John BARNES		2	Earl BARRETT	
16	Michael THOMAS	57	10	Matthias BREITKREUTZ #	
7	Nigel CLOUGH		7	Graham FENTON †	
6	Don HUTCHISON †		8	Stefan BEINLICH ‡	
23	Robbie FOWLER	32	9	Guy WHITTINGHAM	
	Substitutes			*Substitutes*	
1	Bruce GROBBELAAR ‡69		1	Nigel SPINK	
18	Phil CHARNOCK †16 #		14	Dave FARRELL †62	
24	Lee JONES #74		15	Riccardo SCIMECA ‡73	
	Ashley NEAL		12	Bryan SMALL #87	
				Tony DALEY	

FACTFILE

The first of Villa's three games in South Africa... The match is played 6,000 feet above sea level and players report sore throats and lack of breath afterwards... Granada TV show the game live in the North West... Neil Cox takes advantage of a goalkeeping error to lob Villa in front, Dominic Matteo sets up Robbie Fowler to head the equaliser from six yards out and Michael Thomas hits the winner with a fierce drive... Shaun Teale is Villa's skipper.

Tuesday 24th May 1994 • Kings Park, Durban • 8.10pm

MANNING RANGERS 0 ASTON VILLA 1

Half-time 0-0 • Attendance 6,500

Goalscorer Guy WHITTINGHAM (47 mins)

Manning Rangers: BLANKENBERG, LARSEN, RAPEANI ‡, MUIR, CHILOMBO, CHEMBO, NDIMANDE, MUANILE, SAKALA, DU PLESSIS, DHALMINI †. *Substitutes:* KOUMANTARAKIS †53, DAVIES ‡80.

Aston Villa: Mark BOSNICH, Earl BARRETT, Bryan SMALL, Shaun TEALE, Ugo EHIOGU, Kevin RICHARDSON, Neil COX, Dwight YORKE #, Guy WHITTINGHAM, Matthias BREITKREUTZ †, Steve FROGGATT ‡. *Substitutes:* Nigel SPINK, Stefan BEINLICH †45, Dave FARRELL ‡51, Riccardo SCIMECA #80, Tony DALEY, Graham FENTON.

Sunday 29th May 1994 • Ellis Park, Johannesburg • 2.00pm

MOROKA SWALLOWS 0 ASTON VILLA 0

Half-time 0-0 • Attendance 45,000

Moroka Swallows: DE SA, MINE, PSOTSETSI, SIKHONDE, MOLOTSANE, MTAFUDI, MAKABOLE, RAPELEGO, RAMESIKE, LIBO, SEKANO. *Substitute:* MAKGALEDESA.

Aston Villa: Mark BOSNICH, Earl BARRETT, Bryan SMALL, Shaun TEALE, Ugo EHIOGU, Kevin RICHARDSON, Neil COX, Dwight YORKE, Guy WHITTINGHAM, Stefan BEINLICH †, Steve FROGGATT ‡. *Substitutes:* Nigel SPINK, Dave FARRELL ‡65, Riccardo SCIMECA †45, Tony DALEY.

FACTFILE

The South African tour winds up with a record of won one, drew one, lost one... Guy Whittingham scores the only goal of the game in Durban, pouncing onto a weak back pass, and has a 'goal' disallowed for offside in the final game... Moroka Swallows finished their season as runners-up in the National Soccer League, their highest ever placing.

THE MANAGEMENT TEAM

Bodymoor Heath's 'team-behind-the-team', manager **Ron Atkinson's** trusted group of aides, confirmed the effectiveness of their methods as the Coca-Cola Cup landed in the trophy cabinet.

Atkinson's 'hands-on' style of management, still very much of the tracksuit variety, demands that others are delegated to perform their specialist duties in much the same way. For most of the morning and sometimes in the afternoon, Big Ron is out on the training ground doing what he likes most, namely kicking a ball about.

"I'm the oldest, and the best, player manager in the business," he will wisecrack to anyone who cares to listen. He's not slow to tell players what he expects them to do but nor does he make the mistake of being afraid to delegate. **Jim Barron**, his ever-cheerful No.2, spends a similar amount of time on the practice area but he can 'look after the shop' when the gaffer is away on another of his favourite activities as a TV analyst.

Ex-goalkeeper Jim naturally spends some time with the 'keepers but his duties cover almost as diverse a field as the manager's, including supervision of the Reserves.

If, at any time, Big Ron can't handle the welter of media enquiries, then Jim can comfortably step in. Likewise on European trips, Barron is very much Atkinson's right hand, and their personal friendship ensures that it all goes with hardly a hitch.

Direct management of the youth team and YTS scheme has been the combined responsibility of coach **Colin Clarke** and scout **Dave Richardson**, though the latter left the club at the end of the season.

Clarke was once with Atkinson and Barron at Oxford United. Like the other two he feels strongly about the young players being taught discipline and responsibility and insists they take occasional glimpses of the real world, outside of the rather pampered surrounds of pro football.

The coaching set-up is given an extra dimension of experience and quality by the involvement of **Dave Sexton**, now back in the England international fold under Terry Venables.

Sexton's knowledge of football in all its aspects and his gift for imparting styles of play to his charges has made a big contribution to the attractive nature of the football which categorises each of the teams.

Visitors to the training ground, for any length of time, inevitably come to appreciate the relaxed blend of discipline and good humour which pervades the place.

Big Ron's flair for repartee and cutting one-liners sets the tone, though never to the extent of anyone stepping out of line.

Here the smiling, softly-spoken **Jim Walker** gets on with his job as physiotherapist, seemingly unmoved by the queue which can sometimes grow for his services.

Walker, who learned much about the game in his spell under Brian Clough at Derby County, is able to see fitness problems through the eyes of a player rather than as a pure medic. He firmly believes that, with the average footballing injury, as distinct from the very serious type, remedial exercise is as crucial as modern technology.

Jim thus spends a good deal of time away from the treatment room and in the gym or on the practice area helping players back into action.

The fitness factor is supplemented by conditional coach **Paul Barron**, the former Arsenal, Palace, QPR and Albion goalkeeper.

All of which adds to the amount of gear required from kit manager **Jim Paul** whose storeroom looks like a sports good supplier's.

Jim can hold his own with any of the friendly insults dispensed freely by the leg-pulling players whose needs would amaze the parks player.

With homes and aways, long-sleeved and short-sleeved, spare sets, all squad numbers, training gear and leisurewear, plus towels and heaven knows what else, the turn-over in demand is mind-bending.

DALIAN ATKINSON

Born Shrewsbury,
21st March 1968
Joined Villa July 1991,
from Real Sociedad,
£1.6m.
Villa debut v Sheff Wed,
Lge (a), 17/8/91. 1 goal.

Flair for important goals at the right time
was his stock-in-trade once again, with
quality rather than quantity his golden
asset. His nick-of-time strikes in injury
time at Tranmere in the Coca-Cola Cup
semi-final and again to make it 3-1 in
second leg helped take Villa to Wembley.
On the big day his first half opener
paved the way for the trophy and the
return to Europe. Also scored in earlier
rounds at Sunderland (2) and Arsenal.

Career Record:

Season	Club	League Apps	Gls	Cups Apps	Gls
85-86	Ipswich T.	- (1)	-	-	-
86-87	Ipswich T.	3 (5)	-	1 (2)	-
87-88	Ipswich T.	13 (4)	8	1	-
88-89	Ipswich T.	33 (1)	10	5	3
89-90	Sheffield W.	38	10	7	5
90-91	Real Sociedad	29	12		
91-92	Aston Villa	11 (3)	1	3	-
92-93	Aston Villa	28	11	4	2
93-94	Aston Villa	29	8	15	7
Villa record		68 (3)	20	22	9
TOTAL		184 (14)	60	36 (2)	17

★ *England 'B' international (1 cap).*

( ) indicates appearances as a used substitute.

League figures include Play-off games.

Cup figures include FA Cup, League Cup, Full Members' Cup,
Associate Members' Cup, Mercantile Credit Centenary Trophy,
Screen Sport Super Cup, FA Charity Shield, European
Champions' Cup, European Cup Winners' Cup, UEFA Cup,
European Super Cup and World Club Championship.

EARL BARRETT

Born Rochdale,
28th April 1967.
Joined Villa February
1992 from Oldham,
£1.7m.
Villa debut v Man City,
Lge (a), 29/2/92.

Another year of progress for the versatile
defender who continued to shine in any
role selected, mainly right back. Among
his many highlights was his rare feat of
scoring the winner in the Coca-Cola
Cup-tie at White Hart Lane. Appeared for
England against Brazil and Germany in
America last June but made only the first
squad of this term although he was
called up by new boss Terry Venables for
a get-together in April.

Career Record:

Season	Club	League Apps	Gls	Cups Apps	Gls
84-85	Man. City	-	-	-	-
85-86	Man. City	1	-	-	-
(loan)	Chester City	12	-	-	-
86-87	Man. City	1 (1)	-	1	-
87-88	Man. City	-	-	-	-
	Oldham Ath.	16 (2)	-	-	-
88-89	Oldham Ath.	44	-	6	-
89-90	Oldham Ath.	46	2	19	2
90-91	Oldham Ath.	46	3	6	-
91-92	Oldham Ath.	29	2	7	-
	Aston Villa	13	-	-	-
92-93	Aston Villa	42	1	9	-
93-94	Aston Villa	39	-	13	1
Villa record		94	1	22	1
TOTAL		289 (3)	8	61	3

★ *Full England international (3 caps). Also capped
at 'B' and Under-21 levels.*

STEFAN BEINLICH

Born Berlin, Germany, 13th January 1972.·
Joined Villa October 1991 from Bergmann Borsig, £100,000.
Villa debut As substitute v Nott'm. Forest, Zenith Cup (h), 19/11/91.

The 'striker' part of the German duo. Played against Sheffield Wednesday and Wimbledon at Villa Park in mid-season and forced his way back into the reckoning for the last five games. Scored his first senior goal for the club in spectacular fashion at Newcastle in April. Appeared in seven of the ten first-team friendlies this season which involved trips to Japan and South Africa.

Career Record:

Season	Club	League Apps	Gls	Cups Apps	Gls
91-92	Aston Villa	- (2)	-	- (1)	-
92-93	Aston Villa	1 (6)	-	-	-
93-94	Aston Villa	6 (1)	1	-	-
TOTAL		7 (9)	1	- (1)	-

★ *Joined Villa from PFV Bergmann Borsig along with Matthias Breitkreutz in a £200,000 deal.*

★ *Was Villa's top scorer in the Central League this season with 9 goals in 26 games, including a hat-trick against Sheffield United.*

MARK BOSNICH

Born Fairfield, Australia, 13th January 1972.
Joined Villa February 1992 from Sydney Croatia.
Villa debut v Luton Town, Lge (a) 25/4/92.

The charismatic Aussie enjoyed a sensational season as he edged out Nigel Spink from the No.1 goalkeeping place and earned the supporters' Player of the Year award. His penalty saves in the Coca Cola Cup, especially the spectacular semi-final shoot-out against Tranmere at Villa Park, have given him a special place in the club's folklore. Missed the start of the season because of a FIFA ban due to his refusal to play for Australia, although he was later persauded to appear for his country in a World Cup qualifier with Argentina.

Career Record:

Season	Club	League Apps	Gls Ag	Cups Apps	Gls Ag
89-90	Man. United	1	0	-	-
90-91	Man. United	2	2	-	-
91-92	Aston Villa	1	1	-	-
92-93	Aston Villa	17	12	1	0
93-94	Aston Villa	28	28	12 (1)	11
Villa record		46	41	13 (1)	11
TOTAL		49	43	13 (1)	11

★ *Full international with Australia. Appeared in the 1992 Barcelona Olympics. Played just one international this season, a World Cup qualifier against Argentina in in Sydney October.*

★ *Won the club's and the Midland Soccer Writers' 'Player of the Year' awards.*

★ *Saved 5 out 6 penalties faced this season plus three in the Coca-Cola shoot-out with Tranmere.*

● NOTE: *Career records of goalkeepers Mark Bosnich (left) and Nigel Spink (p140) list number of goals conceded in the goals columns.*

MATTHIAS BREITKREUTZ

Born Crivitz, Germany, 12th May 1971
Joined Villa October 1991 from Bergmann Borsig, £100,000.
Villa debut As sub v Sheff Wed, Lge (h), 18/1/92.

German-born midfield player who excelled for the reserves but had limited first-team opportunity because of the overall strength of the squad. Came into the reckoning right at the end of the season when experimental changes were being made due to injuries, but his appearances coincided with poor team performances and heavy defeats at Newcastle and Southampton. Scored three goals in 28(1) Central League games.

Career Record:

Season	Club	League Apps	Gls	Cups Apps	Gls
91-92	Aston Villa	7 (1)	-	-	-
92-93	Aston Villa	2 (1)	-	- (1)	-
93-94	Aston Villa	1 (1)	-	-	-
TOTAL		10 (3)	-	- (1)	-

★ *Joined Villa from PFV Bergmann Borsig along with Stefan Beinlich in a £200,000 deal.*

● *Young professionals* **Chris Boden** *and* **Lee Williams** *also tasted first-team action in 1993-94, but not with Villa.*
Full-back Boden played 4 games on loan with First Division Barnsley in October and November. Midfielder Williams went to Peterborough on loan in February and the move was later made permanent.

GORDON COWANS

Born Durham, 27th October 1958.
Joined Villa July 1974 as an apprentice, and Sept 1976 as a pro.
Villa debut v Man City, Lge (a), 7/2/76.

Jumped at the chance to return for his third spell at Villa Park in June 1993 on a free transfer from Blackburn and add his experience to Villa's European challenge. Moved to Derby for £75,000 in February and helped the Rams to a Wembley play-off final, which they lost to Leicester.

Career Record:

Season	Club	League Apps	Gls	Cups Apps	Gls
75-76	Aston Villa	- (1)	-	-	-
76-77	Aston Villa	15 (3)	3	6 (2)	-
77-78	Aston Villa	30 (5)	7	5 (3)	-
78-79	Aston Villa	34	4	2 (1)	-
79-80	Aston Villa	42	6	10	1
80-81	Aston Villa	42	5	4	-
81-82	Aston Villa	42	6	19	5
82-83	Aston Villa	42	10	15	3
83-84	Aston Villa		-	-	-
84-85	Aston Villa	29 (1)	1	4	1
85-88	With Bari (Italy)				
88-89	Aston Villa	32 (1)	2	9	-
89-90	Aston Villa	34	4	13	-
90-91	Aston Villa	38	1	11	-
91-92	Aston Villa	10 (2)	-	2 (1)	-
	Blackburn	29	2	2	1
92-93	Blackburn	23 (1)	1	7	-
93-94	Aston Villa	9 (2)	-	6	-
	Derby County	22	1	-	-
Villa record		399 (15)	49	106 (7)	10
TOTAL		421 (15)	50	106 (7)	10

★ *Full England international (8 caps). Also capped at 'B' and Under-21 levels.*

NEIL COX

Born Scunthorpe, 8th October 1971. *Joined Villa* February 1991 from Scunthorpe United, £400,000. *Villa debut* v Nott'm F., Zenith Cup (h), 19/11/91.

An invaluable all-rounder and squad man who would have enjoyed far more first-team appearances in a less powerful squad of players. Played usually in the right-back role although he can play midfield and in central defence. Neil came on as a sub in the Coca-Cola Cup Final at Wembley, a well-earned reward for the part he played throughout the season. He made his European debut and added to his collection of England Under-21 caps against Poland in September. He also scored a couple of goals, against Sheffield Wednesday and Manchester United. Frustration at being unable to gain a regular place led to his departure on June 15th, when he joined Middlesbrough in a reported £1m deal.

Career Record:

Season	Club	League Apps	Gls	Cups Apps	Gls
89-90	Scunthorpe	-	-	- (1)	-
90-91	Scunthorpe	17	1	8	-
	Aston Villa	-	-	-	-
91-92	Aston Villa	4 (3)	-	1	-
92-93	Aston Villa	6 (9)	1	3 (2)	1
93-94	Aston Villa	16 (4)	2	7 (2)	-
Villa record		*26 (16)*	*3*	*11 (4)*	*1*
TOTAL		43 (16)	4	19 (5)	1

★ *England Under-21 international.*

★ *Took over in goal when Nigel Spink was sent off 12 minutes from time at Southampton and conceded the fourth goal to Neil Maddison.*

TONY DALEY

Born Birmingham, 18th October 1967. *Joined Villa* May 1983 as an apprentice. May 1985 on professionals forms. v Southampton, Lge (a), 20/4/85.

A mixed season for the likeable Brummie who shone against Manchester United at Wembley and scored the winning goal at Coventry in March. But injury held him back early on before several good performances suggested he was on his way back to his old England form. The possibility of a move to Udinese in Italy fell through when he was looking for a change of clubs in the autumn but he eventually ended his eleven year Villa Park career with a move to Wolves for £1.25m on May 31st.

Career Record:

Season	Club	League Apps	Gls	Cups Apps	Gls
84-85	Aston Villa	4 (1)	-	-	-
85-86	Aston Villa	16 (7)	2	2 (1)	-
86-87	Aston Villa	25 (8)	3	6 (1)	2
87-88	Aston Villa	10 (4)	3	1	-
88-89	Aston Villa	25 (4)	5	8 (1)	1
89-90	Aston Villa	31 (1)	6	11 (1)	2
90-91	Aston Villa	22 (1)	2	8	2
91-92	Aston Villa	29 (5)	7	7	-
92-93	Aston Villa	8 (4)	2	-	-
93-94	Aston Villa	19 (8)	1	9 (1)	-
TOTAL		189 (43)	31	52 (5)	7

★ *Full England international (7 caps), he is the only player to have appeared in the European Championship Finals (Sweden 92) whilst with Villa. Also capped at 'B' and youth levels.*

UGO EHIOGU

Born Hackney, London, 3rd November 1972. *Joined Villa* July 1991 from West Bromwich Albion, £40,000. *Villa debut* v Arsenal, Lge (h), 24/8/91.

Came in ably as central defensive replacement when either Shaun Teale or Paul McGrath were out having already shown his ability as a full back. Ron Atkinson has very high hopes of the quiet, tall and talented young player who looks well groomed to take over when McGrath eventually calls it a day. One of the unlucky ones who missed out on a Coca-Cola Cup final place, particularly as he appeared in the starting line-up in every game afterwards. Captained the England Under-21 side again and scored against Poland at Millwall in September.

Career Record:

Season	Club	League		Cups	
		Apps	Gls	Apps	Gls
90-91	W.B.A.	- (2)	-	-	-
91-92	Aston Villa	4 (4)	-	1 (1)	-
92-93	Aston Villa	1 (3)	-	1	-
93-94	Aston Villa	14 (3)	-	- (2)	-
Villa record		*19 (10)*	*-*	*2 (3)*	*-*
TOTAL		19 (12)	-	2 (3)	-

★ *England Under-21 international.*

★ *Hit the bar with his penalty in the Coca Cola Cup semi-final shoot-out with Tranmere.*

★ *Was on the bench for both of Villa's home UEFA Cup ties.*

★ *Played in 19 Central League games in 93/94.*

DAVE FARRELL

Born Birmingham, 11th November 1971 *Joined Villa* January 1992 from Redditch United, £45,000. *Villa debut* As sub v Oldham, Lge (a), 24/10/92.

A local-born find who has obvious talents on the wing but needs time and matches to establish himself. He played especially well when Villa picked up an invaluable victory over Sheffield United at Bramall Lane and retained his place for the games against Arsenal and Newcastle. Was a member of the Villa party on the end of season tour to South Africa and was due to get married during the close season.

Career Record:

Season	Club	League		Cups	
		Apps	Gls	Apps	Gls
91-92	Aston Villa	-	-	-	-
92-93	Aston Villa	1 (1)	-	-	-
(loan)	Scunthorpe	4 (1)	1	1	-
93-94	Aston Villa	4	-	-	-
Villa record		*5 (1)*	*-*	*-*	*-*
TOTAL		9 (2)	1	1	-

★ *Appeared in 8 of the 10 first-team friendlies and scored at Kidderminster in May.*

★ *Made 29(1) Central League appearances this season, more than any other player, and scored 4 goals.*

MID-SEASON SIGNING:

● ***Scott Murray*** - *Scottish winger who joined Villa from Highland League side Fraserburgh for a £35,000 fee in March 1994. Scored 6 goals in 13 reserve appearances and marked his first-team debut with a goal at Kidderminster in May.*

GRAHAM FENTON

Born Wallsend,
22nd May 1974
Joined Villa July 1990 as
a trainee. February 1992
on professional forms.
Villa debut v Manchester
City, Lge (h), 22/2/94.

The powerful-looking Geordie earned himself a quick recall from The Hawthorns after an impressive loan spell there. He was given the chance to end the scoring problems when injury struck at the end of February and went on as sub in the semi-final second leg against Tranmere. By settling instantly into the first-team pace he then became the surprise selection of the season when he played against Manchester United at Wembley and distinguished himself with honour.

Career Record:

Season	Club	League Apps	Gls	Cups Apps	Gls
92-93	Aston Villa	-	-	-	-
93-94	Aston Villa	9 (3)	1	1 (1)	-
(loan)	W.B.Albion	7	3	-	-
Villa record		*9 (3)*	*1*	*1 (1)*	-
TOTAL		16 (3)	4	1 (1)	-

★ *Scored on loan for West Bromwich Albion against Grimsby, Sunderland and Leicester.*

★ *Scored his first Villa goal in the 2-1 win at Sheffield United in April.*

★ *Won the club's 'Young Player of the Year' award and was runner-up to Julian Joachim for the Midland Soccer Writers' 'Young Player' prize.*

★ *Received an end-of-season call-up to England's Under-21 party for the Toulon Tournament but was forced to withdraw with a groin injury.*

STEVE FROGGATT

Born Lincoln,
9th March 1973
Joined Villa July 1989 as
a trainee. January 1991
on professionals forms.
Villa debut As last minute
substitute v West Ham,
Lge (h), 26/12/91.

Young player whose progress was delayed by injury. It was discovered that he required a built up boot to correct his alignment and now he is all set to continue the form which took him to England Under-21 level. Ron Atkinson was on record once as saying Villa's best performances were when he was in the side supplying width and crossing ability. Made a surprise return to first-team action at left-back against Swindon in February and scored with a lunging header.

Career Record:

Season	Club	League Apps	Gls	Cups Apps	Gls
90-91	Aston Villa	-	-	-	-
91-92	Aston Villa	6 (3)	-	2 (1)	1
92-93	Aston Villa	16 (1)	1	3 (1)	-
93-94	Aston Villa	8 (1)	1	1 (1)	-
TOTAL		30 (5)	2	6 (3)	1

★ *England Under-21 international.*

★ *Was named in the England Under-21 squad for the game with Denmark in March when already injured and was immediately withdrawn.*

★ *Two of his three Villa goals have been against Swindon.*

RAY HOUGHTON

Born Glasgow,
9th January 1962
Joined Villa July 1992
from Liverpool,
£900,000.
Villa debut v Ipswich,
Lge (a), 15/8/92.

By his high standards he spent more time on the bench than he would have liked but set an outstanding example in clubmanship, even when losing his place to Graham Fenton at Wembley. Gave many first-class performances and scored some crucial goals. One of four Villa men in Ireland's World Cup squad.

Career Record:

Season	Club	League Apps	Gls	Cups Apps	Gls
79-80	West Ham	-	-	-	-
80-81	West Ham	-	-	-	-
81-82	West Ham	- (1)	-	-	-
82-83	Fulham	42	5	7	2
83-84	Fulham	40	3	5	-
84-85	Fulham	42	8	4	3
85-86	Fulham	5	-	-	-
	Oxford Utd.	35	4	14	3
86-87	Oxford Utd.	37	5	6	1
87-88	Oxford Utd.	11	1	2	-
	Liverpool	26 (2)	5	7	2
88-89	Liverpool	38	7	14	1
89-90	Liverpool	16 (3)	1	4 (1)	-
90-91	Liverpool	31 (1)	7	7	3
91-92	Liverpool	36	8	15	4
92-93	Aston Villa	39	3	9	1
93-94	Aston Villa	25 (5)	2	8 (3)	3
Villa record		64 *(5)*	5	17 *(3)*	4
TOTAL		423 (12)	59	102 (4)	23

★ *Republic of Ireland full international (57 caps, 3 goals - up to 5/6/94)*

DARIUSZ KUBICKI

Born Warsaw, Poland,
6th June 1963.
Joined Villa August 1991
from Legia Warsaw,
£200,000.
Villa debut
v Southampton, Lge (a),
31/8/91.

A model professional who always gave his best for the reserves despite being third in line behind Earl Barrett and Neil Cox for the right-back position in the first team. Appeared as a sub at Swindon but started just one Premiership game - the home defeat by Southampton in November. Finished the season with an impressive loan spell at Sunderland.

Career Record:

Season	Club	League Apps	Gls	Cups Apps	Gls
91-92	Aston Villa	23	-	7 (1)	-
92-93	Aston Villa	-	-	1	-
93-94	Aston Villa	1 (1)	-	-	-
(loan)	Sunderland	15	-	-	-
Villa record		24 *(1)*	-	8 *(1)*	-
TOTAL		39 (1)	-	8 (1)	-

★ *Full Poland international (46 caps, 1 goal).*

★ *Made 238 appearances (7 goals) for Stal Mielec and Legia Warsaw in the Polish First Division before joining Villa*

★ *Played 19 Central League games in 1993/94.*

OBITUARIES:

● **Tony Barton** - *Villa's European Cup-winning manager died on Friday 20th August 1993 after suffering for a considerable time with heart trouble. A minute's silence was held in his memory before the Villa v Manchester United game.*
● **Danny Blanchflower** - *The former Villa skipper died on Thursday 9th December 1993.*

PAUL McGRATH

Born Ealing, London,
4th December 1959.
Joined Villa August 1989
from Man. United,
£400,000.
Villa debut v Nott'm F.,
Lge (a), 19/8/89.

The Irish international supplemented his reputation as one of Europe's most talented central defenders with yet more magnificent displays despite his well-publicised knee problems. Suggestions that his Villa days were numbered proved premature as he signed a substantial new one-year contract in May, shortly before departing for the World Cup finals.

Career Record:

Season	Club	League Apps	Gls	Cups Apps	Gls
81-82	Man. United	-	-	-	-
82-83	Man. United	14	3	1 (1)	-
83-84	Man. United	9	1	3	-
84-85	Man. United	23	-	7	2
85-86	Man. United	40	3	8	1
86-87	Man. United	34 (1)	2	4 (1)	-
87-88	Man. United	21 (1)	2	2	1
88-89	Man. United	18 (2)	1	5 (1)	-
89-90	Aston Villa	35	1	12	-
90-91	Aston Villa	35	-	9	-
91-92	Aston Villa	41	1	7	-
92-93	Aston Villa	42	4	8	1
93-94	Aston Villa	30	-	14	-
Villa record		*183*	*6*	*50*	*1*
TOTAL		342 (4)	18	80 (3)	5

★ *Republic of Ireland full international (65 caps, 7 goals - up to and including 5/6/94)*

★ *Won the Villa 'Player of the Year' award in 1990, '91, '92 and '93*

MICHAEL OAKES

Born Northwich,
30th October 1973
Joined Villa July 1991 as
a non-contract player,
February 1992 on
professional forms
Villa debut Yet to play

Was substitute goalkeeper on 10 occasions but his only appearances in the first team were as a sub in friendlies at Walsall, Albion and Kidderminster. Gained valuable experience as a member of the squad for the European ties and finally made his league debut against Torquay whilst on loan at Scarborough. Also had a non-playing loan spell at Tranmere towards the end of the season. He won his first England Under-21 cap as a substitute against Denmark in March and claimed an 'assist' by setting up the winning goal. Travelled to the end-of-season Toulon Under-21 tournament as standby 'keeper but came on as sub against France and kept the number one spot for the final three games as England retained the title.

Career Record:

Season	Club	League Apps	Gls	Cups Apps	Gls
91-92	Aston Villa	-	-	-	-
92-93	Aston Villa	-	-	-	-
93-94	Aston Villa	-	-	-	-
(loan)	Scarborough	2	-	-	-
(loan)	Tranmere	-	-	-	-
TOTAL		2	-	-	-

★ *England Under-21 international*

★ *Appeared for Gloucester City and Bromsgrove Rovers on loan in 1992-93*

★ *Father Alan played a club record 669 games for Manchester City*

GARRY PARKER

Born Oxford,
7th September 1965.
Joined Villa November
1991 from Nottingham
Forest, £650,000.
Villa debut v Oldham,
Lge (a), 30/11/91.

One who suffered from the large number of midfield players available by making only a limited number of appearances. He had a couple of spells in the team, was sometimes on the bench and also played a valuable part on occasions in the second team. Among his first-team highlights was the goal which earned a 1-1 league draw at Spurs.

Career Record:

Season	Club	League Apps	Gls	Cups Apps	Gls
82-83	Luton Town	1	-	-	-
83-84	Luton Town	13	2	1	-
84-85	Luton Town	13 (7)	1	4 (4)	1
85-86	Luton Town	4 (4)	-	1 (1)	-
	Hull City	12	-	-	-
86-87	Hull City	37 (1)	-	5	1
87-88	Hull City	33 (1)	8	6	-
	Nott'm. For.	1 (1)	-	-	-
88-89	Nott'm. For.	22	7	14 (1)	6
89-90	Nott'm. For.	36 (1)	6	13	1
90-91	Nott'm. For.	35 (1)	3	15	5
91-92	Nott'm. For.	5 (1)	1	4	-
	Aston Villa	25	1	5	1
92-93	Aston Villa	37	9	9	-
93-94	Aston Villa	17 (2)	2	4	-
Villa record		*79 (2)*	*12*	*18*	*1*
TOTAL		291 (19)	40	81 (6)	15

★ *Capped at England Under-21, Under-19 and youth levels.*

KEVIN RICHARDSON

Born Newcastle-upon-
Tyne, 4th December 1962.
Joined Villa August 1991
from Real Sociedad,
£450,000.
Villa debut v Sheff Wed,
Lge (a), 17/8/91.

The club captain enjoyed a fabulous season highlighted by being named as the Wembley 'Man of the Match' and subsequently being selected for his first England cap in the 5-0 win against Greece in May. Although his 100% appearance record since being signed in 1991 ended in injury in December he missed only two games before returning to his quiet, mature style of leadership.

Career Record:

Season	Club	League Apps	Gls	Cups Apps	Gls
80-81	Everton	-	-	-	-
81-82	Everton	15 (3)	2	1	-
82-83	Everton	24 (5)	3	3 (2)	-
83-84	Everton	25 (3)	4	11 (1)	3
84-85	Everton	14 (1)	4	3 (1)	-
85-86	Everton	16 (2)	3	7	1
86-87	Everton	1	-	1	-
	Watford	39	2	11	-
87-88	Arsenal	24 (5)	4	10 (1)	2
88-89	Arsenal	32 (2)	1	5 (1)	-
89-90	Arsenal	32 (1)	-	7	-
90-91	Real Sociedad	37	-		
91-92	Aston Villa	42	6	9	-
92-93	Aston Villa	42	2	9	1
93-94	Aston Villa	40	5	15	2
Villa record		*124*	*13*	*33*	*3*
TOTAL		383 (22)	36	92 (6)	9

★ *Full England international (1 cap).*

Born Swansea,
21st June 1964.
Joined Villa September
1992 from Liverpool,
£2.3m.
Villa debut v Leeds, Lge
(a), 13/9/92.

The club's leading scorer, including his two in the Coca-Cola Cup Final. Saunders was as mobile and enthusiastic as ever in pursuit of chances and half-chances but the biggest problem for him, and the other strikers, was the difficulty in getting decisive goals in the Premiership games at Villa Park.

Career Record:

Season	Club	League Apps	Gls	Cups Apps	Gls
82-83	Swansea C.	-	-	-	-
83-84	Swansea C.	14 (5)	3	- (1)	-
84-85	Swansea C.	28 (2)	9	4 (1)	-
(loan)	Cardiff City	3 (1)	-	-	-
85-86	Brighton	39 (3)	14	9	5
86-87	Brighton	27 (3)	6	5	-
	Oxford Utd.	12	6	-	-
87-88	Oxford Utd.	35 (2)	12	11 (1)	9
88-89	Oxford Utd.	10	4	2	2
	Derby Co.	30	14	6	1
89-90	Derby Co.	38	11	11	10
90-91	Derby Co.	38	17	8	4
91-92	Liverpool	36	10	18	11
92-93	Liverpool	6	1	1	1
	Aston Villa	35	12	9	4
93-94	Aston Villa	37 (1)	10	14	6
Villa record		72 (1)	22	23	10
TOTAL		388 (17)	129	98 (3)	53

★ *Full international for Wales (44 caps, 14 goals - up to and including 5/6/94).*

Born Birmingham,
15th November 1971.
Joined Villa June 1988
from FA School of
Excellence as a trainee.
July 1990 professional.
Villa debut v Everton,
Lge (a), 19/10/91.

Made his European debut in the 1-1 draw with Deportivo La Coruña in Spain. A valuable squad member whose full appearances spread into double figures but whose chances are somewhat limited because of the settled, solid look of the regular defenders. Played along-side Ugo Ehiogu and Neil Cox in the back four for England's Under 21's against Poland in September.

Career Record:

Season	Club	League Apps	Gls	Cups Apps	Gls
89-90	Aston Villa	-	-	-	-
90-91	Aston Villa	-	-	-	-
91-92	Aston Villa	8	-	4 (1)	-
92-93	Aston Villa	10 (4)	-	1	-
93-94	Aston Villa	8 (1)	-	3	-
TOTAL		26 (5)	-	8 (1)	-

★ *An England Under-21 international, he helped his country to success in the Toulon Tournament last year.*

★ *Also made 23 appearances for the reserves in 1993/94.*

GOALS NOTE

● *Dean Saunders had a goal wiped from his 1992/93 record when a Premier League committee changed his strike against Sheffield United at Villa Park to an 'own goal'. At the time of going to press Deano's goal at Southampton in April 1994 was also under scrutiny by the committee and may yet be changed to an 'og'.*

NIGEL SPINK

Born Chelmsford,
8th August 1958
Joined Villa January 1977
from Chelmsford City
Villa debut v Nott'm
Forest, League (a),
26/12/79.

The popular, dependable veteran revealed great dignity as the inevitable time came for a younger successor to move in. After he had been the 'keeper in possession for the opening ten games injury enabled Mark Bosnich to take his place during the Coca-Cola Cup tie at St. Andrew's and Spink made only half a dozen more appearances.

Career Record:

Season	Club	League		Cups	
		Apps	Gls Ag	Apps	Gls Ag
79-80	Aston Villa	1	2	-	-
80-81	Aston Villa	-	-	-	-
81-82	Aston Villa	-	-	-(1)	0
82-83	Aston Villa	22	23	8	9
83-84	Aston Villa	28	43	13	16
84-85	Aston Villa	19	22	1	3
85-86	Aston Villa	31	53	11	15
86-87	Aston Villa	32	55	7	9
87-88	Aston Villa	44	41	7	11
88-89	Aston Villa	34	52	8	10
89-90	Aston Villa	38	38	13	14
90-91	Aston Villa	34	54	11	13
91-92	Aston Villa	23	21	3	2
92-93	Aston Villa	25	29	8	7
93-94	Aston Villa	14(1)	21	3	1
TOTAL		345(1)	454	93(1)	110

★ *Full England international (1 cap). Also capped at England 'B' level. Member of Villa's European Cup and European Super Cup winning teams.*

STEVE STAUNTON

Born Drogheda, Ireland,
19th January 1969.
Joined Villa August 1991
from Liverpool, £1.1m.
Villa debut v Sheff. Wed.
League (a), 17/8/91.
Scored the winner.

A difficult season for the influential Irish Republic international as a groin injury kept him out for two lengthy spells. Fortunately he recovered just in time to play at Wembley, though a little short of match practice. Staunton, who was a member of Jack Charlton's World Cup squad, signed a new Villa Park contract before leaving for America thus silencing rumours of a return to Liverpool.

Career Record:

Season	Club	League		Cups	
		Apps	Gls	Apps	Gls
86-87	Liverpool	-	-	-	-
87-88	Liverpool	-	-	-	-
(loan)	Bradford City	7(1)	-	3	-
88-89	Liverpool	17(4)	-	8	1
89-90	Liverpool	18(2)	-	4(2)	3
90-91	Liverpool	20(4)	-	9	2
91-92	Aston Villa	37	4	6	-
92-93	Aston Villa	42	2	9	-
93-94	Aston Villa	24	3	9	-
Villa record		103	9	24	-
TOTAL		165(11)	9	48(2)	6

★ *Full Republic of Ireland international (47 caps, 5 goals - up to and including 5/6/94). Scored important goals against Albania and Lithuania last summer which helped Ireland on the road to World Cup qualification.*

● NOTE: *Career records of goalkeepers Nigel Spink (left) and Mark Bosnich (p131) list number of goals conceded in the goals columns.*

SHAUN TEALE

Born Southport,
10th March 1964.
Joined Villa July 1991
from Bournemouth,
£300,000.
Villa debut v Sheff Wed,
Lge (a), 17/8/91.

Once again he was a tenacious central defensive partner for Paul McGrath and was one of Villa's star performers at Wembley having scored one of the goals in the dramatic semi-final comeback against Tranmere. When he was subsequently named in Terry Venables' England training squad in April it completed a remarkable five-year rise from non-League football. Missed three games through suspension, including vital cup games at Tranmere and Bolton, after being sent off for the first time in his career, at Grimsby in the FA Cup.

Career Record:

Season	Club	League		Cups	
		Apps	Gls	Apps	Gls
88-89	Bournemouth	19 (1)	-	-	-
89-90	Bournemouth	34	-	6	-
90-91	Bournemouth	46	4	10	1
91-92	Aston Villa	42	-	9	1
92-93	Aston Villa	39	1	8	1
93-94	Aston Villa	37 (1)	1	13	1
Villa record		*118 (1)*	*2*	*30*	*3*
TOTAL		217 (2)	6	46	4

★ *Joined Everton as an apprentice in January 1980 but was released and spent eight months with Huddersfield Town. Then came spells with non-league clubs Burscough, Ellesmere Port, Southport, Northwich Victoria and Weymouth before joining Bournemouth for £50,000 in January 1989.*

ANDY TOWNSEND

Born Maidstone,
27th July 1963.
Joined Villa July 1993
from Chelsea, £2.1m.
Villa debut v Queen's
Park Rangers, Lge (h),
14/8/93.

The close season signing arrived from Chelsea stressing how much he wanted to win his first major honours in football, having been an unsuccessful semi-finalist on five occasions with three different clubs. The Republic or Ireland World Cup skipper was held back by injury for much of his early spell at the club but was a powerful and outstanding midfield driving force as he realised his ambition in the Coca Cola Cup Final.

Career Record:

Season	Club	League		Cups	
		Apps	Gls	Apps	Gls
84-85	Southampton	5	-	-	-
85-86	Southampton	25 (2)	1	5 (5)	-
86-87	Southampton	11 (3)	1	2 (1)	-
87-88	Southampton	36 (1)	3	5	-
88-89	Norwich	31 (5)	5	7 (1)	2
89-90	Norwich	35	3	9	-
90-91	Chelsea	34	2	11	3
91-92	Chelsea	35	6	10	1
92-93	Chelsea	41	4	7	3
93-94	Aston Villa	32	3	15	1
TOTAL		285 (11)	28	71 (7)	10

★ *Republic of Ireland international (44 caps, 5 goals - up to and including 5/6/94).*

★ *Played non-League football for Welling United and Weymouth before joining Southampton for £35,000 in January 1985. Made his Football League debut for Southampton against Villa in April 1985, the same game in which Tony Daley made his Villa debut.*

GUY WHITTINGHAM

Born Evesham,
10th June 1964.
Joined Villa August 1993
from Portsmouth,
£1.1m.
Villa debut As sub v Man.
Utd, Lge (h), 23/8/93.

Found it hard to make his impact on the top division with slightly limited opportunity after his million-pound signing from Pompey, which involved Mark Blake moving to Fratton Park. It was when he went on loan to Wolves in the latter part of the season that the ex-soldier began to find his former Fratton Park goal touch. Scored in his first two games for Villa, friendlies at Walsall and Wigan, and netted in his first full Premiership game at Everton.

Career Record:

Season	Club	League Apps	Gls	Cups Apps	Gls
89-90	Portsmouth	39 (3)	23	4	1
90-91	Portsmouth	34 (3)	12	5 (1)	8
91-92	Portsmouth	30 (5)	11	4 (4)	2
92-93	Portsmouth	46	42	10	5
93-94	Aston Villa	13 (5)	3	3	-
(loan)	Wolves	13	8	1	-
TOTAL		175 (16)	99	27 (5)	16

★ *His next league goal will be his 100th.*

★ *His 47 goals for Portsmouth in 1992-93 broke Pompey's 66-year-old club record by four and put him way ahead of any other player in the country that season.*

★ *Scored 4 goals in 7 first-team friendlies and 6 in 9 reserve team outings in 1993-94.*

DWIGHT YORKE

Born Canaan, Tobago,
3rd November 1971.
Joined Villa December
1989 from Signal Hill in
Tobago, £120,000.
Villa debut v C.Palace,
Lge (a), 24/3/90.

A frustrating season for the cheerful West Indian but happily marked with a spectacular ending. Injury kept him out of the side until around Christmas and even after that he was largely employed as a substitute. This meant that he missed out on Europe and the Wembley Final but he had scored the winning goal as sub in the fourth round FA Cup-tie at Grimsby. Yorke's big moments came in the second half of the final match when he went on as sub to get the two goals which beat Liverpool.

Career Record:

Season	Club	League Apps	Gls	Cups Apps	Gls
89-90	Aston Villa	- (2)	-	-	-
90-91	Aston Villa	8 (10)	2	3	-
91-92	Aston Villa	27 (5)	11	8	6
92-93	Aston Villa	22 (5)	6	6 (2)	1
93-94	Aston Villa	2 (10)	2	- (2)	1
TOTAL		59 (32)	21	17 (4)	8

★ *Full international with Trinidad & Tobago.*

★ *Scored the last two goals in front of the Holte End terrace before it's demolition in May.*

● *All international records are up to and including 5th June 1994.*

FIRST TEAM APPEARANCES & GOALSCORERS

	LEAGUE		FA CUP		LGE CUP		UEFA CUP		TOTAL	
	Apps	Gls	Apps	Gls	Apps	Gls	Apps	Gls	Apps	Gls
Dalian ATKINSON	29	8	3	-	8	6	4	1	44	15
Earl BARRETT	39	-	3	-	7	1	3	-	52	1
Stefan BEINLICH	6 (1)	1	-	-	-	-	-	-	6 (1)	1
Mark BOSNICH	28	-	3	-	7 (1)	-	2	-	40 (1)	-
Matthias BREITKREUTZ	1 (1)	-	-	-	-	-	-	-	1 (1)	-
Gordon COWANS	9 (2)	-	-	-	2	-	4	-	15 (2)	-
Neil COX	16 (4)	2	2 (1)	-	4 (1)	-	1	-	23 (6)	2
Tony DALEY	19 (8)	1	2	-	5 (1)	-	2	-	28 (9)	1
Ugo EHIOGU	14 (3)	-	- (1)	-	- (1)	-	-	-	14 (5)	-
Dave FARRELL	4	-	-	-	-	-	-	-	4	-
Graham FENTON	9 (3)	1	-	-	1 (1)	-	-	-	10 (4)	1
Steve FROGGATT	8 (1)	1	1	-	- (1)	-	-	-	9 (2)	1
Ray HOUGHTON	25 (5)	2	3	1	4 (2)	2	1 (1)	-	33 (8)	5
Dariusz KUBICKI	1 (1)	-	-	-	-	-	-	-	1 (1)	-
Paul McGRATH	30	-	2	-	8	-	4	-	44	-
Garry PARKER	17 (2)	2	1	-	3	-	-	-	21 (2)	2
Kevin RICHARDSON	40	5	3	-	8	2	4	-	55	7
Dean SAUNDERS	37 (1)	10	3	1	7	4	4	1	51 (1)	16
Bryan SMALL	8 (1)	-	-	-	1	-	2	-	11 (1)	-
Nigel SPINK	14 (1)	-	-	-	1	-	2	-	17 (1)	-
Steve STAUNTON	24	3	2	-	5	-	2	-	33	3
Shaun TEALE	37 (1)	1	2	-	7	1	4	-	50 (1)	2
Andy TOWNSEND	32	3	3	-	8	-	4	1	47	4
Guy WHITTINGHAM	13 (5)	3	-	-	2	-	1	-	16 (5)	3
Dwight YORKE	2 (10)	2	- (2)	1	-	-	-	-	2 (12)	3
Own Goal	-	1	-	-	-	-	-	-	-	1

Unused Substitutes:
Nigel Spink 37, Neil Cox 14, Guy Whittingham 13, Ugo Ehiogu 10, Michael Oakes 10,
Mark Bosnich 8, Garry Parker 6, Ray Houghton 4, Tony Daley 3, Bryan Small 3,
Dwight Yorke 3, Stefan Beinlich 2, Gordon Cowans 1, Dave Farrell 1, Dean Saunders 1.

Goalscorers in friendly games:
Dalian Atkinson 4, Guy Whittingham 4, Tony Daley 2, Neil Cox 1, Ugo Ehiogu 1,
Dave Farrell 1, Steve Froggatt 1, Paul McGrath 1, Scott Murray 1, Dean Saunders 1,
Andy Townsend 1, Own Goal 1.

FA CARLING PREMIERSHIP STATISTICS 1993-94

FINAL TABLE

		Pl	Home					Away					Total					Pts
			W	D	L	F	A	W	D	L	F	A	W	D	L	F	A	
1	Manchester United	42	14	6	1	39	13	13	5	3	41	25	27	11	4	80	38	92
2	Blackburn Rovers	42	14	5	2	31	11	11	4	6	32	25	25	9	8	63	36	84
3	Newcastle United	42	14	4	3	51	14	9	4	8	31	27	23	8	11	82	41	77
4	Arsenal	42	10	8	3	25	15	8	9	4	28	13	18	17	7	53	28	71
5	Leeds United	42	13	6	2	37	18	5	10	6	28	21	18	16	8	65	39	70
6	Wimbledon	42	12	5	4	35	21	6	6	9	21	32	18	11	13	56	53	65
7	Sheffield Wednesday	42	10	7	4	48	24	6	9	6	28	30	16	16	10	76	54	64
8	Liverpool	42	12	4	5	33	23	5	5	11	26	32	17	9	16	59	55	60
9	Queen's Park Rangers	42	8	7	6	32	29	8	5	8	30	32	16	12	14	62	61	60
10	Aston Villa	42	8	5	8	23	18	7	7	7	23	32	15	12	15	46	50	57
11	Coventry City	42	9	7	5	23	17	5	7	9	20	28	14	14	14	43	45	56
12	Norwich City	42	4	9	8	26	29	8	8	5	39	32	12	17	13	65	61	53
13	West Ham United	42	6	7	8	26	31	7	6	8	21	27	13	13	16	47	58	52
14	Chelsea	42	11	5	5	31	20	2	7	12	18	33	13	12	17	49	53	51
15	Tottenham Hotspur	42	4	8	9	29	33	7	4	10	25	26	11	12	19	54	59	45
16	Manchester City	42	6	10	5	24	22	3	8	10	14	27	9	18	15	38	49	45
17	Everton	42	8	4	9	26	30	4	4	13	16	33	12	8	22	42	63	44
18	Southampton	42	9	2	10	30	31	3	5	13	19	35	12	7	23	49	66	43
19	Ipswich Town	42	5	8	8	21	32	4	8	9	14	26	9	16	17	35	58	43
20	Sheffield United	42	6	10	5	24	23	2	8	11	18	37	8	18	16	42	60	42
21	Oldham Athletic	42	5	8	8	24	33	4	5	12	18	35	9	13	20	42	68	40
22	Swindon Town	42	4	7	10	25	45	1	8	12	22	55	5	15	22	47	100	30

ROLL OF HONOUR

Champions: Manchester United
Runners-up: Blackburn Rovers
Relegated: Sheffield United, Oldham Athletic and Swindon Town
FA Cup winners: Manchester United
Coca-Cola Cup winners: Aston Villa

FACTS & FIGURES

Of the 462 games played, 192 resulted in home wins, 128 in away wins and 142 in draws. A total of 1,195 goals were scored, that's an average of 2.58 per game, 663 by the home clubs and 532 by the away clubs.

Most goals: 82, Newcastle United
Most home goals: 51, Newcastle United
Most away goals: 41, Manchester United
Least goals: 35, Ipswich Town
Least home goals: 21, Ipswich Town
Least away goals: 14, Ipswich Town and Manchester City

Least goals conceded: 28, Arsenal
Least home goals conceded: 11, Blackburn R.
Least away goals conceded: 13, Arsenal
Most goals conceded: 100, Swindon Town
Most home goals conceded: 45, Swindon Town
Most away goals conceded: 55, Swindon Town

Highest goals aggregate: 147, Swindon Town
Lowest goals aggregate: 81, Arsenal

Best home record: 48pts, Man United
Best away record: 44pts, Man United
Worst home record: 19pts, Swindon Town
Worst away record: 11pts, Swindon Town

Highest home score:
Newcastle Utd. 7 Swindon Town 1, 12.3.94

Highest away scores:
Swindon Town 0 Liverpool 5, 22.8.93
Swindon Town 0 Leeds United 5, 7.5.94
Everton 1 Norwich City 5, 25.9.93
Ipswich Town 1 Arsenal 5, 5.3.94
Oldham Ath. 2 Manchester Utd. 5, 29.12.93
Norwich City 4 Southampton 5, 9.4.94

GOALSCORERS & ATTENDANCES

LEADING SCORERS

(Including Cup & European games)

41 Andy Cole (Newcastle United)
34 Alan Shearer (Blackburn Rovers)
34 Ian Wright (Arsenal)
28 Chris Sutton (Norwich City)
27 *Mark Stein (Chelsea)
25 Eric Cantona (Manchester United)
25 *Sean McCarthy (Oldham Athletic)
25 Matthew Le Tissier (Southampton)
24 Peter Beardsley (Newcastle United)
24 Dean Holdsworth (Wimbledon)
23 Mark Bright (Sheffield Wednesday)
22 *Nathan Blake (Sheffield United)
21 Mark Hughes (Manchester United)
19 Kevin Campbell (Arsenal)
19 Tony Cottee (Everton)
19 Ian Rush (Liverpool)
18 Les Ferdinand (Queens Park Rangers)
18 Robbie Fowler (Liverpool)
18 *Keith Scott (Swindon Town)
17 Ryan Giggs (Manchester United)
17 Rod Wallace (Leeds United)
16 Dean Saunders (Aston Villa)
16 Trevor Morley (West Ham United)
15 Dalian Atkinson (Aston Villa)
15 Ian Marshall (Ipswich Town)
15 Teddy Sheringham (Tottenham Hotspur)
15 *Paul Walsh (Manchester City)
Includes goals for other clubs

Most Goals in a Match:
4 Efan Ekoku (Norwich) v Everton 25.9.93
3 Mick Quinn (Coventry) v Arsenal 14.8.93
3 Tony Cottee (Everton) v Sheff U. 21.8.93
3 Kevin Campbell (Arsenal) v Ipswich 11.9.93
3 Alan Shearer (Blackburn) v Leeds 23.10.93
3 Peter Beardsley (Newcastle) v W'don 30.10.93
3 Robbie Fowler (Liverpool) v Soton 30.10.93
3 Bradley Allen (QPR) v Everton 20.11.93
3 Andy Cole (Newcastle) v Liverpool 21.11.93
3 Kevin Campbell (Arsenal) v Swindon 27.12.93
3 Tony Cottee (Everton) v Swindon 15.1.94
3 Jan Fjortoft (Swindon) v Coventry 5.2.94
3 Dean Saunders (A.Villa) v Swindon 12.2.94
3 Matthew Le Tissier (Soton) v L'pool 14.2.94
3 Andy Cole (Newcastle) v Coventry 23.2.94
3 Ian Wright (Arsenal) v Ipswich 5.3.94
3 Ian Wright (Arsenal) v Soton 19.3.94
3 Matthew Le Tissier (Soton) v N'wich 9.4.94
3 Dean Holdsworth (W'don) v Oldham 26.4.94

THE GATE LEAGUE

	Best	Average
Manchester United	44,751	44,243
Liverpool	44,601	38,503
Leeds United	41,125	34,506
Newcastle United	36,388	33,792
Arsenal	36,901	30,531
Aston Villa	45,347	28,962
Tottenham Hotspur	33,130	27,255
Sheffield Wednesday	34,959	27,082
Manchester City	35,155	26,709
Everton	38,157	22,901
West Ham United	28,832	20,588
Sheffield United	30,044	19,567
Chelsea	37,064	19,211
Norwich City	21,181	18,179
Blackburn Rovers	21,462	17,319
Ipswich Town	22,559	16,411
Swindon Town	18,102	15,010
Southampton	19,105	14,761
Queens Park Rangers	21,267	14,133
Coventry City	17,020	13,559
Oldham Athletic	16,708	12,564
Wimbledon	28,553	10,467

Highest Attendance:
45,347 Aston Villa v Liverpool, 7.5.94

Lowest Attendance:
4,739 Wimbledon v Coventry City, 26.12.93

PONTIN'S LEAGUE DIVISION ONE TABLE

	P	W	D	L	F	A	Pts
Manchester United	34	22	7	5	77	38	73
Aston Villa	34	18	9	7	61	29	63
Bolton Wanderers	34	15	10	9	88	65	55
Wolverhampton W.	34	15	9	10	45	38	54
Derby County	34	14	8	12	55	51	50
Nottingham Forest	34	14	8	12	55	51	50
Sunderland	34	12	13	9	47	53	49
Blackburn Rovers	34	14	7	13	40	47	49
Leeds United	34	13	8	13	42	48	47
Coventry City	34	13	7	14	42	41	46
Sheffield United	34	12	9	13	57	60	45
Notts County	34	12	8	14	43	50	44
Everton	34	12	7	15	54	50	43
Liverpool	34	10	11	13	42	51	41
Newcastle United	34	10	8	16	46	53	38
Sheffield Wed.	34	7	12	15	46	63	33
Leicester City	34	8	7	19	37	58	31
York City	34	6	10	18	36	67	28

VILLA FACTS & FIGURES 1993-94

HIGHEST AND LOWEST

Highest home attendance:
45,347 v Liverpool, 7.5.94
Lowest home attendance:
16,180 v Southampton, 24.11.93
Highest away attendance:
77,231 v Manchester U. (CCC Final), 27.3.94
Lowest away attendance:
7,533 v Wimbledon, 21.8.93

Biggest victory:
5-0 v Swindon Town (home), 12.2.94
Heaviest defeat:
1-5 v Newcastle United (away), 27.4.94

Most goals in a match:
3, Dean Saunders v Swindon (a), 12.2.94

Most goals against:
2, Lee Sharpe (Man Utd), 23.8.93
2, Matthew Le Tissier (Southampton), 24.11.93
2, Eric Cantona (Man Utd), 19.12.93
2, Ian Wright (Arsenal), 23.4.94
2, Peter Beardsley (Newcastle Utd.), 27.4.94
2, Matthew Le Tissier (Southampton) 30.4.94

Clean sheets: 18
Failed to score: 17

Villa scored first: 25
Scored first and won: 19
Scored first and drew: 4
Scored first and lost: 2

Opponents scored first: 25
Lost after opponents scored first: 16
Drew after opponents scored first: 3
Won after opponents scored first: 6

Highest League position: 1st
Lowest League position: 11th

● *This statistical review of 1993-94 covers all of the 57 League, FA Cup, League Cup and UEFA Cup games played.*

SEQUENCE RECORDS

Most matches undefeated:
8, Aug 28 - Sep 29
Most home matches undefeated:
5, Jan 15 - Feb 27
Most away matches undefeated:
12, Aug 18 - Nov 6
Most wins in succession:
3, Oct 23 - 30, Jan 8 - 15 & Jan 29 - Feb 12
Most home wins in succession:
3, Jan 15 - Feb 12
Most away wins in succession:
3, Oct 26 - Nov 6 & Dec 29 - Jan 12
Longest run without a win:
4, Dec 4 - 19 & Mar 30 - Apr 11
Longest run without a home win:
5, Mar 12 - Apr 4
Longest run without an away win:
3, Feb 16 - Mar 2
Most defeats in succession: 3
Goals for in successive matches:
8, Jan 8 - Feb 16
Goals against in successive matches:
6, Dec 4 - Jan 1 & Apr 11 - May 7
Longest run without scoring:
384 minutes, Mar 27 - Apr 16
Longest run without conceding a goal:
385 minutes, Aug 23 - Sep 18
Most consecutive appearances:
128 - Kevin Richardson, 17.8.91 - 4.12.93
42 - Earl Barrett, 19.10.93 - end of season
Ever-presents: None

DEBUTANTS

Three players made their Villa first team debuts in 1993/94 - Andy Townsend, Guy Whittingham and Graham Fenton.

RED CARDS

Shaun Teale (v Grimsby) and Nigel Spink (v Southampton) were both sent-off for the first time in their careers. Opposition players to receive their marching orders were Paul Tait (Bitmingham), Steve Livingstone (Grimsby) and Andrei Kanchelskis (Man United).

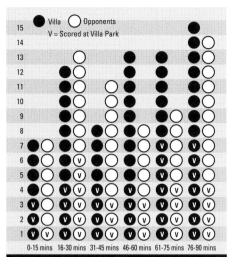

GOAL TIME GRAPH

GOAL TIMES

Villa have conceded just two goals at home in the first 15 minutes of a match in the last two seasons. Only Roy Keane, for Forest in 92-93, and Ipswich's Gavin Johnson, in 93-94, have given the opposition an early advantage.

QUICK OFF THE MARK

Dalian Atkinson scored Villa's fastest goal of the season, after just five minutes of the Coca-Cola Cup tie at Arsenal. Tranmere's Ian Nolan scored the earliest goal conceded by Villa, also after five minutes.

HOLTE v WITTON

Of the 50 goals scored at Villa Park 26 were netted at the Holte End (13 for Villa, 13 against) and 24 at the Witton End (16 for, 8 against).

PENALTIES

There were 17 penalties, 11 scored, 5 saved (all by Mark Bosnich) and 1 missed:

Game	Mins	Taker v Goalkeeper	Outcome
v Tottenham (h)	71	Steve Staunton v Erik Thorstvedt	Goal
v Birmingham (a)	36	John Frain v Mark Bosnich	Saved
v Newcastle (h)	46	Malcolm Allen v Nigel Spink	Goal
v Deportivo (a)	3	Bebeto v Mark Bosnich	Saved
v Swindon (a)	32	Paul Bodin v Nigel Spink	Goal
v Arsenal (a)	43	Ian Wright v Mark Bosnich	Saved
v Sheffield Wed. (h)	53	Dean Saunders v Kevin Pressman	Goal
v Exeter City (a)	59	Dean Saunders v Peter Fox	Goal
v Swindon Town (h)	66	Dean Saunders v Jon Sheffield	Goal
	84	Dean Saunders v Jon Sheffield	Goal
v Manchester C. (h)	82	Dean Saunders v Tony Coton	Missed
v Tranmere Rov. (h)	29	John Aldridge v Mark Bosnich	Goal
v Tottenham (a)	44	Darren Anderton v Mark Bosnich	Saved
	52	Nick Barmby v Mark Bosnich	Saved
v Man Utd (CCCF)	89	Dean Saunders v Les Sealey	Goal
v Arsenal (h)	30	Ian Wright v Nigel Spink	Goal
v Newcastle (h)	23	Peter Beardsley v Nigel Spink	Goal

There was also the penalty shoot-out with Tranmere (see page 88) when Mark Bosnich saved 3 out of 7 kicks and Villa scored 5 out of 7.

SCORELINES

1-0 wins - 10
2-1 wins - 9
3-1 wins - 3
4-1 wins - 2
5-0 wins - 1

0-0 draws - 7
1-1 draws - 4
2-2 draws - 3

0-1 defeats - 6
0-2 defeats - 3
0-3 defeats - 1
1-2 defeats - 4
1-3 defeats - 2
1-4 defeats - 1
1-5 defeats - 1

PONTIN'S CENTRAL LEAGUE

Aug	19	H	Leeds United	1-0	Fenton
Aug	26	A	Sheffield Wednesday	2-0	Whittingham 2
Sep	8	A	Sunderland	3-1	Daley 2, Crisp
Sep	16	H	Everton	2-1	Daley 2
Sep	23	H	Wolverhampton W.	0-1	
Sep	30	A	York City	4-2	Beinlich, Berry, Yorke 2
Oct	7	A	Newcastle United	1-0	Yorke
Oct	13	H	Manchester United	1-1	Farrell
Oct	21	A	Nottingham Forest	1-2	Whittingham
Oct	28	H	Liverpool	4-0	Davis, Beinlich, Fenton 2
Nov	1	A	Sheffield United	0-1	
Nov	10	H	Leicester City	3-1	Whittingham 2, Farrell
Nov	17	H	Notts County	4-0	Browne, Parker 2, Beinlich
Nov	23	A	Derby County	1-1	Fenton
Dec	2	H	Blackburn Rovers	1-0	Fenton
Dec	15	H	Sheffield Wednesday	3-0	Daley, Farrell, Berry
Jan	5	H	Coventry City	4-0	Fenton 2, Breitkreutz, Yorke
Jan	19	H	Newcastle United	3-0	Beinlich 2, Yorke
Feb	2	H	Nottingham Forest	2-0	Whittingham, Farrell
Feb	8	A	Everton	0-3	
Feb	17	H	Sunderland	1-1	Boden
Mar	3	H	Bolton Wanderers	3-1	Murray 3
Mar	9	A	Blackburn Rovers	1-2	Beinlich
Mar	17	A	Wolverhampton W.	1-3	Breitkreutz
Mar	23	H	York City	0-0	
Mar	29	A	Coventry City	1-1	Crisp
Apr	5	A	Leeds United	1-1	Murray
Apr	13	H	Sheffield United	6-0	Beinlich 3, Scimeca 2, Breitkreutz
Apr	20	A	Leicester City	2-0	Murray 2
Apr	23	A	Liverpool	1-1	Scimeca
Apr	25	A	Manchester United	1-1	Boden
Apr	28	H	Derby County	0-2	
May	3	A	Notts County	1-1	Browne
May	11	A	Bolton Wanderers	2-1	Cowe, Scimeca

BIRMINGHAM SENIOR CUP

Nov	15	A	Willenhall (Rnd 2)	2-2	Davis, Fenton
Dec	9	A	Willenhall (Rnd 2 Rep)	3-2	Yorke 2, Davis
Jan	8	H	Halesowen T. (Rnd 3)	2-0	Scimeca, Davis *(Played at Bodymoor Heath)*
Jan	31	A	Hednesford T. (Rnd 4)	1-2	Scimeca

Top two finish for the seconds, Young Lions roar to cup success

The Reserve and Youth teams continued to provide a solid potential back-up to the first team with a hint of success at both levels.

In the Pontins' Central League the second team were runners-up to Manchester United having finished as champions in 1992-93.

During the season there were many outstanding individual and collective displays including an opening spell in August of four successive victories in their role as defending champions.

The true yardstick of success at this level is, however, the production of individuals for the first team and in this regard Graham Fenton's achievement was the highlight of the season.

His promotion after his spell on loan to West Bromwich Albion, culminating in his winning a Coca Cola Cup Winners' medal was an inspiration to all of the young players who have joined the club on YTS terms.

The winning of the Southern Junior Floodlit Cup by the youth team, in a two-legged Final against Spurs, was also a great incentive for the first-team players of the future.

At the end of the season the club's Director of Youth, Dave Richardson, decided to move on. Many good players were brought to the club in Richardson's two spells with Villa and he was not easily replaced.

The constant process of introducing new quality YTS players was not interrupted, however, as plans were quickly in place for 1994-95.

SOUTHERN JUNIOR FLOODLIT CUP

Sep	1	H	**Fulham** (Rnd 1)	2-1	Byfield, Hendrie
Sep	27	A	Bournemouth (Rnd 2)	2-1	Hendrie, Petty
Dec	20	H	**Bristol City** (Rnd 3)	2-0	Hendrie, Byfield
Mar	9	H	**Brighton** (S/F)	2-2	Hendrie, Byfield
Mar	14	A	Brighton (S/F Replay)	2-1	Farrelly, Byfield
May	5	H	**Tottenham** (Final 1L)	1-0	Hendrie
May	11	A	Tottenham (Final 2L)	2-2	Walker, Brown

FA YOUTH CUP

Oct	26	A	Cambridge Utd. (Rnd 1)	4-1	Burchell 2, Byfield, Farrelly
Dec	6	A	Watford (Rnd 2)	3-1	Byfield 2, Brown
Jan	26	A	Bristol City (Rnd 3)	4-1	Walker 2, Byfield, Hendrie
Feb	9	H	**West Ham U.** (Rnd 4)	1-2	Byfield

MIDLAND YOUTH CUP

Oct	4	A	Hereford Utd. (Prelim.)	3-2	Burchell, Hendrie, Mitchell
Nov	1	A	Leicester City (Rnd 1)	2-1	Farrelly, Burchell
Feb	17	A	Stoke City (Rnd 2)	1-4	Walker

MIDLAND PURITY YOUTH LEAGUE

Aug	7	H	**Birmingham City**	0-3	
Aug	14	A	Coventry City	0-3	
Aug	21	H	**Derby County**	2-4	Aston, Byfield
Aug	27	A	Grimsby Town	1-1	Boxall
Sep	4	H	**Leicester City**	1-1	Byfield
Sep	10	A	Lincoln City	6-2	Byfield 3, Moore, Impey, McAuley
Sep	25	A	Northampton Town	1-1	Hendrie
Oct	2	H	**Notts County**	0-1	
Oct	9	A	Nottingham Forest	3-1	Byfield, Brown, Hendrie
Oct	23	A	Port Vale	1-0	Hines
Oct	30	A	Leicester City	4-1	Burgess 3, Barratt
Nov	6	H	**Shrewsbury Town**	1-1	Byfield
Nov	13	A	Stoke City	3-5	Senior, Boxall, Brown
Nov	27	A	West Bromwich Albion	1-0	Hines
Dec	11	H	**Wolverhampton W.**	6-3	Byfield 2, Hendrie 2, Aston, Burchell
Dec	18	A	Wolverhampton W.	0-2	
Jan	15	H	**Coventry City**	1-2	Boxall
Jan	29	A	Derby County	1-1	Boxall
Feb	5	H	**Grimsby Town**	3-1	Brown, Peters (pen), Devlin
Feb	12	H	**Lincoln City**	0-1	
Feb	19	A	Mansfield Town	1-1	Walker
Mar	5	A	Notts County	0-1	
Mar	12	H	**Walsall**	3-2	Peters, Burgess, Miles
Mar	19	H	**Nottingham Forest**	0-1	
Mar	25	A	Peterborough United	4-1	Byfield 2, Hines, Hendrie
Mar	30	H	**Peterborough Utd.**	1-1	Mooney
Apr	9	A	Shrewsbury Town	3-0	Mooney 2, Brown
Apr	16	H	**Stoke City**	1-2	Collins
Apr	20	A	Birmingham City	2-1	Burgess, Byfield
Apr	23	A	Walsall	4-1	Hendrie 3, Byfield
Apr	26	H	**Port Vale**	1-0	Byfield
Apr	30	H	**West Bromwich A.**	1-1	Byfield
May	7	H	**Mansfield Town**	2-0	Brown, Byfield
May	18	H	**Northampton Town**	4-1	Burgess 2, Walker, Hendrie

MIDLAND PURITY YOUTH LEAGUE CUP

Oct	16	H	**Walsall** (Rnd 2)	1-2	Hendrie

RESERVE & YOUTH TEAM APPEARANCES

	CENTRAL LGE		SENIOR CUP		YOUTH LGE		YOUTH CUPS	
	Apps	Gls	Apps	Gls	Apps	Gls	Apps	Gls
Lee ASTON	-	-	-	-	11 (2)	3	3 (1)	-
Stefan BEINLICH	26	9	1	-	-	-	-	-
Trevor BERRY	10 (9)	2	4	-	-	-	-	-
Chris BODEN	21 (1)	2	3	-	-	-	-	-
Mark BOSNICH	3	-	-	-	-	-	-	-
Mike BOXALL	-	-	-	-	16 (2)	4	1 (4)	-
Matthias BREITKREUTZ	28 (1)	3	-	-	-	-	-	-
Stuart BROCK	1	-	2	-	17	-	8	-
Ian BROWN	-	-	1 (2)	-	29 (2)	5	15	2
Paul BROWNE	13	2	3	-	-	-	-	-
Lee BURCHELL	-	-	-	-	27	1	15	4
Darren BYFIELD	- (1)	-	-	-	24 (1)	16	14	9
Steven COWE	2 (2)	1	-	-	-	-	-	-
Gordon COWANS	4	-	-	-	-	-	-	-
Neil COX	13	-	-	-	-	-	-	-
Richard CRISP	12 (4)	2	4	-	-	-	-	-
Tony DALEY	4	5	-	-	-	-	-	-
Neil DAVIS	10 (5)	1	4	3	-	-	-	-
Ugo EHIOGU	19	-	-	-	-	-	-	-
Darren EVANS	15	-	4	-	-	-	-	-
Dave FARRELL	29 (1)	4	2	-	-	-	-	-
Gareth FARRELLY	3 (1)	-	1	-	19	-	12	3
Graham FENTON	12 (4)	7	2	1	-	-	-	-
Steve FROGGATT	1	-	-	-	-	-	-	-
Lee HENDRIE	1	-	-	-	24 (1)	9	15	8
Leslie HINES	-	-	-	-	20 (5)	3	9 (2)	-
Dariusz KUBICKI	19	-	-	-	-	-	-	-
Andrew MITCHELL	-	-	-	-	21 (4)	-	11 (1)	1
David MOORE	-	-	-	-	27 (3)	1	13 (1)	-
John MURPHY	-	-	-	-	21 (3)	-	14	-
Scott MURRAY	14	6	-	-	-	-	-	-
Michael OAKES	16	-	2	-	-	-	-	-
Garry PARKER	15	2	-	-	-	-	-	-
Dennis PEARCE	7 (4)	-	4	-	-	-	-	-
Mark PETERS	-	-	-	-	15 (5)	2	2 (3)	-
Ben PETTY	-	-	-	-	16 (5)	-	12	1
Adam RACHEL	-	-	-	-	16	-	6	-
Riccardo SCIMECA	9 (2)	4	3	2	-	-	-	-
Marc SENIOR	-	-	-	-	19 (3)	1	1	-
Bryan SMALL	23	-	-	-	-	-	-	-
Nigel SPINK	14	-	-	-	-	-	-	-
Steve STAUNTON	1	-	-	-	-	-	-	-
Richard WALKER	-	-	-	-	6 (2)	2	11 (1)	4
Guy WHITTINGHAM	9	6	-	-	-	-	-	-
Lee WILLIAMS	5 (3)	-	3	-	-	-	-	-
Dwight YORKE	11	5	1	2	-	-	-	-

Also played for the reserves: Crawford 1app (Lge); West 3 apps (Lge).
Also played for the youth team (triallists/schoolboys): Barratt 1(1) app 1 gl (Lge); Bluck 1 app (Lge); Bowler 2 apps (Lge);
Burgess 9(2) apps, 7 gls (Lge); Chaliner 1 app (Lge); Coles 1 app (Lge); Collins 7(2) apps 1 gl (Lge); Coulter -(1) app (Cup);
Cross 1 app (Lge); Devlin -(2) apps 1 gl (Lge); Doherty -(1) app (Cup); Dunn 1 app (Lge); Glover 1 app (Lge);
Hughes 1 app (Lge); Impey 1 app 1 gl (Lge); Jaczeszun 7 apps (Lge); Kearn 1 app (Cup); Kelly 1(1) app (Lge); King 1 app (Lge);
Lonsdale 3 apps (Lge); McAuley -(2) apps 1 gl (Lge); Miles 1 (2) apps 1 gl (Lge); Miley 3(2) apps (Lge);
Mooney 2 apps 3 gls (Lge), 2 apps (Cup); Peet 1 app (Lge); Ramsey -(1) app (Lge).

VILLA'S ALL-TIME LEAGUE RECORD

Season	Div	Teams	Pos	P	W	D	L	F	A	W	D	L	F	A	Pts	Cup Honours
1888-89	1	12	2nd	22	10	0	1	44	16	2	5	4	17	27	29	*(FAC Winners in 1886-87)*
1889-90	1	12	8th	22	6	2	3	30	15	1	3	7	13	36	19	
1890-91	1	12	9th	22	5	4	2	29	18	2	0	9	16	40	18	
1891-92	1	14	4th	26	10	0	3	63	23	5	0	8	26	33	30	*FAC Runners-up*
1892-93	1	16	4th	30	12	1	2	50	24	4	2	9	23	38	35	
1893-94	**1**	**16**	**1st**	**30**	**12**	**2**	**1**	**49**	**13**	**7**	**4**	**4**	**35**	**29**	**44**	
1894-95	1	16	3rd	30	12	2	1	51	12	5	3	7	31	31	39	*FAC Winners*
1895-96	**1**	**16**	**1st**	**30**	**14**	**1**	**0**	**47**	**17**	**6**	**4**	**5**	**31**	**28**	**45**	
1896-97	**1**	**16**	**1st**	**30**	**10**	**3**	**2**	**36**	**16**	**11**	**2**	**2**	**37**	**22**	**47**	*FAC Winners*
1897-98	1	16	6th	30	12	1	2	47	21	2	4	9	14	30	33	
1898-99	**1**	**18**	**1st**	**34**	**15**	**2**	**0**	**58**	**13**	**4**	**5**	**8**	**18**	**27**	**45**	
1899-00	**1**	**18**	**1st**	**34**	**12**	**4**	**1**	**45**	**18**	**10**	**2**	**5**	**32**	**17**	**50**	
1900-01	1	18	15th	34	8	5	4	32	18	2	5	10	13	33	30	*FAC Semi-finalists*
1901-02	1	18	8th	34	9	5	3	27	13	4	3	10	15	27	34	
1902-03	1	18	2nd	34	11	3	3	43	18	8	0	9	18	22	41	*FAC Semi-finalists*
1903-04	1	18	5th	34	13	1	3	41	16	4	6	7	29	32	41	
1904-05	1	18	4th	34	11	2	4	32	15	8	2	7	31	28	42	*FAC Winners*
1905-06	1	20	8th	38	13	2	4	51	19	4	4	11	21	37	40	
1906-07	1	20	5th	38	13	4	2	51	19	6	2	11	27	33	44	
1907-08	1	20	2nd	38	9	6	4	47	24	8	3	8	30	35	43	
1908-09	1	20	7th	38	8	7	4	31	22	6	3	10	27	34	38	
1909-10	**1**	**20**	**1st**	**38**	**17**	**2**	**0**	**62**	**19**	**6**	**5**	**8**	**22**	**23**	**53**	
1910-11	1	20	2nd	38	15	3	1	50	18	7	4	8	19	23	51	
1911-12	1	20	6th	38	12	2	5	48	22	5	5	9	28	41	41	
1912-13	1	20	2nd	38	13	4	2	57	21	6	8	5	29	31	50	*FAC Winners*
1913-14	1	20	2nd	38	11	3	5	36	21	8	3	8	29	29	44	*FAC Semi-finalists*
1914-15	1	20	13th	38	10	5	4	39	32	3	6	10	23	40	37	
First World War																
1919-20	1	22	9th	42	11	3	7	49	36	7	3	11	26	37	42	*FAC Winners*
1920-21	1	22	10th	42	11	4	6	39	21	7	3	11	24	49	43	
1921-22	1	22	5th	42	16	3	2	50	19	6	0	15	24	36	47	
1922-23	1	22	6th	42	15	3	3	42	11	3	7	11	22	40	46	
1923-24	1	22	6th	42	10	10	1	33	11	8	3	10	19	26	49	*FAC Runners-up*
1924-25	1	22	15th	42	10	7	4	34	25	3	6	12	24	46	39	
1925-26	1	22	6th	42	12	7	2	56	25	4	5	12	30	51	44	
1926-27	1	22	10th	42	11	4	6	51	34	7	3	11	30	49	43	
1927-28	1	22	8th	42	13	3	5	52	30	4	6	11	26	43	43	
1928-29	1	22	3rd	42	16	2	3	62	30	7	2	12	36	51	50	*FAC Semi-finalists*
1929-30	1	22	4th	42	13	1	7	54	33	8	4	9	38	50	47	
1930-31	1	22	2nd	42	17	3	1	86	34	8	6	7	42	44	59	
1931-32	1	22	5th	42	15	1	5	64	28	4	7	10	40	44	46	
1932-33	1	22	2nd	42	16	2	3	60	29	7	6	8	32	38	54	
1933-34	1	22	13th	42	10	5	6	45	34	4	7	10	33	41	40	*FAC Semi-finalists*
1934-35	1	22	13th	42	11	6	4	50	36	3	7	11	24	52	41	
1935-36	*1*	*22*	*21st*	*42*	*7*	*6*	*8*	*47*	*56*	*6*	*3*	*12*	*34*	*54*	*35*	
1936-37	2	22	9th	42	10	6	5	47	30	6	6	9	35	40	44	
1937-38	**2**	**22**	**1st**	**42**	**17**	**2**	**2**	**50**	**12**	**8**	**5**	**8**	**23**	**23**	**57**	*FAC Semi-finalists*
1938-39	1	22	12th	42	11	3	7	44	25	5	6	10	27	35	41	
Second World War																
1946-47	1	22	8th	42	9	6	6	39	24	9	3	9	28	29	45	
1947-48	1	22	6th	42	13	5	3	42	22	6	4	11	23	35	47	
1948-49	1	22	10th	42	10	6	5	40	36	6	4	11	20	40	42	
1949-50	1	22	12th	42	10	7	4	31	19	5	5	11	30	42	42	

SEASON-BY-SEASON

Season	Div	Teams	Pos	P	W	D	L	F	A	W	D	L	F	A	Pts	Cup Honours
1950-51	1	22	15th	42	9	6	6	39	29	3	7	11	27	39	37	
1951-52	1	22	6th	42	13	3	5	49	28	6	6	9	30	42	47	
1952-53	1	22	11th	42	9	7	5	36	23	5	6	10	27	38	41	
1953-54	1	22	13th	42	12	5	4	50	28	4	4	13	20	40	41	
1954-55	1	22	6th	42	11	3	7	38	31	9	4	8	34	42	47	
1955-56	1	22	20th	42	9	6	6	32	29	2	7	12	20	40	35	
1956-57	1	22	10th	42	10	8	3	45	25	4	7	10	20	30	43	*FAC Winners*
1957-58	1	22	14th	42	12	4	5	46	26	4	3	14	27	60	39	
1958-59	*1*	*22*	*21st*	*42*	*8*	*5*	*8*	*31*	*33*	*3*	*3*	*15*	*27*	*54*	*30*	*FAC Semi-finalists*
1959-60	2	22	1st	42	17	3	1	62	19	8	6	7	27	24	59	*FAC Semi-finalists*
1960-61	1	22	9th	42	13	3	5	48	28	6	4	11	30	49	43	*LC Winners*
1961-62	1	22	7th	42	13	5	3	45	20	5	3	13	20	36	44	
1962-63	1	22	15th	42	12	2	7	38	23	3	6	12	24	45	38	*LC Runners-up*
1963-64	1	22	19th	42	8	6	7	35	29	3	6	12	27	42	34	
1964-65	1	22	16th	42	14	1	6	36	24	2	4	15	21	58	37	*LC Semi-finalists*
1965-66	1	22	16th	42	10	3	8	39	34	5	3	13	30	46	36	
1966-67	1	22	21st	42	7	5	9	30	33	4	2	15	24	52	29	
1967-68	2	22	16th	42	10	3	8	35	30	5	4	12	19	34	37	
1968-69	2	22	18th	42	10	8	3	22	11	2	6	13	15	37	38	
1969-70	*2*	*22*	*21st*	*42*	*7*	*8*	*6*	*23*	*21*	*1*	*5*	*15*	*13*	*41*	*29*	
1970-71	3	24	4th	46	13	7	3	27	13	6	8	9	27	33	53	*LC Runners-up*
1971-72	**3**	**24**	**1st**	**46**	**20**	**1**	**2**	**45**	**10**	**12**	**5**	**6**	**40**	**22**	**70**	
1972-73	2	22	3rd	42	12	5	4	27	17	6	9	6	24	30	50	
1973-74	2	22	14th	42	8	9	4	33	21	5	6	10	15	24	41	
1974-75	2	22	2nd	42	16	4	1	47	6	9	4	8	32	26	58	*LC Winners*
1975-76	1	22	16th	42	11	8	2	32	17	0	9	12	19	42	39	
1976-77	1	22	4th	42	17	3	1	55	17	5	4	12	21	33	51	*LC Winners*
1977-78	1	22	8th	42	11	4	6	33	18	7	6	8	24	24	46	
1978-79	1	22	8th	42	8	9	4	37	26	7	7	7	22	23	46	
1979-80	1	22	7th	42	11	5	5	29	22	5	9	7	22	28	46	
1980-81	**1**	**22**	**1st**	**42**	**16**	**3**	**2**	**40**	**13**	**10**	**5**	**6**	**32**	**27**	**60**	
1981-82	1	22	11th	42	9	6	6	28	24	6	6	9	27	29	57	*EC Winners*
1982-83	1	22	6th	42	17	2	2	47	15	4	3	14	15	35	68	*ESC Winners*
1983-84	1	22	10th	42	14	3	4	34	22	3	6	12	25	39	60	*LC Semi-finalists*
1984-85	1	22	10th	42	10	7	4	34	20	5	4	12	26	40	56	
1985-86	1	22	16th	42	7	6	8	27	28	3	8	10	24	39	44	*LC Semi-finalists*
1986-87	*1*	*22*	*22nd*	*42*	*7*	*7*	*7*	*25*	*25*	*1*	*5*	*15*	*20*	*54*	*36*	
1987-88	2	23	2nd	44	9	7	6	31	21	13	5	4	37	20	78	
1988-89	1	20	17th	38	7	6	6	25	22	2	7	10	20	34	40	
1989-90	1	20	2nd	38	13	3	3	36	20	8	4	7	21	18	70	*FMC Area Finalists*
1990-91	1	20	17th	38	7	9	3	29	25	2	5	12	17	33	41	
1991-92	1	22	7th	42	13	3	5	31	16	4	6	11	17	28	60	
1992-93	P	22	2nd	42	13	5	3	36	16	8	6	7	21	24	74	
1993-94	P	22	10th	42	8	5	8	23	18	7	7	7	23	32	57	*LC Winners*

	P	W	D	L	F	A	Pts
Home	1872	1088	402	382	3953	2139	2712
Away	1872	505	446	921	2397	3407	1522
Total	3744	1593	848	1303	6350	5546	4234

2pts for a win up to season 1980-81
3pts for a win from season 1981-82

Other honours: World Club Championship runners-up 1982-83 FA Charity Shield joint winners 1981-82 FA Charity Shield runners-up 1910-11, 1957-58, 1972-73

FAC = FA Cup; LC = League Cup; FMC = Full Members' Cup; EC = European Champions' Cup; ESC = European Super Cup. Championship seasons in **bold** type, relegation seasons in *italics*.

SUBSCRIBERS ROLL CALL

1 Neil Gallagher	63 Brian C. Seadon	125 David Poole
2 Philip R. Haynes	64 A. Rogers	126 James A. Flynn
3 Rob Rodway	65 Adam 'One-Arm Villa'	127 Katie Flynn
4 Nigel Iwanski	66 Carol Smith	128 Mark H. Whitehouse
5 Keith Taylor	67 Craig S. Putman	129 Ian R. Wilson
6 Eddie McNeill	68 Gerald Leek	130 Darren Woodfield
7 David Hodges	69 Christopher Dennis	131 Alison & Vic Clements
8 Mr J. R. Onyon	70 Susan Pudge	132 Warren H. McDivitt
9 Roger Nicklin (Tamworth)	71 Anthony Harold	133 Adrian Sussex Thorne
10 Gregory Upton	72 Charles Keenan	134 Keith Powell
11 R. H. Rose	73 Neil Cooper	135 Adrian Goddard
12 Ross Griffith	74 Teresa Ecija	136 Neil A. Powell
13 Sue & Mick Tilt	75 Alison Jones	137 Robert Bartlett
14 Dave Nicholson	76 Rachel Townsend	138 Mark Napier
15 Pete Abrahams	77 Gary Cowdrill	139 Martin K. James
16 Simon 'Wilf' Wheeler (Tamworth)	78 Daniel M. W. Nash	140 David Michael Buttery
17 Andrew K. Clark	79 Susan Glaves	141 Craig Vigurs
18 John Stammers	80 Simon Padmore	142 Stephen Lynch
19 Ralf Schulz	81 Stephen C. Tovey	143 Helen Freeman
20 Stephen Murphy	82 Saul C. Gray	144 Stuart J. Freeman
21 John Hadgkiss	83 Robert York	145 Graham Coggins
22 Edward Mills	84 Christopher Dicken	146 Gary Coggins
23 Mr T. D. Measey	85 Nick Marple	147 Eric Norman Farmer
24 Ruth Simmons	86 Sara Tovey	148 Liam Rollason
25 Chris Riordan	87 Simon Lawrie Turner	149 Alan Gee
26 Kevin Portley	88 Wizard of Oz	150 N. J. Orton
27 Paul Perry	89 R. O. Evans	151 Stephen Hill
28 Therese Barrow	90 Rob Smith	152 Oliver Keats
29 Frank McNally	91 Jason 'Nobby' Crowley	153 Mickey Gorman
30 Colin Askey	92 John Fairfield	154 Ramon Halford
31 Jamie Cash	93 Nick & John Timothy	155 Ben A.V. Halford
32 Peter Harrold	94 David John Peachey	156 Thomas Deakin
33 Dean Measey	95 Paul Woodford	157 Daniel Arrowsmith
34 Michael Barr	96 Matthew Book	158 Alison K. Francis
35 Matthew Green	97 Darren Hudson-Wood	159 Jon Broad
36 Neil Hansen	98 Christopher Drew	160 Aaron Davie
37 Paul Sheehy	99 Nicholas Cox	161 Paul Arnold
38 Rob Hale	100 Amy Hunter	162 Robert John Lee Allison
39 Neal Sawyer	101 Paul Hooton	163 Stephen James Allison
40 Gary Walden	102 Barry Geddis	164 Mark Stoneman
41 Mr A. Nicholls	103 Paul John Hinkley	165 Chris Dingley
42 Chris & David Morey	104 Andy Seal (Telford)	166 Martin J. Jackson
43 Stephen & James Williams	105 Darren Paul Hunt	167 Jacqueline Boston
44 Barbara Coll	106 Mark Glyn Jones	168 Lee Pendrey
45 Andrew, James, Paterson	107 Jackson Hunt	169 H. C. Gee
46 Vince Kiely	108 Becky Willis	170 Alan West
47 Carol Maguire	109 Richard Linley	171 Darren Harness
48 Peter Nicholls	110 Oliver Eagle	172 Philip Gray
49 Derek, Kerry, Carly Day	111 Wally Baylis	173 Rob & Penny
50 Mark Whorton	112 Charles R. J. Clarke	174 Tony A. Bill
51 Steve Matthews	113 Terry Wright	175 Matthew Stephen Allen
52 Sharron Philpot	114 Matthew John Collinge	176 M. G. Taylor
53 Mick Turner	115 Caroline Crutchley	177 Neil Alcock
54 Pauline A. Holloway	116 Gordon Parton	178 Richard Ian Stait
55 Andrew & Adam Morgan	117 Richard Lee Goodwin	179 Paul Tierney
56 Keith & Graham Rickett	118 Paul Ford	180 Geoffrey Wright
57 Brett Rotheroe	119 Helen Sutton	181 Jane Dormer
58 Kevin A. W. Williams	120 Kev Buttery	182 Clive & Michele Platman
59 R. E. Garratt	121 Mark Lench	183 Terence McGeough
60 Martin Weaver	122 Sean Christopher Edkins	184 Lara Swann
61 Craig Ramsey	123 Paul Anderton	185 Stuart T. Swann
62 David Woodley	124 Louise Bowdler	186 Stewart Ray

187 Graham Watkiss	259 Christine & Ian Rossiter	321 Richard Winter
188 Richard Court	260 Brian Flanagan	322 Andrew Williams
189 Ann Curtis	261 Paul Palmer	323 R. A. Jones
190 Andrew Oates	262 Dave Skinner	324 Harry W. McDivitt
191 Steve Webb	263 Gareth Humpage	325 Clive Nicholls
192 Jack David Roberts	264 Andrew Webster	326 Bob Nicholls
193 Carl John Roberts	265 Colin R. Walster	327 Gido Kirfel
194 John Lane	266 Ross Martin	328 Mathew John Chapman
195 John O'Brien	267 Greg Martin	329 Stephen Sturman
196 Noritoshi Tateno	268 Ruth Edwards	330 Mr I. M. Rollitt
197 David Yeomans	269 Adrian Archer	331 A. Hooper
198 Jane Bowyer	270 Michael Shrimplin	332 Andy Downes
199 David M. Edwards	271 Alex Perkins	333 P. J. Hadoulis
200 Lindsey Roberts	272 Paul Aldhouse	334 Tim Cotter
201 Liam Murray	273 M. A. Cooper	335 Phil Cotter
202 Susan Higginbotham	274 David Tansey	336 Kevin Stratford
203 S. F. Randle	275 Paul Groves	337 Sheena Meredith
204 Joe Ridout	276 Adam Coles	338 Matthew Dale
205 R. D. Widdowson	277 Emma Pritchard	339 Martin Greenslade
206 Emma Rock	278 Brig Flounders	340 Sarah Burch
207 Daniel Reeves	279 Sarah Wilkes	341 Matthew Idoine
208 Vincent J. McKenna	280 Dominic Kavanagh	342 Nick Allman
209 Alexis Jackson Wagner	281 Robert A. Clarke	343 Julie Richardson
210 Adrian John Miles	282 Mick Cooper	344 Paul Burke
211 Lee Coton	283 Andrew Fitter	345 Malcolm Philip Price
212 Jason Wardle	284 Peter Houghton	346 Gordon Wilfred Price
213 Mark Hamblett	285 Jürgen Hohmann	347 Neil Brailsford
214 Stephen J. Lammas	286 Steven Coleman	348 Adrian Spray
215 Craig Winstone	287 Peter Curry	349 Paul Rostance
216 Julian Smith	288 Andrew G. Harris	350 Adam France
217 Simon Daykin	289 James W. Johnstone	351 Christopher Newman
218 Mark Randle	290 B. M. Dain	352 Graham Anderson
219 Adrian Batsford	291 Paul & Jenny Bailey	353 Gary & Jackie Hodges
220 C. R. Brown	292 Gordon Reynolds	354 Liam Foley
221 Andrew Phillips	293 Anthony Woolley	355 Karen Green
222 Ian Stringer	294 P. W. Taylor	356 Rod Snelson
223 Adrian J. Hill	295 John A. Gould (1934)	357 Ian A. Swindell
234 Mr Philip John Shakespeare	296 Nigel Thompson	358 High C. Swindell
235 David Smith	297 John Peter Reidy	359 Gina Lynch
236 Pamela Bridgewater	298 Peter Brett	360 Robert Bowker
237 David Bridgewater	299 S. J. Lavery	361 Garry J. Moore
238 Mark H. Homer	300 Thomas Johansson	362 Michael Alfred Milne
239 Stewart J. Draper	301 Steve Knott	363 Jennifer Blake
240 Bill Marron	302 Peter, Margaret & Gary James	364 Simon Blake
241 John, David & Peter Hitchman	303 P. L. Bullock	365 Philip J. Etheridge
242 Trevor John Baker	304 Mr S. James-Dyke	366 Lisa Robinson
243 Mrs B. R. Warman	305 David Smart	367 Scott Hemmens
244 David Warman	306 Tony Spraggon	368 D. H. Perry
245 'Doskit'	307 Leni D. Ward	369 W. A. Harvey
246 Ashley Goodwin	308 Raymond Warr	370 James & Colin Daly
247 Dawn McCarrick	309 Miss Lucy Randolph	371 Jennifer Beale
248 AV Norwegian Supporters Branch	310 Lee Moreton	372 Martin A. Bird
249 Wendy Jordan	311 Nicholas Lovell	373 Andy Cole
250 Stephen Morris (France)	312 Derek Wisdom	374 Paul & Denise Allibone
251 Matthew Alan Hipkiss	313 Ben Sedgwick	375 CJ, Miranda & Helen Turner
252 P. Pilkington	314 Claire Cooper	376 Richard Moss
253 Richard Pallot	315 Kevi McGovern	377 Tony C. Dacey
254 Dr Mark Wilson	316 Lorna Summers	378 Debbie & Kevin Joynes
255 Sarah Kinsman	317 P. R. Jones	379 L. N. E. Barlow
256 J. R. Meek	318 Chris Rigby	380 Peter Lee Maddocks
257 Graham L. Garvey	319 Paul Jarvis	381 D. S. Mitchell
258 Bob Peach	320 Mr C. J. Lally	382 Daniel P. Bytheway

383	Robert & Liza Giles	445	Lee Day	507	Peter J. Charles
384	John Michael Derry	446	Sara Burton	508	Catherine Guest
385	J. Gaitskell	447	Iain Fenwick	509	Steve A. Heath
386	B. R. Veal	448	Michael J. F. Doyle	510	David Jasper
387	Mr Jonathan Stratford	449	Gareth C. Jones	511	Caroline Gaitskell
388	Mark Howes	450	Richard Jones	512	Mark Stanford
389	Michael Paul Field	451	Kevin Whittick	513	Darren Sheffield
390	Richard Atkins	452	Reine Bladh	514	Anton Tarabilda
391	John Atkins	453	Keith Gerald Wilkinson	515	G. A. Dixon
392	Paul Parker	454	Andrew Webb	516	Andrew Worrall
393	Paul Biddlestone	455	Tracy Haines	517	Ian Barton
394	Jim Foat	456	Bernard R. Bemand	518	Ian & Philip Pestridge
395	Cliff Paget	457	Simon Peter Rawlins	519	Steven Heywood
396	Adrian Chamberlain	458	R. F. Rea	520	David Mann
397	Bryan Harte	459	J. C. Noden	521	Chris Deakin
398	Miss Marie Connaughton	460	Mrs Sarah Reynolds	522	Ross McCarthy
399	Benito De Rosa	461	Miss Tracie Peagram	523	Hayden Wakeling
400	Tracey B. & Roy H.	462	Alan F. Jasper	524	Gary Chamberlain
401	Keith A. Birch	463	Simon Kerr-Edwards	525	Gavin Spybey
402	Mark Keylock	464	Anthony Richard Joyner	526	Peter W. Giles
403	David & Martin George	465	Ian Nicholls	527	Scott Ratcliffe
404	David Whitlock	466	Clive W. Cross	528	James S. T. Brown
405	Rob Davis	467	John Treadwell	529	Tracey Cox
406	Phillip Raymond Bassett	468	Alan & Thomas Green	530	Richard Keble
407	Neil Hemming	469	Brian Moloney	531	Lee J. Wilkins
408	Andrew Smith	470	Jon G. Jones	532	Jamie Duggan
409	Kevin Fowler	471	Nicola Friel	533	Kevin Cox
410	Michelle Walters	472	Jonathan Giffin	534	Lloyd Hutchings
411	Andrew Mark Neale	473	Mark T. Lowndes	535	Michael J. Reidy
412	Keeley Grain	474	Sean Escritt	536	Martin Hodson
413	Christopher Hearn	475	Hannah Dosanjh	537	Ben Sutherland
414	Antonio Durante (Italy)	476	Derek Hollis	538	James Dagley
415	John Collins	477	Anthony J. C. Hughes	539	Jason Badham
416	Nicola Chapman	478	David & Kathryn Knight	540	Jamie Willetts
417	Simon Giles	479	Russell Brown Jnr.	541	Chris Harris
418	Steve Hughes	480	Darren Bray	542	Peter Moon
419	Nick Walker	481	Robert Cooley	543	Paul Lawrence
420	John Mannifield	482	Chris Newton	544	Colin Glynn
421	A. J. Moore	483	Jens Martin	545	Richard Henman
422	Paul John Geraghty	484	John Lacey	546	James Aldridge
423	Morten Esbjerg	485	Gary Lacey	547	Mark Jenkins
424	J. A. Porter	486	Jonathan Andrew James Cox	548	Michael & Nicholas English
425	Jason Kennedy	487	Richard Allen	549	Leanne Bedford
426	Ian Campbell	488	Aston & Graham Perry	550	David Lock
427	Anthony Baker	489	Daniel Carlile	551	Heather Sidwell
428	Karl Linder	490	Tim Parker	552	Andy Lareen
429	Neal Strange	491	Christopher Biggs	553	G. E. Telfer
430	Andy & Tracey Orton	492	Des Suckling	554	Angela Guoite
431	Dixie Woodhams	493	Nikki Long	555	Aaron Hickman
432	David Wardrop	494	John Doyle	556	David Hitchins
433	Ian Harrison	495	David Aston	557	Roger Moore
434	Simon Harrison	496	John S. Brown	558	Charlotte Hanslow
435	Paul Shelley	497	Zoe E. Gough	559	Carolyn Sheridan-Jones
436	Brian Marshall	498	Adam S. G. Mullins	560	Andrew Steward
437	Kevi Marshall	499	David John Stuart	561	Martin Jeffrey
438	Martyn R. Smith	500	Lisa Whitmore	562	Bill Gubb
439	B. J. Curnock	501	Terry Whitmore	563	Mark Alders
440	Leo Osborn	502	Mark Lohan	564	Adam Thomas Barrett
441	Debbie Bennett	503	Philip Bennett	565	Matthew & Effie Randall
442	James Perry	504	Nicholas T. Watts	566	Brian Haggitt
443	Anthony Madigan	505	Adam Clarke	567	Jonathan L. Whitlock
444	Clare Beswick	506	Colin Hann	568	Matthew Robert Oakes

SUBSCRIBERS ROLL CALL

569	Ross Underhill	631	Mark Ferriday	693	R. K. Pearson
570	Jonathan Morgan	632	Stephen Drew	694	Mick Brown
571	Andy, Bradley & Rachel Armstrong	633	John A. Tooth	695	Dominic James 'Pongo' Moore
572	Ben Redding	634	Jonathan Starbuck	696	Patrick F. J. O'Reilly
573	J. E. S. Cook	635	Ian Lane	697	Matthew Bond
574	Nigel Ainge	636	Martin Lane	698	A. L. Brusch
575	Sam Podmore	637	Gary & Debbie Wood	699	Alan Robert Wilkinson
576	Barry Wall	638	Beth Lury	700	David John Edward Clayton
577	Paul Vidler	639	Ali Green	701	Ashley Ward
578	Peter Beardshaw	640	Danny Green	702	Martell Beckford (11)
579	David England	641	Julia Greenfield	703	Pele Tomic
580	Adele & Rod Ross	642	Paul Cummins	704	Robin & Oliver Peck
581	Lee Keith Chapman	643	Jason Davis	705	Eamonn Christopher Smith
582	F. J. Cox	644	Andy Perry	706	David Clarkson
583	David & Trish	645	Andrew Wiseman	707	Mark & Alex Smith
584	Jimmy Smith	646	Carl Thornton	708	Simon Phillips
585	John Arthur Westwood	647	Alice McPake	709	Barrie Bailey (Plymouth)
586	The Wardle Family	648	Robert Gough	710	Roger Bailey (Nottingham)
587	Philip Goldie	649	Simon J. Lane	711	Brian Bailey (Plymouth)
588	Keith Stubbs	650	Alex Ashford	712	Derek Anthony Price
589	Nigel Sadler	651	Gavin Harris	713	Michael Louis Wilde
590	Jack Pinnock	652	The Jones Family (Walsall)	714	Matthew Seymour
591	Tony 'Fant' Green	653	Vera Ellen Ragsdale	715	Alex Wier
592	Neil Byrne	654	Ian Smith	716	Theresa Donner
593	S. Walton	655	Kris Long	717	Joanne Barber
594	Paul Hughes	656	Michelle Diggins	718	Roy Stringer
595	Sharon Thickett	657	Andrea Warren	719	Harvey Stringer
596	Melvin Thickett	658	Martin Lockley	720	Rowan Stringer
597	Anthony Thickett	659	David Ostojitsch	721	Craig Nichols
598	M. Cox	660	Michael Knight	722	Carly Nichols
599	Tom Kirk	661	Dean Strange	723	Andrea Hall
600	Geoff Elkington	662	Stuart Bailey	724	Amanda Ann Evans
601	Adam Robins	663	Richard & Steven Baker	725	Andy Congrave
602	Martin Colin Roberts	664	Paul Emes	726	John A. Hinton
603	Charlotte Louise Briggs	665	Michael C. Wedge	727	Derek Hinton
604	WP. SA. FA. Duff	666	Maria, Emma, Clare Ganner	728	Brian Horner
605	G. Padmore	667	Robert Patterson	729	Mike Manley
606	Mr N. J. Bindoff	668	Paul Jones	730	David Ennis
607	Mr B. Bindoff	669	John Donohoe	731	Andy Knight
608	Master G. A. Bindoff	670	Brian Thomas Berry	732	Mark Whale
609	Mark Wheeler	671	Tony Shanley	733	Nathan Collins
610	Chris Messer	672	Sam Gamble	734	Michael Shelton
611	Vicky Bennett	673	Becky Lowe	735	Debbie Jones
612	Neil F. Jones	674	Antony McAllister	736	Adrian Guy
613	Mark S. Waldron	675	Phillip Bagnall	737	Mark Harrell
614	Michael P. McTiernan	676	John Clayton	738	Nicholas Majer
615	Jessica & Alex Wright	677	Ian Clayton	739	Louise Barnsley
616	Keith Potter	678	Christopher Tamburro	740	Doe & Norman Hood
617	Martyn Jones	679	Erica Jessop	741	Cyril Hood
618	Stephanie Julie Jones	680	Kevin & Wilma	742	Dave Silver
619	Tracy Donna Jones	681	Mark Pitcher	743	Elizabeth Macwillson
620	I. J. Walker	682	Ian Checkley	744	Peter (Holte-Ender) Caunt
621	Andrew Dawes	683	Neil F. Ingram	745	Andrew & Kate Harris
622	Paul Gilks	684	Shaun, Craig, John Harris	746	Bill Willcox
623	Sue & Steve Daly	685	K. W. Brookin	747	Ken Marriott
624	D. Byrne	686	Mark Slater	748	C. J. Whitaker
625	S. Myatt	687	Daniel Stefan O'Gorman	749	David Foster
626	N. Watts	688	B. W. Hughes	750	John Alan Dunn
627	Stuart Sturmey	689	Alan Bowdler	751	Mark Dodd
628	Dave Alan Turner	690	Vincent R. Green	752	Darren Bedford
629	Michael Morgan	691	Helen Hollywell	753	Robert Hughes
630	David Barron	692	Paul Randle	754	Graham N. Willetts

SUBSCRIBERS ROLL CALL

755	Alexander Berwick	817	Cathryn Evans	879	Graeme Reid
756	Robert A. Taylor	818	Margaret Downey	880	John Foster
757	Robert L. Taylor	819	Jason Russell Perry	881	Paul Fitzpatrick
758	Pam Harris	820	Sid Jeewa	882	Dennis Rebbeck
759	Gingerpud – R.I.P.	821	Tony Broadhurst	883	Nick Harper
760	M. Pond	822	Frank MacDonald	884	Stephen Hood
761	John Haynes	823	Adrian Rogers	885	Gerald Roberts
762	Richard Shutt	824	Dave, Marg & Paul Buet	886	Sid Conway
763	Jean & Diane Gledhill	825	Gareth Stokes	887	Thomas Fraser
764	Tony Kiely	826	Derek T. Hough	888	Elizabeth Medcraft
765	Ian David Parkes	827	Carl Danson	889	Christopher Ashmore
766	Ashley Sargeant	828	Peter Aldridge	890	Gavin W. Handley
767	Craig Anthony Sargeant	829	Nicola Royles	891	Brendan Shields
768	Moscow Lions	830	Alison Royles	892	Matthew Sparrow
769	Roger Levicki	831	Michael Ireland	893	Michael David Bromwich
770	Tim Levicki	832	Thomas Blomberg (Sweden)	894	Scott Davidson
771	Andrew Levicki	833	Geoff Baker	895	Lee Symonds
772	Gary Pritchett	834	Mathew Kendrick	896	Neil Reading
773	Alison Harding	835	Russell Turvey	897	Craig Reading
774	Charles Stratton	836	Kevin Lowbridge	898	Ian Murphy
775	D. A. Lewis	837	Luke John Clarke	899	Paul Taylor
776	Jonathan Handley	838	Martha Osborne	900	Alan S. Johnson
777	Rebecca Smith	839	Peter J. Nally	901	Richard Wilson
778	Andrew Bateman	840	Linda Kim Smith	902	S. A. Underhill
779	Miss Diane Swales	841	Gary Arthurs	903	G. Holloway
780	Stephen Naylor	842	Paul Virgo	904	Gwyn Brewer
781	Steven J. Giles	843	Scott Marsden	905	Joseph Michael Hopkins
782	Steven McDermott	844	Richard T. Merrick	906	Donald Grisdale
783	Nathan Rose	845	Carl Davies	907	Sioned Enlli & Siôn Ynyr
784	Katie Prestwich	846	Graham Carlin	908	Stephen Marshman
785	David Francis	847	Elliott Jauncey	909	Ted Geary
786	Andrew Homer	848	Alistair Hudson	910	Joanne Hunt
787	Aden Cole	849	Trevor Bragg	911	Dawn Mann
788	Peter John Richmond	850	Owen Suter	912	Robert Taylor
789	James Howl	851	Peter J. Ball	913	D. Higgins
790	Billy Howl	852	Mary, John & Shaun Smith	914	Jackie & Iain Rawlings
791	Neil Clark	853	Matthew Shrimpton	915	Bryan Reid
792	Peter Clark	854	Philip Shrimpton	916	Simon K. Green
793	Robert Bryan	855	Ian Edward Beesley	917	Christopher John Reed
794	Jamie 'Bazza' Barrett	856		918	Jason Michael Smith
795	S. D. Lewis	857	Mark Pugh	919	Tony & Liam Hall
796	Julie Ann Harrison	858	Bruce Veitch	920	Pamela Pedley
797	Alyx Sara Pleaden	859	Keith 'Wendy' Griffin	921	Alex Patterson
798	Robin Nicholas Pleaden	860	Philip, Kevin, Tracy Piper	922	Brent Aston
799	Stuart Hughes	861	Christopher Hageney	923	Brian J. Maybury
800	Christopher Homewood	862	Matthew Woodhouse	924	Richard A. Hales
801	Nina Williams	863	Charles Southby	925	Sue Smith
802	Becky Houghton	864	Ed Knott	926	Ralph & Wendy
803	Mark Rogers	865	Robert Meadows	927	David Bray
804	Ray Marshall	866	Dan Taylor	928	John Millward
805	Adam G. Petersen	867	Mark McCormack	929	Thomas Algernon Taylor Snr
806	Si Fairlcough	868	David Daniel	930	Thomas Algernon Taylor
807	Tony Kenny	869	Bully, Lisa & Leanne	931	Thomas Algernon Taylor Jnr
808	Daron Howe	870	Chris Russell	932	P. J. Stocker
809	Ben Goldspink	871	Martin J. Watson	933	Peter Wildrianne
810	Kelly Sutton	872	Gavin & Craig Roberts	934	Peter Davies
811	Glyn Harries	873	Kevin Gledhill	935	Keith Gleadall
812	Robert Scott Watson	874	Peter Gledhill	936	John Brealey
813	Richard D. Webb	875	J. M. Richmond	937	Ben Ashford
814	Ray Troth	876	Carl Dickens	938	Martin Attwood
815	Nigel Snowden	877	Darren Wilkins	939	Martin Primmer
816	Antony Morris	878	Paddy Fenlon	940	Mr Leonard Stanton

SUBSCRIBERS ROLL CALL

941 Spencer Alan Malpass (AVFC)	1003 Gary & David Foster	1065 Dave Williams
942 Simon & Karen Hassall	1004 Mr R. J. Bunn	1066 Adrian J. Mullis
943 Derek Michael Ford	1005 Ian Shave	1067 Mrs S. M. Scott
944 Ian Hoskison	1006 Sue Glenton	1068 Allen Souch
945 Keir Hardy	1007 Steven McCabe	1069 Gerald H. Lodwick
946 Robert Mark Feasey	1008 Chris Hartshorne	1070 Warren Rees
947 Frank Francies	1009 C. Duncan T. Brown	1071 Andy Dale
948 I. Levell	1010 Mandy, Julie & Pam	1072 Scott Bradley (Evesham)
949 John Bannister	1011 Ian Thrupp	1073 David Sims (Australia)
950 Robert Lerner	1012 Barry Glaudot	1074 Christopher Swann
951 Jonathan Grossman	1013 Andrew John Bemand	1075 Lucy Audrey Evans
952 Collett Kids	1014 Neil A. Pearson	1076 James Powell
953 Richard Prvulovich	1015 Mark A. J. Ward	1077 C. Stephens
954 Nick Becenna	1016 Robert John Kench	1078 Carrie M. P. Fisher
955 Frank Allen	1017 Robert Aston	1079 H. E. Holman
956 Daniel Wigham	1018 Robert Butler	1080 Craig Holman
957 Mr C. G. Michell	1019 Anna & Roisin Mendoca	1081 Tony Lennon
958 Richard R. Carter	1020 Shaun Clarke	1082 Kevin Lennon
959 Laura Partington	1021 Andrew Clayton	1083 Andrew John Francis
960 John Holmes	1022 Michael Bergin	1084 Andrew Mateer
961 Miss J. Cox	1023 Peter Rodgers	1085 Andrew James Harper
962 Ben Moseley	1024 Kelly Neal	1086 Mark Freer
963 Sheila Bourke	1025 Anthony Ayre	1087 Miss Jayne Elson
964 Angus Rae	1026 R. L. Elwell	1088 D. P. Shipley
965 Andrew Rollason	1027 Esther & Ray Rawlings	1089 Colin Holmes
966 Harry Gatward	1028 Jim McDonald	1090 Craig Millard
967 Holte-Enders Chris, Guy & Steve	1029 David Fortnam	1091 McWilliams Family
968 Simon J. Rawlings	1030 Paul Webb	1092 G. M. Howard
969 E. T. Smyth	1031 J. A. Powell	1093 Geoff Blick
970 Chris du Bois	1032 Mark David Goodwin	1094 Tony D. Wilkes
971 Andrew Smart	1033 Nicholas Blewer	1095 Mark Barrington Stewart
972 Nicholas Smart	1034 Jonathon Paul Burton	1096 Stuart Baker
973 Emma & Lucy Wearden	1035 Stanley T. T. Jones	1097 Jonathan Muir
974 Pattison Family	1036 Terence Stone	1098 Natalie Langford
975 Emma Hurcombe	1037 Nick Morton	1099 Mark I. Kane
976 Reza Bodiat (South Africa)	1038 Jonathan Tebbutt	1100 Terence Anthony Barker
977 Julian Turner (South Africa)	1039 Neil Harris	1101 Andrew Hart
978 Nigel Renshaw	1040 Miss Karen A. Cousins	1102 Mark Lees
979 Stephen Renshaw	1041 Jeff Winters	1103 Simon Foxhall
980 Simon & Tim Bull	1042 D. S. Willetts	1104 Jeff Corfield
981 Pamela Wood	1043 Mark Clews	1105 Corrina Ansbro
982 Richard Hinton	1044 John Adkins	1106 Mark Rowland (Skully)
983 Mr Clifford Knight	1045 Michael Weller	1107 W. H. J. Ward
984 Andrew Paul Beard	1046 Karyn Hasson	1108 Steve Ewer
985 Talia Homer	1047 John W. Daw	1109 Liam & Michael Kiernan
986 Darren Fisher	1048 David French	1110 Gary Corbett
987 Graham & Neil Jinks	1049 Andrew & John Gillingham	1111 Michelle Angela McDonough
988 Craig Crossley	1050 Andrew R. Owen	1112 James H.W.T. Soden
989 Colin Roy Pheasant	1051 Richard Bennett	1113 Daren Reynolds
990 William J. Mottram	1052 Samantha Gough	1114 Fred Gray
991 Geoff Underhill	1053 Nanette Abberley	1115 Suzanne & James French
992 Christopher K. Devey	1054 Premier Entertainments	1116 Janet Farren
993 P. L. Day (Tenby)	1055 Ellena Burchell	1117 Charles Wesley
994 Robert Abbotts	1056 Sean Christopher Starrs	1118 Nicola Stonehouse
995 Martin S. Buck	1057 Paul Hawkins	1119 Michelle Wesley
996 Daniel Perry	1058 Gwen Bunce	1120 A. A. Bent
997 Nick Yates	1059 R. F. Harris	1121 Dave Cox (Toronto)
998 Gary Sinnott	1060 B. T. Harris	1122 John Simmonds
999 Jack Stephen Wright	1061 S. M. Goodall	1123 Joe Ward
1000 Chris & Jim Marcantonio	1062 Dave Crathorne	1124 Phil Gautrey
1001 Lucie Michelle Winspur	1063 Tom Holland (The Guard)	1125 Michael Murphy
1002 Clive Foster	1064 Jim Stelfox	1126 Matthew Plant

1127 Andrew Summers	1189 P. N. Harris	1251 Anthony Middleton
1128 Michael Bishop	1190 Frank Croft	1252 Simon Burchell
1129 David Halford	1191 Michael & Nicholas Heaven	1253 David Widgery
1130 David Alyn Harris	1192 Mark Preston	1254 David W. Goodyear
1131 Liam & Mary Davis	1193 Steve & Gary Woodrow	1255 Simon D. Goodyear
1132 Christopher Howdle	1194 Matthew John Curley	1256 Robert Brooke
1133 Roger W. Linney	1195 Mark Deeley	1257 Tom Ryan
1134 Mike Taylor	1196 Miss Elizabeth May Alsop	1258 Richard Ryan
1135 T. M. Newcombe	1197 Gordon Cull	1259 Darran Boulter
1136 Neil Edwards	1198 C. J. Mercier	1260 Martin Montgomery
1137 Adam Peter O'Connor	1199 Ken Noon	1261 Vernon Grove
1138 Robert Cooper	1200 Paul Noon	1262 Sylvia Holden
1139 Ronald R. Vincent	1201 Peter Noon	1263 Mark Lakin
1140 Christopher Pritchard	1202 Caroline James	1264 Iain Jones
1141 Gareth Jackson	1203 Leslie James Odley	1265 R. A. Clarkson
1142 Steve Bowden	1204 Steven Wright	1266 Desmond Brennan
1143 Peter Goode	1205 Stephen Donnelly	1267 Robin Dean
1144 Matthew Campbell	1206 Vicky Lee	1268 N. M. Salter
1145 Eric Cartwright	1207 Karen Jeffery	1269 Peter T. Vos
1146 Geoffrey & Jeremy Foden	1208 Robert Bell	1270 T. A. Forbes
1147 Terry Hall (South Africa)	1209 A. R. Miller	1271 Leonard Rawlings Layton
1148 Maurice Carter	1210 Mark Thornley	1272 David Hockenhull
1149 Paul Michael Trilloe	1211 Paul Gray-Davis	1273 Nicola Bullivant
1150 Kirk Wheeler	1212 Mark Pearce	1274 Leighton Bullivant
1151 Lynn May	1213 Roger Harrison	1275 Steve Farr
1152 Hugh Thomas	1214 Julie A. Empson	1276 Karl Hosea
1153 Mike Coleman	1215 David Pinner	1277 Emma Brannigan
1154 Angela Weir	1216 Andrew Wibberley	1278 Brian Cowling
1155 Richard Pike	1217 Keith Puttick	1279 Nigel Rose
1156 Richard Morley	1218 H. John De Saulles	1280 James Michael Deeley
1157 Tony Benbow	1219 Jamie Lockley	1281 Martyn Bacchus
1158 Warren Enon	1220 Suzanne Moloney	1283 Peter L. Styler
1159 Claire Enon	1221 Amanda & Gordon Grove	1284 Peter Goakes
1160 Anthony Ellis	1222 Philip Chandler	1285 Neil P. Gaskell
1161 Thomas Eric Cole	1223 M. E. C. Wilson	1286 Paul Kenna
1162 Gavin Jones	1224 Mike & Mary Ruston	1287 Stefan Wally
1163 Adam Rooke	1225 David Cleminson	1288 Jo Rutherford
1164 Ian Drew	1226 Robbie Lloyd Daniel Marsden	1289 John Randall Feely
1165 Sam Jones	1227 Roger Ahluwalia Timmins	1290 Raymond John Paul Feely
1166 Siân Nolan	1228 D. W. I. Thomas	1291 Chris M. Pritchard
1167 J. Bellfield	1229 G. R. Powell	1292 D. P. Bellis
1168 Paul Edwards	1230 George Guest	1293 Luke Farrington
1169 Greg Rose	1231 Mark Green	1294 Simon Booker
1170 Mrs B. Kitley	1232 Ron Gumbley	1295 M. C. Walker
1171 Keith T. Smith	1233 Tina Clay	1296 A. Jeffery
1172 Jonathan Betts	1234 Edmund Gajny	1297 T. Freeman
1173 Kris Michael Hinde	1235 Kevin Clews	1298 S.J. Curry
1174 Christopher C. Fleming	1236 John S. Griffiths	1299 Daniel Richard Evans
1175 Dave Tiller	1237 Les Stoddart	1300 John A. Williams
1176 J. D. Close	1238 N. C. Geldard-Williams	1301 Mr & Mrs Chris Taylor
1177 Sam Smith	1239 Darren Seaton	1302 Frank Beach
1178 Mervyn Aston Arscott	1240 James C. Flood	1303 Phil Lees
1179 Paul Mervyn Arscott	1241 David A. Jones	1304 Trevor Hartley
1180 Darren Whitehouse	1242 Paul Richard Webb	
1181 Robin D. Wilkes	1243 Neil Ian Walker	
1182 Ronald Cooksey	1244 Nick Bevan	
1183 Duncan K. S. Law	1245 Craig Marriott	
1184 Nigel Groves	1246 Robert Head	
1185 Geoff Clarke	1247 L. Davies	
1186 Jack Robert Welch	1248 Kieran Sheridan	
1187 Michael O'Brien	1249 Philip Kimberley	
1188 Steven John Green	1250 Joanne Dacosta